TENANTS' RIGHTS
IN NEW YORK

TENANTS' RIGHTS IN NEW YORK

———

Brette McWhorter Sember
Attorney at Law

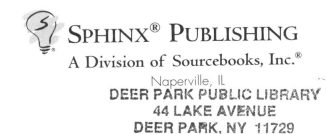
SPHINX® PUBLISHING
A Division of Sourcebooks, Inc.®
Naperville, IL

First edition, 2000

Published by: **Sphinx® Publishing, A Division of Sourcebooks, Inc.®**

Naperville Office
P.O. Box 4410
Naperville, Illinois 60567-4410
630-961-3900
Fax: 630-961-2168

Interior and Cover Design: Sourcebooks, Inc.®
Interior and Cover Production: Amy S. Hall and Mark Warda, Sourcebooks, Inc.®

This publication is designed to provide accurate and authoritative information in regard to the subject matter covered. It is sold with the understanding that the publisher is not engaged in rendering legal, accounting, or other professional service. If legal advice or other expert assistance is required, the services of a competent professional person should be sought.

From a Declaration of Principles Jointly Adopted by a Committee of the American Bar Association and a Committee of Publishers and Associations

Library of Congress Cataloging-in-Publication Data
Sember, Brette McWhorter
    Tenants' rights in New York / Brette McWhorter Sember.
        p.   cm.
    Includes index.
    ISBN 1-57248-122-6 (pbk.)
        1. Landlord and tenant--New York (State)--Popular works. I. Title.
    KFN5145.Z9 S455 2000
346.74704'34--dc21

00-028505

Printed and bound in the United States of America.
HS Paperback — 10 9 8 7 6 5 4 3 2 1

CONTENTS

For Erma and Bill who marked me on their wall,

For Dublin and Sam who are always in my heart,

and for Terry, Quinne, and Zayne who are The Reason.

Many thanks to Mark Warda, a wonderful friend, for his insight
and advice and for making that fateful phone call.

Using Self-Help Law Books

Before using a self-help law book, you should realize the advantages and disadvantages of doing your own legal work and understand the challenges and diligence that this requires.

THE GROWING TREND

Rest assured that you won't be the first or only person handling your own legal matter. For example, in some states, more than seventy-five percent of the people in divorces and other cases represent themselves. Because of the high cost of legal services, this is a major trend and many courts are struggling to make it easier for people to represent themselves. However, some courts are not happy with people who do not use attorneys and refuse to help them in any way.

We write and publish self-help law books to give people an alternative to the often complicated and confusing legal books found in most law libraries. We have made the explanations of the law as simple and easy to understand as possible. Of course, unlike an attorney advising an individual client, we cannot cover every conceivable possibility.

COST/VALUE ANALYSIS

Whenever you shop for a product or service, you are faced with various levels of quality and price. In deciding what product or service to buy, you make a cost/value analysis on the basis of your willingness to pay and the quality you desire.

When buying a car, you decide whether you want transportation, comfort, status, or sex appeal. Accordingly, you decide among such choices as a Neon, a Lincoln, a Rolls Royce, or a Porsche. Before making a decision, you usually weigh the merits of each option against the cost.

When you get a headache, you can take a pain reliever (such as aspirin) or visit a medical specialist for a neurological examination. Given this choice, most people, of course, take a pain reliever, since it costs only pennies; whereas a medical examination costs hundreds of dollars and takes a lot of time. This is usually a logical choice because it is rare to need anything more than a pain reliever for a headache. But in some cases, a headache may indicate a brain tumor and failing to see a specialist right away can result in complications. Should everyone with a headache go to a specialist? Of course not, but people treating their own illnesses must realize that they are betting on the basis of their cost/value analysis of the situation. They are taking the most logical option.

The same cost/value analysis must be made when deciding to do one's own legal work. Many legal situations are very straight forward, requiring a simple form and no complicated analysis. Anyone with a little intelligence and a book of instructions can handle the matter without outside help.

But there is always the chance that complications are involved that only an attorney would notice. To simplify the law into a book like this, several legal cases often must be condensed into a single sentence or paragraph. Otherwise, the book would be several hundred pages long and too complicated for most people. However, this simplification necessarily leaves out many details and nuances that would apply to special or unusual situations. Also, there are many ways to interpret most legal questions. Your case may come before a judge who disagrees with the analysis of our authors.

Therefore, in deciding to use a self-help law book and to do your own legal work, you must realize that you are making a cost/value analysis. You have decided that the money you will save in doing it yourself outweighs the chance that your case will not turn out to your satisfaction. Most people handling their own simple legal matters never have a problem, but occasionally people find that it ended up costing them more to have an attorney straighten out the situation than it would have if they had hired an attorney in the beginning. Keep this in mind while handling your case, and be sure to consult an attorney if you feel you might need further guidance.

LOCAL RULES   The next thing to remember is that a book which covers the law for the entire nation, or even for an entire state, cannot possibly include every procedural difference of every jurisdiction. Whenever possible, we provide the exact form needed; however, in some areas, each county, or even each judge, may require unique forms and procedures. In our state books, our forms usually cover the majority of counties in the state, or provide examples of the type of form which will be required. In our national books, our forms are sometimes even more general in nature but are designed to give a good idea of the type of form that will be needed in most locations. Nonetheless, keep in mind that your state, county, or judge may have a requirement, or use a form, that is not included in this book.

CHANGES IN   You should not necessarily expect to be able to get all of the informa-
'THE LAW   tion and resources you need solely from within the pages of this book. This book will serve as your guide, giving you specific information whenever possible and helping you to find out what else you will need to know. This is just like if you decided to build your own backyard deck. You might purchase a book on how to build decks. However, such a book would not include the building codes and permit requirements of every city, town, county, and township in the nation; nor would it include the lumber, nails, saws, hammers, and other materials and tools you would need to actually build the deck. You would use the book as your guide, and then do some work and research involving such matters as whether you need a permit of some kind, what type and grade of wood are available in your area, whether to use hand tools or power tools, and how to use those tools.

Before using the forms in a book like this, you should check with your court clerk to see if there are any local rules of which you should be aware, or local forms you will need to use. Often, such forms will require the same information as the forms in the book but are merely laid out differently or use slightly different language. They will sometimes require additional information.

Besides being subject to local rules and practices, the law is subject to change at any time. The courts and the legislatures of all fifty states are constantly revising the laws. It is possible that while you are reading this book, some aspect of the law is being changed.

In most cases, the change will be of minimal significance. A form will be redesigned, additional information will be required, or a waiting period will be extended. As a result, you might need to revise a form, file an extra form, or wait out a longer time period; these types of changes will not usually affect the outcome of your case. On the other hand, sometimes a major part of the law is changed, the entire law in a particular area is rewritten, or a case that was the basis of a central legal point is overruled. In such instances, your entire ability to pursue your case may be impaired.

To help you with local requirements and changes in the law, be sure to read the section in chapter 1 on "Finding the Law: Legal Research."

Again, you should weigh the value of your case against the cost of an attorney and make a decision as to what you believe is in your best interest.

Introduction

A tenant who is educated about what New York landlord/tenant laws require of tenants can avoid costly problems. A tenant who also knows what New York laws require of landlords is doubly prepared. He or she not only understands what tenant responsibilities are, but is also armed with the knowledge of what responsibilities the landlord has to the tenant. You cannot stand up for your rights until you know what they are. This book is written to help you, the tenant, understand your rights and obligations as a tenant, but also to show you what your landlord is required to provide to you. The book contains valuable information about how you can protect and enforce your rights as well as how you can expect your landlord to enforce his rights.

Laws are passed to create specific rules for specific situations. Unfortunately, this means they are not always easily understandable for the average reader. This book explains those complex laws in simple words so that New York tenants can understand their rights and responsibilities. If you would like more detail about a law, check the statutes in appendix A or research the court cases as explained in chapter 2.

New York landlord/tenant law is constantly changing. The legislature passes new laws each year and courts are constantly writing more opinions. These events mean that the law is not a fixed set of rules, but a creature in constant motion.

No book of this type can be expected to cover every situation. The laws change yearly and judges can interprets laws in different ways. Only a lawyer experienced in this area of the law can give you a dependable, legal opinion about your individual case. This book can be an important tool for you as a tenant. It can help you understand your rights and help you avoid making costly mistakes. Knowledge is power and this book is can offer you that.

This book contains explanations of the law and step by step procedures for enforcing your rights as a tenant. As you read this book and follow the procedures described, you should know that different counties have different customs and different judges have individual ways of doing things. Court clerks and judge's law clerks cannot give you legal advice, but often they can tell you what is needed to proceed with your case. Before filing any forms in court, check to see if your court provides its own set of forms or has any special requirements.

We at Sourcebooks hope that you find this book useful and we welcome your comments on this or any of our books.

GENERAL CONSIDERATIONS 1

RELATIONSHIPS

As a tenant, it is in your best interest to maintain a workable business relationship with your landlord or manager and a friendly relationship with other tenants in your building. The most important rule of thumb, no matter who you are dealing with, is to be pleasant and friendly whenever possible. People are more willing to help you if you are non-threatening and calm.

DEALING WITH YOUR LANDLORD

Your landlord owns your building as a moneymaking venture. He or she is trying to make a profit, or to at least cover the bills on the property until the mortgage is paid off. Most decisions a landlord makes come down to a bottom line profit or loss decision. From the start of your relationship with your landlord, you need to remember that this is a business. Your landlord is not interested in being your friend. This does not mean you must be rivals. You and your landlord both want you to stay in the unit. It is much easier for a landlord to keep a current tenant than to find a new one. Keep this in mind when you make requests of the landlord. It is much easier for your landlord to fix something in your apartment than to have to rent the unit to someone else. When you approach your landlord with repairs or other problems, do so in a friendly, yet confident, manner.

Your landlord has a set of responsibilities to you that must be honored (as discussed throughout this book). As a tenant, you need to learn to ask for what you are entitled. Everyone has heard horror stories about absentee landlords who let buildings fall apart. In all likelihood, your landlord is not part of this group. Learn how to get in touch with your landlord and don't be afraid to request that the landlord comply with the law!

DEALING WITH A MANAGER

Some landlords hire a manager (who is paid or allowed to live rent free in the building) to handle tenant relationships. Managers perform all of the things landlords do: renting out the units, arranging for repairs, collecting rent, and dealing with complaints. Treat a manager in the same way you would a landlord. Some managers handle many buildings or units and may be difficult to reach. If you are having a problem and the manager is unable or unwilling to solve it, contact the landlord directly.

DEALING WITH OTHER TENANTS

It is to your advantage to get to know the other tenants in your building. If you are having a problem with the landlord, find out if the other tenants have the same or a similar problem. See chapter 5 for more information on tenant organization.

You and the other tenants share a building. You are neighbors, not strangers. Treat them as you would like to be treated. There is nothing worse than living next door to someone with whom you are having a feud. If you are new in a building, other tenants can give you a lot of information about the landlord, the manager, the building, and the neighborhood. They are an important resource.

Dealing with Roommates

If you have a roommate, the two of you are partners of a sort and should try to work together. The best way to ensure that your relationship goes smoothly is to have a complete understanding about how rent, utilities, and other expenses will be shared before you move in together. Use the Roommate Agreement, form 14, to spell out the terms of your agreement.

You and your roommate will be living together like family even though you may be strangers to each other. Your arrangement will succeed if you are considerate of each other and each other's property. Before you take on a roommate, be sure that you will be able to share your living space with someone else comfortably. If you are very private, a roommate may not be for you. See chapter 9 for more information on roommates.

LAWS & REGULATIONS THAT APPLY TO RENTALS

2

NEW YORK LANDLORD/TENANT LAWS

There are many laws that deal with landlord/tenant issues in New York. The New York legislature passes statutes, municipalities (*a.k.a.* cities) have codes, and courts decide cases and issue opinions (*a.k.a.* decisions) about landlord/tenant issues. The codes and laws provide rules and procedures that must be followed, and the courts' opinions interpret or clarify the laws and decide how they are applied.

It is not unusual for laws, codes, and court opinions to conflict. If you are in a situation where you cannot understand how the laws apply to your situation, you should consider the advantage of consulting an attorney versus the cost.

NEW YORK STATE LAWS

Landlord/tenant law in New York is spread out through different statutes. State laws mentioned in this book are located in the Consolidated Laws of New York. You might find it helpful to use *McKinney's Consolidated Laws of New York Annotated*, which not only lists the laws, but also summarizes judicial opinions that explain them.

The following sections of the law contain provisions governing landlord/tenant law:

- ☞ Real Property Law (RPL)
- ☞ Real Property Actions and Proceedings (RPAPL)
- ☞ Multiple Residence Law (MRL)
- ☞ Multiple Dwelling Law (MDL)
- ☞ Energy Law (Ener. L.)
- ☞ Executive Law (Exec. L.)
- ☞ Civil Practice Law and Rules (CPLR)
- ☞ General Obligations Law (GOL)
- ☞ Lien Law (LL)
- ☞ Unconsolidated Laws (Unconsol. L.)
- ☞ New York Codes, Rules and Regulations (NYCRR)

LOCAL LAWS

Laws governing real property are passed by both counties and cities. Many New York City ordinances are discussed in this book. Be sure to check with your county and city to see if there are any ordinances which apply to your situation.

FEDERAL LAWS

Landlord/tenant relations are governed by rules of the Environmental Protection Agency and the Department of Housing and Urban Development, federal laws such as the Civil Rights Act and the American with Disabilities Act. Some of the rules provided by the agencies list above are discussed in this book. If you need to contact a federal agency, look in the United States government section of the phone book. A free *Public Housing Handbook* is available from the local office of the Department of Housing and Urban Development. Other HUD rules are available as well.

CONDOMINIUM AND CO-OP RULES

If you are living in, or are considering, a co-op or condo, you should be aware that there are rules that apply to your tenancy which may not be spelled out in your lease. Ideally, you should review them before you rent such a unit because they might conflict with your plans.

CONDOMINIUMS

Condominiums are owned by the people who live in them. Each person owns the individual unit he or she lives in and owns an interest in the common areas. Condominiums are governed by the Condominium Act (Real Property Law § 339-d). Condominiums have a board of managers who run the building. There are by-laws, or rules, that all owners and tenants in the building must follow. If you do not follow these rules, you can be fined or evicted. Your tenancy in the unit may need to be approved by the management and go to an interview prior to approval. The New York State Attorney General's office has a free publication entitled *How to Handle Problems with a Condominiums Board of Directors*. Look in your phone book for your local office.

CO-OPS

Co-ops are owned by a corporation. Each resident is given ownership of his unit and stock in the corporation. Each must make a capital contribution (or big up front payment of cash when moving in) and pay a monthly amount. Co-ops have a board of managers who manage the building. Like a condominium, you may need to be approved by the building management before your tenancy is approved. The New York State Attorney General's office has a free publication entitled *How to Handle Problems with a Co-op's Board of Managers*. Look in your phone book for your local office.

DEED RESTRICTIONS

Like condos and co-ops, subdivisions may have rules which affect the use of the property. These may be called deed restrictions, restrictive covenants, or covenants and conditions.

Despite the fact that nothing may be in the lease, your tenancy is subject to any restrictions placed on the property prior to your tenancy. You could be sued by a neighborhood association, developer, or other group which has the power to enforce the restrictions.

If the restrictions conflict with your lease, or if your lease does not subject you to the restrictions, then you might have a claim against your landlord if the restrictions impair your use of the property as intended in the lease.

Deed restrictions you might run across could include restrictions on where vehicles can be parked, what kinds of lawn ornaments are permitted, what types of structures can be placed on the property, etc. If you will be renting in a subdivision, check with your landlord to find out if there are any such restrictions. If you know there is a neighborhood association, check with them to learn about restrictions.

LEGAL RESEARCH

This book provides summaries of many laws and opinions. Some laws are included in full in appendix A. You may want or need to read an entire law or case summarized in this book. If you become involved in a court case, you may find that you need to do some research to support your position. Every county has a law library open for public use. Check the county government listings in your phone book for the location of the law library in your area. Law schools also have libraries that may permit public use. Do not hesitate to ask a law librarian to help you find something.

To find a state law, get the volume of the New York Statutes that contains the title of the law you need and look for the section number. For example, to find RPL § 101, get the volume for Real Property Law and find section 101.

To locate a particular court opinion, such as *Brainard Mfg. Co. v. Dewey Garden Lanes, Inc.*, 78 A.D.2d 365, 435 N.Y.S.2d 417 (4th Dept., 1981) you need to understand how to read the citation (the numbers following the name of the case). First is the title of the case. There are two sets of numbers and letters that are separated by a comma. The first one in our example, 78 A.D.2d 365, tells you to go to volume 78 of the Appellate Division Reports, Second Series, and look on page 365 to find the case. The second one, 435 N.Y.S.2d 417, tells you another place where you can find the same case, in volume 435 of the New York Supplement, Second Series, on page 417. The information in the parentheses (4th Dept., 1981) tells you that the case was decided by the Appellate Division in the Fourth Department in 1981. It may be a big boost for your case if you can find a case in your favor decided by the same department (the state is divided into districts called *departments*) in which your case is being heard (ask the court clerk if you don't know your local department number).

Many Internet sites that can help you obtain information as well. Several are listed below:

☞ For access to all current New York state statutes:
http://www.assembly.state.ny.us/cgi-bin/claws

☞ For access to New York City ordinances:
http://www.council.nyc.ny.us

☞ For access to Court of Appeals decisions from 1992 to the present:
http://www.law.cornell.edu/ny/ctap/overview/html

☞ New York City Housing Court cases and a wealth of other helpful information:
http://www.tenant.net/court/hcourt

☛ The New State Attorney General's site:

http://www.oag.state.ny.us/business/tenantgu

☛ The New York State Division of Housing and Community Renewal which can provide Fact Sheets and other information:

http://www.dhcr.state.ny.us

☛ The *Community Training and Resource Center (CTRC)* is a non-profit agency that helps New York City tenants. They offer many publications and can be reached at 212-964-7200.

To learn more about doing legal research, read *Legal Research Made Easy*, by Suzan Herskowitz, available at your local or online bookstore or directly from Sphinx Publishing (1-800-226-5291).

OBTAINING ASSISTANCE

If you have read this book and have done some research or do not want to have to do any research but still need more information, there is help available. Look in the state government pages in your phone book for the nearest office for the Attorney General or call the Division of Housing and Community Renewal at 718-739-6400. If you still have questions, contact your local legal aid office. While you might not qualify for them to represent you, you often can get answers to some simple questions over the phone.

If you cannot obtain the answers to your questions in the above ways, you may be able to have an attorney explain your rights in a single consultation, even if you cannot afford to hire one to handle your whole case. For the name of an attorney in your area who is skilled at these types of cases, contact the New York State Bar Association Lawyer Referral Service at 1-800-342-3661. Your county bar association may also have a referral service.

BEGINNING THE LANDLORD/TENANT RELATIONSHIP

3

THE APPLICATION PROCESS

Most landlords require tenants to complete an application that requests information about the tenant's employment, salary, previous addresses, and references. You should complete this form honestly. If there is information requested with which you are not comfortable, you can refuse to answer, but risk being denied the rental. You may be asked to give your social security number, bank account information, copies of pay stubs or tax returns and contact information for your employer. For references, list only people who will say good things about you. If the application asks for information about race or religion, you should not complete the section unless you don't mind sharing that information or want the place so desperately that you don't want to risk losing it. When you fill out an application, be sure to do so neatly. You really want to make a good impression. You might also want to provide the landlord with extra information that was not requested. Some tenants ask employers or former landlords to write reference letters that begin with "To Whom It May Concern." This letter can be provided to the prospective landlord.

YOUR CREDIT REPORT

Your landlord may want to obtain a copy of your credit report, mostly to verify that you are able to pay the rent and that you have not had credit problems in the past. The landlord must get your permission to obtain the report. He can also charge you for the cost of obtaining your report. Ask the landlord which credit bureau he or she will be using. You can call and verify the cost of the report and you can also verify that the landlord actually did order one.

If the landlord rejects your application based on the information in the credit report, you can request a free copy of the report yourself within sixty days of the rejection by sending a written request.

You are also entitled to other information on which the landlord based your rejection, such as information from a reference or from an employer.

DISCRIMINATION

Housing discrimination occurs when someone does not let you rent property because of your race, religion, sex, national origin, number of children, or handicapped status. There are federal, state, and local laws that protect tenants against discrimination. If you believe someone has discriminated against you, you can contact an attorney who has experience in housing discrimination about filing a lawsuit or call the United States Department of Housing and Urban Development's hotline at 1-800-669-9777. You may be able to collect damages for your losses as well as punitive damages. The New York State Division of Human Rights should also be contacted. Look under Human Rights in the New York State government listings in the phone book for the number of your local office.

Be aware that just because you fall into a protected category (for example if you are of Mexican descent or if you are a woman) and are turned down for a rental or charged a higher rate than other tenants, this does not automatically mean the landlord has discriminated against you. You must be able to prove to a court that you were turned down because you are a member of that group. The best way to prove this is to show that someone, who is not in a typically discriminated against group, was accepted when you were rejected or was offered a lower rent than you.

FEDERAL LAWS   Congress has enacted several laws that protect minorities against housing discrimination.

The *Civil Rights Act of 1968* prohibits any policy that has a discriminatory effect. A complaint must be filed within 180 days and does not apply to single family homes if the landlord has three or fewer of them. It also does not apply to rental units of four or fewer units if the landlord lives there.

The *Civil Rights Act of 1982* prohibits actions taken with the intent to discriminate.

The *Civil Rights Act, 1988 Amendment* prohibits discrimination against handicapped people, families with children, or someone because of his age. A complaint must be filed within two years. This does not apply to single-family homes if the landlord owns three or less or to buildings of four or fewer units if the landlord lives there.

The *Federal Fair Housing Act of 1968* prohibits sexual harassment of tenants by landlords or managers (sexual harassment includes offensive sexual comments, offensive sexual touching, and rape).

The *Federal Fair Housing Act Amendments of 1991* requires that buildings of four or more units that were first occupied after March 1991, be handicap accessible. All units on the ground level and all units that can be reached by elevator must be accessible. Doorways must be wide enough to accommodate wheelchairs and light switches and thermostats must be close enough to the ground to be reached from a wheelchair. The kitchens and bathrooms in these units must meet certain other requirements to make them accessible.

NEW YORK LAWS

New York has its own discrimination laws that are similar to the federal laws. Executive Law § 296 makes it illegal to discriminate based on marital status or because someone is handicapped. Real Property Law §§ 236* (make sure section 236 has an asterisk, § 236 without an asterisk is completely different) and 237 make it illegal to discriminate against people with children (except where the landlord lives in the duplex or if the housing is designed for the elderly) and to refuse to allow tenants to have children during the lease.

Executive Law § 292(21) uses a definition of discrimination that is similar to the federal one. The landlord must provide reasonable accommodations for handicapped persons as long as it does not create undue hardship for the landlord.

LOCAL LAWS

The New York City Administrative Code (N.Y.C. Admin. Code) prohibits discrimination on the basis of actual or perceived sexual orientation, the tenant's occupation, alienage, or citizenship [N.Y.C. Admin. Code § 8-107 (5) (a-c)]. You may wish to check with your city or county to find out if they have discrimination laws of their own.

HOME BUSINESSES

Today, many people work at home and most of these businesses are little noticed and not problems, but some home businesses violate laws or regulations. If you are caught, you can be fined or put out of business. You should check with the town clerk, city hall, or county zoning department to see if what you plan to do is legal under the zoning regulations. You should also check with the county clerk's office to see if there are any covenants or restrictions on the property which prohibit what you are planning.

Of course, if what you are planning does not affect your neighborhood, for example, if you are painting pictures, writing books or making phone calls from your home you won't have to worry. But if customers or clients often come to your home, or if they make pickups and deliveries each day, you may have trouble.

You should also make sure that your renter's insurance (if you carry it) covers you if you run a business. Some policies are void if the home is used for commercial purposes.

PETS

A landlord may refuse to allow tenants to have pets, but under the Civil Rights Law, guide dogs for hearing and vision impaired tenants must be allowed. In New York City, if a tenant keeps a pet openly for at least three months and the landlord does not object, the landlord forfeits the right to object to the pet. If the pet creates a nuisance to other tenants or causes damage, the landlord may require that the pet be removed [N.Y.C. Admin. Code § 27-2009 (1)]. Similar rules have been applied by judges throughout the state. If your landlord allows you to have a pet, make sure you get permission in writing as part of the lease or as a separate written agreement.

INSPECTING THE UNIT

Before you move into a rental unit, you should inspect it carefully. You should never sign a lease without first inspecting the unit. Ideally, this would be done with the landlord or the landlord's agent. Check all appliances, turn on all faucets, and check the operation of the windows, smoke alarms, doors, and toilets.

If you notice defects (or problems) with the unit, like a stain on the carpet or a large crack in the plaster, you can handwrite these in on the lease as pre-existing defects that were present when you moved in, so you will not be held responsible for them.

You may wish to take some photographs and date them. Having an acquaintance with you when you take the photos would be helpful if you ever have to present them in court and need a witness to verify when they were taken.

Many landlords have inspection checklists, but if yours does not, you can use form 1 in appendix C. It is best if you can get your landlord to sign a copy, but if you cannot, at least give or send a copy to your landlord as soon as you move into the unit.

Rent Regulation 4

Rules that Apply to Rent

A landlord is usually free to charge whatever rent he or she feels is appropriate. *Rent control* laws are the only laws New York has governing rent control. These laws are only in some cities and are discussed later in this chapter.

Date Due

Rent is due on the date specified in the lease. If it is not specified in the lease, it is not due until after it is earned, at the end of the term (which is usually a month). *DeSimone v. Canzonieri*, 246 A.D. 735, 283 N.Y.S. 860 (2d Dept., 1935). If the due date falls on a Saturday, Sunday, or legal holiday, the rent is due the next business day. If you mail your rent, it must be *received* by the landlord on or before the due date, although some landlords may be flexible about this. The landlord must provide you with a written receipt if you pay any way other than a personal check. If you pay by personal check, the landlord must provide you with a receipt if you request one.

Place Due

If the lease does not specify where payment is to be made, then it is payable at the leased premises. This generally means the landlord will come and collect it or that you will have to give it to the landlord or manager who lives on site. If you and your landlord agree that you can mail the rent, you should get this in writing.

RAISING RENT   If you have a lease for a specific period of time (like one or two years), the landlord cannot raise the rent during the time period in the lease unless the lease specifically allows the rent to be raised. Once your lease ends and you seek to renew it, the landlord can decide to raise it as a condition of renewal. If your landlord tries to raise the rent during the term of a lease which does not provide for raises, this is a breach by the landlord and you are not legally obligated to pay the additional amount.

If you have a month-to-month tenancy, the landlord can raise the rent by giving you thirty days notice. If you do not agree to the new amount, your tenancy is terminated. If you are in a rent stabilized unit, read the provisions described later in this chapter and consult DHCR Fact Sheets # 11, 12, and 26.

LATE FEES   Most leases provide for a late penalty if rent is not received within a certain time after it is due. If your lease does not mention a late fee, your landlord cannot impose one. A lease may provide a grace period, such as three days after the due date, during which the rent can be paid without penalty. There is no grace period unless your lease specifically says so. If the penalty is too harsh, a court may rule that it is *unconscionable*, and therefore illegal. Under New York law [RPL § 233(r)], mobile home leases always have a ten day grace period and a limit of five percent on the amount of the late fee.

If your unit is rent-regulated and you are having a problem with rent overcharges or increases or want your rent reduced due to a decrease in services, contact the DHCR.

If you pay your rent late and the landlord accepts it, you cannot be evicted for nonpayment. See chapter 12 for more information about this. If you know you are going to be late on your rent, send your landlord a letter explaining why, when you will have the money, and how grateful you will be if he will make an exception and accept the rent late this one time without a late fee.

ACCELERATION   *Acceleration* occurs when future rent becomes due ahead of time. The lease may provide that all the rent for the rest of the rental term becomes due when there is nonpayment. *Fifty States Management Corp. v. Pioneer Auto Sales, Inc.*, 46 N.Y.2d 573, 415 N.Y.S.2d 800 (1979). A lease provision requiring rent acceleration when the landlord terminates the lease was found to be enforceable. *Holy Properties Ltd. v. Kenneth Cole Productions*, 87 N.Y.2d 130, 637 N.Y.S.2d 964 (1995).

LAWS LIMITING RENT

In New York City and some parts of Nassau, Rockland, and Westchester counties, as well as some other municipalities across the state, the amount of rent a landlord can charge is regulated by law. There are two ways rent can be regulated. One is called *rent control* and one is called *rent stabilization*.

Rent regulation began as a way to ease the housing crisis in New York City in the 1940s. At the time, there was a housing shortage which sky-rocketed prices. The legislature stepped in and set up rules by which rent could be controlled.

Rent control exists in buildings built before 1947 with three or more units in which the same tenant has lived continuously since before July 1, 1971. Rent stabilization exists in any rent control unit that becomes vacant, as well as buildings built before 1974 with six or more units.

The Division of Housing and Community Renewal (DHCR) is the state agency that regulates rent control and rent stabilized units in New York State. If you have a rent regulated apartment, you should locate the nearest DHCR office. A list of DHCR offices is given at the end of this chapter. The DHCR can be reached at (718) 739-6400 or at www.dhcr.state.ny.us. *Fact Sheets* are available at no cost from the DHCR, which discuss specific rent regulation topics in detail in a way that cannot be covered in this book. You may wish to request the entire packet of fact sheets to keep as a reference aid. All forms discussed in this chapter are DHCR forms. Should you need to use any, complete them and file them with your local DHCR office.

The Community Training and Resource Center (212-964-7200) can also provide assistance to New York City tenants.

RENT CONTROL

Rent control exists in fifty-one municipalities in New York State, but most rent control units are in New York City. In New York City, rent control applies to buildings with three or more units built before 1947 that were used as or converted to residential use prior to February 1, 1947, and continuously occupied by the same tenant or his or her successor (i.e., a family member who has lived with the tenant for the last two years and has made this his or her primary residence; non-traditional family members can qualify for this as well if the relationship can be proven) since July 7, 1971 (9 NYCRR § 2104.6).

Government housing, units used for charitable or educational purposes by not-for-profit institutions, motor courts, mobile homes, hotels, and furnished rooms are exempt from this legislation. Most rent control units are occupied by the elderly. Once the unit becomes vacant, it is then governed by rent stabilization laws, or becomes deregulated.

Rent control units are statutory tenancies. Once the lease has expired, there is a statutory tenancy governed by applicable laws (the Local Emergency Rent Control Act, beginning at Unconsol.L. § 8601 for New York City; and the Emergency Housing Rent Control Law, beginning at Unconsol. L. § 8581 for areas outside New York City).

SUBLEASING

Rent control units may be subleased only if subleasing was allowed in the original lease.

RENT AMOUNTS

The laws governing rent control units set the maximum rent (*Maximum Base Rent* or *MBR*) that can be charged for the unit. The amount is determined using a formula that considers the taxes, water expense, sewer costs, and operating and maintenance expenses of the building; and deducts losses from vacancies (9 NYCRR § 2201.4). The MBR can be changed every two years to reflect changes in operating costs, but cannot be raised in excess of 7.5% in New York City. Outside New York City the DHCR determines the maximum allowable rates of rent increase (9 NYCRR §§ 2201.5 and 2201.6). A landlord must apply to the DHCR for an Order of Eligibility to raise rent. This cannot be done without DHCR approval.

Rent may also be raised in the following circumstances, upon the landlord's application to the DHCR:

☛ Major capital improvements are made to the building which benefit all tenants, such as a new boiler. There is a fifteen percent limit per year on increases due to this.

☛ Improvements or enlargements to the unit, including increase in services, furniture or equipment. The tenant's consent is required.

☛ The landlord and tenant agree to use another formula due to substantial improvements to the building or unit (9 NCRR § 2202.5).

☛ The tenant subleases the unit without the landlord's consent.

☛ Current operating and building expenses are not currently being met (9 NYCRR §§ 2202.8 through 2202.11).

☛ Unique circumstances cause the maximum rent to be lower than that for comparable units (9 NYCRR § 2202.7).

☛ The tenant agrees to a two year lease that includes an increase of services, furniture, or equipment (9 NYCRR § 2202.5).

Rent can be decreased by the DHCR if the tenant can show a reduction in services; such as an inoperative elevator, *Jemrock Realty v. Anderson*, 228 A.D.2d 355, 644 N.Y.S.2d 263 (1st Dept., 1996).

DEREGULATION A rent control unit can become deregulated (that is no longer subject to rent control) if:

☛ the tenant or tenant's successor (a family member who also shares the unit) vacates the unit; or

☛ the maximum rent is $2,000 on or after July 7, 1993, and the tenant's annual income is over $175,000 for each of the past two years [Unconsol. L. 8582(2)].

EVICTION   It is very difficult to be evicted if you are a rent control tenant. Before an eviction, the landlord must apply for a Certificate of Eviction from the DHCR and properly notify the tenant. The only grounds for eviction are:

☞ the tenant's failure to pay rent (9 NYCRR § 2104.1);

☞ the tenant commits nuisance or objectionable conduct [Unconsol. L. § 8585(1)];

☞ the tenant's occupancy is illegal under law [Unconsol. L. § 8585(1)];

☞ the tenant uses the unit for illegal or immoral use [Unconsol. L. § 8585(1)];

☞ the tenant refuses to provide access for necessary repairs or improvements [Unconsol. L. § 8585(1)];

☞ the landlord needs the unit for himself or herself or for his or her immediate family (this must be an immediate and compelling need) (Unconsol. L. § 8585.2);

☞ the landlord is a not-for-profit institution and needs the property for a charitable or educational purpose;

☞ the landlord wishes to demolish the building or withdraw it from the rental market;

☞ the landlord wishes to subdivide or substantially alter the unit or building; or

☞ the tenant refuses to renew at the end of the rental period.

The landlord may evict the tenant without applying for a Certificate of Eviction if:

☞ tenant did not use the unit as his or her primary residence (9 NYCRR § 2504.4), or

☞ the tenant breached the lease [Unconsol. L. § 8585(1)].

RENT STABILIZATION

With over one million units in New York State, rent stabilization is much more common than rent control. *Rent stabilization* applies to the following buildings:

In New York City:

☛ Buildings of six or more units built between February 1, 1947, and January 1, 1974

☛ Buildings of six or more units built before February 1, 1947, and the current tenant moved in after June 30, 1971

☛ Buildings of thirty or more apartments built or substantially renovated since 1974 and which are receiving special tax benefits

Outside of New York City:

☛ Buildings of six or more units built before January 1, 1974, in localities that adopted the Emergency Tenant Protection Act (ETPA)

☛ Apartments in areas that enacted the ETPA

☛ Rent controlled apartments vacated after June 30, 1971

The following units are excluded from rent stabilization:

☛ Rent control units

☛ Government housing

☛ Buildings completed or substantially rehabilitated after 1974

☛ Units owned or operated by charitable or educational institutions

☛ Hotel rooms

☛ Units not used by the tenant as his or her primary residence

LEASE When you first move into a rent stabilized apartment, you sign what is called a *vacancy lease*. When your current lease expires and you renew, you sign a *renewal lease*. All leases for rent stabilized units in New York City must have a Rent Stabilization Lease Rider attached to them by the landlord. The DHCR has a required form for a rent stabilization renewal lease. All leases in New York City must have a Window Guard Rider attached (for more information about window guards, see chapter 7).

RENT AMOUNT

Rent stabilized units must be registered initially and yearly with the DHCR by the landlord, and a copy of the registration must be provided to the tenant. This registration contains the legal regulated rent or base rent, which is the rent that has been charged for the past four years. All increases and adjustments are added to this amount. A new tenant has ninety days to appeal the base amount [use Challenge Re: Maximum Base Rent Order (form 6)] and prove that it exceeds the fair market value (FMV) of the unit (there can be no appeal if the first rent-stabilized tenant moved in between 1971 and 1974) [Unconsol. L. 8629(b)]. FMV is equal to the average of: the Maximum Controlled Rent or the Maximum Base Rent, whichever is higher, and the rents of qualifying comparable apartments, with an addition for any new equipment.

If you believe you are being overcharged, read the DHCR's Fact Sheet #26 and use the Tenant's Complaint of Rent and/or Other Specific Overcharges in Rent Stabilized Apartments in New York City (form 5) and Rent Overcharge Application—Information (form 4).

Tenants have a choice of a one or two year lease under either a vacancy or renewal lease. There is a vacancy bonus of twenty percent of two year's rent under a vacancy lease. This is an additional amount that can be charged by the landlord. Renewal increases may be collected when a lease is renewed. Additional rent increases are set yearly by the local rent guidelines boards in New York City, and Nassau, Westchester, and Rockland counties.

If you are not offered a renewal lease or have problems with its terms, use Tenant's Complaint of Owner's Failure to Renew Lease and/or Failure to Furnish a Copy of a Signed Lease (form 2) or Mediation Program—Lease Renewal Violation(s) (form 3).

In New York City, there is a fuel cost adjustment that may be added to the rent, based on the increase or decrease of fuel costs [N.Y.C. Admin. Code § 26-405(n)]. To challenge a landlord's fuel cost adjustment, read

DHCR's Fact Sheet #13 and use Tenant's Challenge to Owner's Report and Certification of Fuel Cost Adjustment (form 8).

If your landlord has not provided adequate heat or hot water (see chapter 7 for a discussion of minimum requirements), use Failure to Provide Heat and/or Hot Water—Tenant Application for Rent Reduction (form 7).

Rent increases can also occur when major improvements or enlargements have been made to the unit. The consent of the tenant is required unless the work is done during vacancy. Ordinary maintenance and repairs do not qualify for a rent increase. *Linden v. New York State Div. Of Housing and Community Renewal*, 217 A.D.2d 407, 629 N.Y.S.2d 32 (1st Dept., 1995).

Major capital improvements (sometimes called *MCIs*) to the entire building, which benefit all the tenants, also warrant a rent increase. An installation of something like a new boiler would qualify (Unconsol. L. § 8584.3, 9 NYCRR § 2522.4). There is a limit of six percent per year in New York City on MCI increases. Outside New York City, there is a fifteen percent limit. Rent may also be increased due to an increase in building services if seventy-five percent of the tenants consent. Fifty-five percent consent is required if the addition is part of an overall improvement [9 NYCRR § 2102.3(b)].

An increase may also occur when normal increases do not offset the landlord's increased operating expenses [Unconsol. L. § 8626(d)]. Provisions for New York City are contained in 9 NYCRR § 2522.4, and provisions for outside New York City are contained in 9 NYCRR § 2502.4. There is a limit of six percent per year for this type of increase.

Landlords are not required to raise rents and sometimes a landlord can be persuaded to make a concession for you. If the landlord does not specify that the concession is to apply to a certain lease term, he will be required to offer you this concession with each renewal. *Century Operating Corp. v. Popolizio*, 90 A.D.2d 731, 455 N.Y.S.2d 7789 (1st Dept., 1982).

DEREGULATION	At the time this book was written, a rent stabilized unit is deregulated if the rent reaches $2,000 and the tenant's income for the past two years exceeds $175,000; or if the unit becomes vacant and the rent reaches $2,000.
HARASSMENT	If you are harassed by your landlord or your landlord attempts to retaliate against you by cutting off services or evicting you, the DHCR can provide you with assistance. File Tenant's Statement of Complaint(s)—Harassment (form 11).
EVICTION	It is difficult for a landlord to evict you when you are a rent-stabilized tenant. The standards are the same as for rent control tenants. Refer to the earlier section regarding eviction of rent control tenants.
LITIGATION	Should you take your landlord to court and win, you will need to complete DHCR forms, including Judgment (form 9) and Notice of Rent Stabilized Tenant Concerning Payment of Penalties Which Landlord Has Been Directed to Pay by an Administrator's Order (form 10).

LOFTS

Lofts, or *Interim Multiple Dwellings (IMDs)*, are units made out of large spaces that were used for manufacturing or commercial purposes and then occupied by residential tenants before a Certificate of Occupancy was obtained and before renovations were made to convert the units to residential use. Lofts were another answer to the housing crisis in New York City and first became popular during the 1970s. Lofts in New York City are governed by the Multiple Dwelling Law and are regulated by the Loft Board.

Improvements to lofts that are made and paid for by tenants are owned by the tenants.

Rent increases are not permitted until the unit is in compliance with the safety requirements in the Multiple Dwelling Law. Once there is compliance, rent may be raised based on the owner's costs involved in meeting the requirements. When the Certificate of Occupancy is obtained, another increase is permitted. At this point, a lease must be offered to the tenant, the rent stabilization guidelines apply, and the unit becomes regulated by the rent guidelines board (MDL 286).

Rent Regulation does not apply if the space is used for commercial or manufacturing purposes again or if the owner buys the tenant's improvements when the tenant vacates.

SINGLE ROOM OCCUPANCIES

A *Single Room Occupancy (SRO)* is a single room with a private kitchen or private bathroom, but not both. SROs are governed by the ETPA. Buildings with six or more SROs are rent stabilized unless they are used for transient renters (those who have no permanent residences, but rent rooms on a daily or weekly basis). There is no regulation of rent charged to transients. However, transient residents cannot be denied the right to become permanent residents.

The eviction rules for rent regulation apply to permanent residents, except there is no eviction for a tenant's refusal to sign a renewal lease.

**Division of Housing and Community Renewal
District Rent Offices**

Bronx Borough Rent Office:
    One Fordham Plaza, 2nd Floor - Suite 210
    Bronx, NY 10458
    (718) 563-5678

Brooklyn Borough Rent Office:
    55 Hanson Place, 7th Floor
    Brooklyn, NY 11217
    (718) 722-4778

Buffalo Rent Office:
    Statler Towers
    107 Delaware Avenue, Suite 600
    Buffalo, NY 14202
    (716) 842-2244

Central Office for Rent Administration and Queens Rent Office:
92-31 Union Hall Street
Jamaica, NY 11433
(718) 739-6400

Harassment Unit:
25 Beaver Street, 5th Floor
New York, NY 10004
(212) 480-6238 and (212) 480-6239

Lower Manhattan Borough Rent Office:
(South Side of 110th St. and below)
25 Beaver Street, 5th Floor
New York, NY 10004
(212) 480-6238 and (212) 480-6239

Upper Manhattan Borough Rent Office:
(North Side of 110th St. and above)
Adam Clayton Powell, Jr. Office Bldg.
163 West 125th St., 5th Floor
New York, NY 10027
(212) 961-8930

Nassau County Rent Office:
50 Clinton Street, 6th Floor - Room 605
Hempstead, NY 11550
(516) 481-9494

Rockland County Rent Office:
94-96 North Main Street
Spring Valley, NY 10977
(914) 425-6575

Staten Island Borough Rent Office:
60 Bay Street, 7th Floor,
Staten Island, NY 10301
(718) 816-0278

Westchester County Rent Office:
55 Church Street, 3rd Floor
White Plains, NY 10601
(914) 948-4434

THE RENTAL AGREEMENT 5

LEASES AND RENTAL AGREEMENTS

A *rental agreement* is a broad term that means any type of agreement to rent a premises, whether it is a verbal month-to-month, or a written five year lease. A *lease* is a rental agreement for a specific period of time.

ORAL AND WRITTEN LEASES

A lease does not have to be in writing to be valid. Courts have found leases to exist even where the parties did not clearly verbally agree on one.

📖 A lease was found to exist where the landlord sent a letter with the proposed terms of the lease as an offer and the tenant accepted, but never signed a lease. *Kalker v. Columbus Properties, Inc.*, 111 A.D..2d 117, 489 N.Y.S.2d 495 (1st Dept., 1985).

📖 A lease was found to exist where the tenant simply paid rent and moved into the unit. *Galante v. Hathaway Bakeries, Inc.*, 6 A.D.2d 142, 176 N.Y.S.2d 87 (4th Dept., 1958).

Leases can be implied from the parties' intentions, their behavior, and their negotiations. New York law requires that a lease for more than one year be in writing, indicate the amount of the rent, and be signed by both parties (General Obligations Law § 5-703).

You will need to weigh the pros and cons of your situation to decide if you are going to insist on a written lease. An unwritten lease is generally easier to break; whereas a written lease clearly binds you for the period of time indicated, but clearly sets out the agreement. In most cases, it is in your best interest to have a written lease.

A lease for less than one year may be oral. The problem with oral leases is that if you end up in court, the case will depend on whether you or the landlord is more believable. An oral lease for more than a year will not usually be upheld unless there is a written note or memorandum signed by the parties stating that they made an oral agreement but not including the terms (GOL § 5-701).

LENGTH OF THE LEASE OR AGREEMENT

Your agreement with your landlord may be for a set period of time (such as one year) or may be a month-to-month tenancy, where both you and your landlord have the option of ending your agreement each month. Month-to-month leases give you a lot of flexibility, but also some uncertainty, since you could be asked to leave with only one month's notice.

LEASE PROVISIONS

A complete lease should contain the following minimum provisions:

- ☛ Name of landlord
- ☛ Name of tenant
- ☛ Description of the premises being rented (usually by address, including unit number, if any)

☞ Amount of rent

☞ Starting date

☞ Granting clause (a clause saying that the premises "is hereby rented to tenant" or similar words)

☞ Length of the rental period (how long the tenant is renting it for)

☞ Signatures of both tenant and landlord

New York law requires that leases be clear and legible and be in print of at least eight points (THIS IS PRINTED IN EIGHT POINT TYPE). Leases also must include captions or subheadings that divide the lease into sections (CPLR § 4544; GOL § 5-702).

LEAD-BASED
PAINT DISCLOSURE

If your rental unit was built before 1978, your landlord is required to provide you with a notice that there may be lead-based paint in the unit as well as a pamphlet from the U.S. Government, *Protect Your Family From Lead in Your Home*. Lead-based paint has been proven to pose health hazards to children. If you receive one of these notices, read the pamphlet carefully and call the National Lead Information Clearinghouse (1-800-424-5323) if you have any questions.

In New York City, multiple dwellings rented to tenants with a child or children under age six must have peeling lead paint removed or covered [N.Y.C. Health Code § 173(14)]. Contact the New York City Department of Health if your unit has peeling lead paint and your landlord is not handling the problem. This is a hazard you should take seriously. See chapter 7 for more details about lead paint and other environmental hazards.

WINDOW GUARD
RIDER

In New York City, a Window Guard Rider must be attached to all leases. See chapter 7 for more information on window guards.

PROBLEMS WITH THE LEASE

Some lease provisions are void and unenforceable, even though both the landlord and tenant agreed to them in writing because of either state statutes or court decisions. If you are negotiating a lease and spot one of these clauses, you should not sign the lease until the clause is deleted. Even though the law currently holds such provisions to be void, you never know when the law could change or you could get a judge who has a unique interpretation of the law. If your current lease contains one of these clauses, relax because it is likely that if you ever had to go to court, the clause would be found to be void.

UNCONSCIONABILITY

If a judge decides a lease is extremely unfair, he or she may decide it is *unconscionable* (so unfair that it cannot be enforced in court) and choose not to enforce all of it or parts of it (RPL § 235-c). A provision requiring the tenant to pledge household furniture as security for payment of rent is considered unconscionable and is void (RPL § 231). When you negotiate a lease, if there is a clause in the lease that you find to be very unfair, you should try to get the landlord to delete it. However, if he or she refuses and you really want the unit, consider that if the landlord tries to enforce it, it may be declared void.

WAIVER OF LIABILITY OR RIGHTS

Certain waivers in the following types of clauses are void and you can recover damages if you have any losses caused by one of these clauses:

Warranty of Habitability. A clause waiving the Warranty of Habitability is void (RPL § 235-b). See chapter 7 for a full discussion of the Warranty of Habitability.

Security Deposit. A waiver of the requirement that the landlord hold your security deposit in an interest-bearing account is void (GOL § 7-103). See chapter 6 for more information about security deposits.

Negligence. A waiver of the landlord's liability for negligence (GOL § 5-321; RPL § 259-c). See chapter 8 for more information about landlord negligence.

Jury Trial. Waiver in a lease of the right to a jury trial is void (GOL § 5-321; RPL § 259-c).

Attorney's Fees. If the lease gives the landlord the right to collect attorney's fees from you in a lawsuit that the landlord wins, you are also entitled to collect attorney's fees if you win. This cannot be waived (RPL § 234).

Rent Regulation. A waiver by a rent-regulated tenant of rent regulation protections is void. See chapter 4 for more information on rent regulation.

Bankruptcy. A clause prohibiting a tenant from filing bankruptcy or from including the landlord as a creditor in the bankruptcy is void [11 USCA 365 (e) (1)] (Note: this is a federal law.).

Subletting. A clause waiving your right to sublet with the reasonable consent of the landlord is unenforceable (RPL § 226-b). See chapter 9 for a full discussion of subletting.

Tenants' Association. You cannot waive the right to form or join a tenant's association (RPL § 230). See chapter 11 for more information on tenant organizations.

How to Get out of a Lease

Once you sign a lease, you cannot change your mind. Unlike some types of contracts, there is no "three-day right of recision" with a lease. A lease is a legally binding document and cannot just be disregarded by either the landlord or the tenant. However, you may be able to reach an agreement with your landlord should you need to end the lease early. See chapter 12 for more information.

In certain instances, a lease may not be enforced by the courts, so you could ignore it with no penalties:

Fraud. If the landlord knew the truth and fraudulently misrepresented a material fact about the lease, then it may be unenforceable. *Barclay Arms, Inc. v. Barclay Arms Associates*, 74 N.Y.2d 644, 542 N.Y.S.2d 512

(1989). An example would be if the landlord told you that the lease said that the apartment came furnished and this was not true. A mistake by the landlord that is not intentional fraud does not count.

Impossibility. If the lease says the unit is rented for a certain purpose and it is impossible to use the unit for that purpose, then the lease may be unenforceable.

   📖 A landlord's failure to obtain a certificate of occupancy is not enough to void the lease. *Kosher Konveniences, Inc. v. Ferguson Realty Corp.*, 171 A.D.2d 650, N.Y.S.2d 131 (2d Dept., 1991).

Unavailability. The unit must be available on the first day of the period for which it is rented. If it is not, you may cancel the lease (RPL § 223-a).

OPTIONS

Some leases contain clauses that give you the right to renew the lease or to buy the property if it is ever put up for sale.

OPTION TO RENEW

An *option to renew* gives you the right to extend the lease at the end of the rental period.

An automatic renewal provision is unenforceable unless the landlord gives the tenant written notice fifteen to thirty days before the end of the lease term (GOL § 5-905).

   📖 The amount of rent for a renewal period cannot be left as "to be negotiated" and must be clearly stated. A formula or guideline that will be used to determine the amount is acceptable in place of a dollar amount. *Seiden v. Francis*, 184 A.D.2d 904, 585 N.Y.S.2d 562 (3d Dept., 1992); *Sunrise Mall Associates v. Import Alley of Sunrise Mall*, 211 A.D.2d 711, 621 N.Y.S.2d 662 (2d Dept., 1995).

   📖 Any changes to the terms of the lease in a renewal must be stated in the option clause. *Kay-Bee Toy and Hobby Shops v. Pyramid Company of Plattsburgh*, 126 A.D.2d 703, 511 N.Y.S.2d 308 (2d Dept., 1987).

OPTION TO PURCHASE   An *option to purchase* usually gives you the irrevocable right to purchase the property during or at the end of the lease. A *right of first refusal* requires the landlord to offer the property to you first if he ever decides to sell. Usually you will need to meet the terms of any offer the landlord receives from another party.

  📖 The terms of an option must be clear, definite, and a price or guideline must be given for determination. *Cobble Hill Nursing Home, Inc. v. Henry and Warren Corporation*, 548 N.Y.S.2d 920 (1989).

  📖 The lease and option to purchase are considered to be separate documents, and even if the lease is breached (broken), the option will still exist. *Curry Road Ltd. v. Rotterdam Realties Inc.*, 195 A.D.2d 780, 600 N.Y.S.2d 339 (3d Dept., 1994).

Your Security Deposit 6

Security deposits are not required under New York law (except in some rent regulated instances), but almost all landlords require them. A security deposit is usually equal to one month's rent and is paid when the lease is signed or an agreement is made. In some rent regulated units, the amount of the security deposit is regulated. Security deposits are taken by landlords as a kind of insurance against damage caused by the tenant. The cost of repairs made necessary by damage the tenant creates can be taken out of the security deposit by the landlord at the end of the rental. Any amount left over must be returned to the tenant.

If you do not have a written lease or if your lease does not contain a clause about the security deposit, be sure to get a receipt from the landlord for the deposit, clearly stating it to be a security deposit. You do not want there to be any question as to the amount when you ask to have it returned at the end of the tenancy.

Landlord's Method of Holding

If a property has six or more units, the security deposits must be kept in a separate interest bearing bank account (except in certain rent regulated situations) [GOL § 7-103(2)]. The landlord may not keep any of his or her own money in this account and (putting other money in the account is called *commingling*).

Many people (including landlords!) are not aware of these requirements. When you sign the lease, you can ask whether the landlord will be placing the deposit into an existing account or opening a new one. You can request that he or she do so. However, if your landlord does not, it is unlikely to be considered a major violation by a court.

    📖 If commingling occurs, courts have allowed the landlord to correct it without requiring an immediate return of the deposit to the tenant. *Purfield v. Kathrane*, 73 Misc.2d 194, 341 N.Y.2d 376 (Civ.Ct. N.Y. City, 1973).

    📖 Even though the tenant breached the lease, the landlord was still required to maintain the deposit in a separate account and not commingle funds. *In re Perfection Svcs. Press, Inc.*, 18 N.Y.2d 644, 273 N.Y.S.2d 71 (1966).

The State Attorney General has the power to sue landlords who fail to place security deposits in bank accounts. However, this may only occur when there has been "repeated or persistent fraud or illegality." *State v. Wolowitz*, 96 A.D.2d 47, 468 N.Y.S.2d 131 (2d Dept., 1983). If your landlord fails to put your deposit in the bank, the Attorney General probably will not help you, but if your landlord does this with all the tenants in a one hundred unit building, there may be assistance available.

In rent regulated units, the Department of Housing and Community Renewal can provide assistance with problems with security deposits (see chapter 4 for more information).

NOTICE

When your landlord deposits your security deposit in a bank account, he or she must notify you in writing as to the name and location of the bank and the amount deposited [GOL § 7-103(2)].

    When a landlord wrote "For Deposit Only" on the back of the tenant's check it was not considered to be sufficient notice. *LeRoy v. Sayers*, 217 A.D.2d 63, 635 N.Y.S.2d 217 (1st Dept., 1995).

    Failure by a landlord to give the tenant notice of the name and location of the bank was found to be inconsequential and did not entitle the tenant to a return of the deposit. *Purfield v. Kathrane*, 73 Misc.2d 194, 341 N.Y.S.2d 376 (Civ. Ct. N.Y. City, 1973).

INTEREST

As explained earlier, when a property has six or more units, the landlord must keep any security deposits in an interest-bearing account. The account must earn interest at the prevailing rate at the time. The interest that accrues to your deposit belongs to you and must be paid to you at the end of the tenancy, or annually if you so request. Your landlord may keep one percent of the security deposit as an annual administrative fee.

If your landlord did not keep the deposit in an interest-bearing account, technically, you are still owed the interest it would have earned. However, if he refuses, it would likely be more trouble than it is worth to try to force him to pay you. However, you might try contacting your local Attorney General's office for assistance.

GETTING YOUR DEPOSIT BACK

If you leave the rental unit in acceptable condition when you move out and do not owe back rent, the landlord is required to refund the deposit. *Kaplan v. Shaffer*, 112 A.D.2d 369, 491 N.Y.S. 821 (2d Dept., 1985). The landlord may deduct unpaid rent and damage from the deposit. *Rivertower Associates v. Chalfen*, 153 A.D.2d 196, 549 N.Y.S.2d 719 (1st Dept., 1990).

You are not responsible for paying for damage caused by normal wear and tear; however, it can be difficult to define what that includes. A need for painting after five years would be normal wear and tear. A hole in the wall would not be. If there is any damage to your unit, you should photograph it so that you can prove exactly what damage occurred. If you broke a window, you will be responsible for it; but you do not want to be held responsible for replacing the entire window sill and frame.

Before leaving, go through the unit with the landlord and fill out the inspection checklist (form 1 in this book) so that you and your landlord are in agreement as to whether there were any damages caused by you. If you filled one out when you began your lease, be sure to point out the items which were damaged when you moved into the unit.

If repairs are necessary, request that the landlord provide you with receipts and invoices to verify the amount spent. If the landlord intends to do the repairs himself or herself, request a record of them. If you get an estimate of the cost of a repair, that may protect you against the landlord overcharging you. If you believe the prices are inflated, call the person who did the work and ask what was charged. Call and get estimates from other companies to compare the cost. You can sue your landlord in small claims court if you are overcharged for repairs.

Some leases have clauses that allow the landlord to keep part of the deposit if the tenant leaves before the lease expires. These clauses have been upheld when they are found to be compensation for the landlord's income loss, but not when they are a way to penalize the tenant.

Sometimes landlords and tenants agree to use the security deposit as payment for the last month's rent if there are no damages to be paid. This has been permitted by the courts and relieves the tenant of the responsibility for paying the final month's rent. *Walker v. 18th Street Holding Corp.*, 267 A.D.2d 141, 44 N.Y.S.2d 866 (1st Dept., 1943).

When you move out, send your landlord a letter requesting the return of your security deposit within thirty days of the day you leave. Be sure to give the address to which it should be sent. If you did an inspection together before leaving, gently remind him or her that there was no damage to the unit and you would like your deposit back in the full amount. If the landlord fails to return it, you need to bring a small claims case to get it back. Keep the original inspection sheet and your security deposit receipt to use as evidence.

SPECIAL RULES

RENEWALS

When a lease is renewed, the landlord will keep the security deposit as the deposit for the new lease. If the rent increases, an additional security deposit may be required.

SALE OF THE PREMISES

If the property is sold during the tenancy, the security deposit and an accounting must be given to the new owner within five days of the sale. The tenant must be notified of the sale and transfer of deposits in writing by certified or registered mail. The notice given to the tenant must include the new owner's name and address. Failure to do this is a misdemeanor (GOL § 7-105). In rent controlled or rent stabilized buildings, and in buildings where at least six tenants have a written lease, the new owner is responsible to you for your security deposit even if the seller never transferred it.

PREPAID RENT

If you prepay rent, such as paying the last month at the beginning of the term, the advance rent must be held by the landlord in a separate interest-bearing account and you are entitled to the interest.

.

MAINTENANCE AND REPAIRS 7

LANDLORD'S RESPONSIBILITIES FOR MAINTENANCE AND REPAIRS

The Multiple Dwelling Law, which applies to buildings of three or more units in cities with a population of 325,000 or more, and the Multiple Residence Law, which governs cities with populations under 325,000 as well as all towns and villages, set out maintenance guidelines that landlords must follow, including garbage removal, locks and keys, clean and safe conditions in common areas, extermination of vermin, heat, and hot and cold running water (MDL 78, 80, MRL 174). Other requirements which are found in court cases, as well as other statutes and regulations are as follows (MDL cites are for cities of 325,000 or more and MRL cites are for smaller cities; unless otherwise indicated, all other provisions are applicable to all size cities):

☞ Self-closing and self-locking doors must be installed in buildings built prior to 1968 if requested by the majority of tenants. Without a request by the tenants, minimal precautions must be taken. Doors must be kept locked at all times unless there is an attendant (MDL § 50-a).

☞ Landlord must maintain the premises free of any known defects or any that would be reasonably known (MDL 78, RPL 235-b).

☞ Landlord must comply with all health, housing and building codes. Check with your local health or building inspector.

☞ Two way intercoms with buzzers must be installed and maintained in buildings built after 1968 that have eight or more units (MDL 50-a).

☞ Generally, there is no requirement for a landlord to remove snow or ice from sidewalks, unless it is bumpy or rough. *Greenstein v. Springfield Development Corp.*, 22 Misc.2d 740, 204 N.Y.S.2d 518 (Civ.Ct., New York County, 1960). However, in New York City, snow must be removed no more than four hours after snow stops falling (N.Y.C. Admin. Code §§ 16-123, 19-152).

☞ Smoke detectors must be installed and maintained in each unit (MDL §§ 68, 15, MRL § 15). In New York City, one smoke detector must be installed near each room used for sleeping. The tenant can be charged up to $10 for each smoke detector. If the smoke detector needs repair or replacement in the first year of use, the landlord must repair or replace it (N.Y.C. Admin. Code 27-2045, 27-2046).

☞ Landlords must provide exterior lighting above the front entrance of the building only in cities with populations of 325,000 or more (MDL 35). Interior lighting must be provided in the vestibule, halls, and stairs (MDL 37).

☞ Lead paint must be removed or covered in New York City (N.Y.C. Admin Code 27-2023h1).

☞ There are restrictions on the removal and handling of asbestos (12 NYCRR § 56-1.7).

☞ In New York City, window guards (metal bars on windows to prevent falls) must be installed in hallway windows and in units with children age ten and younger. They also must be installed upon the request of any tenant. Windows accessing fire escapes are excluded. Tenants must be given annual notice of their right to window guards and a lease rider must be provided. Rent control and rent stabilized tenants may be charged for the guards. (N.Y.C. Admin. Code 17-123, N.Y.C. Health Code § 131.15).

☞ In New York City, apartments must be painted at least every three years (sooner if the lease requires) unless the owner never provided the service. See DHCR fact sheet #28.

☞ U.S. Postal regulations require that buildings with three or more units have secure mailboxes for each unit unless management distributes the mail to the tenants. The mailboxes must be kept in good repair.

☞ Elevators must have mirrors that allow people to see who is on the elevator before entering it (MDL 51-b, N.Y.C. Admin. Code 27-2042).

☞ Peepholes are required in all units (MDL 51-c) and door chains are required in New York City (N.Y.C. Admin. Code 27-2043).

☞ In New York City, between October 1 and May 31, apartments must be heated to at least sixty-eight degrees between 6 A.M. and 10 P.M. if the outside temperature falls below fifty-five degrees; and must be heated to at least fifty-five degrees between 10 P.M. and 6 A.M. if the outside temperature falls below forty degrees (MDL 79).

☞ Electrical, plumbing, sanitary, heating, and ventilating systems and appliances installed by landlords must be maintained in safe and working order (MDL 78, 80, MRL 174).

SINGLE FAMILY HOMES AND DUPLEXES

There are no requirements for maintenance for single family homes and duplexes; however, the landlord must comply with all local ordinances and meet the warranty of habitability discussed below.

WARRANTY OF HABITABILITY

The *warranty of habitability* is a guarantee every tenant receives from his or her landlord that the premises being rented is in safe and habitable condition and will be kept in that condition during the rental period.

This warranty is not actually written in your lease but it was made an unwritten part of every residential lease by state law. RPL 235-b states that every lease contains an implied warranty of habitability, whether or not it is written in the lease, that cannot be waived by the tenant. The warranty applies to each unit as well as all common areas. The warranty of habitability requires:

☛ That the premises be fit for human habitation. The unit must have essential services and features that a tenant would reasonably expect it to have. This not only includes heat and water but also services such as garbage collection, working smoke detectors, working elevators, and that it is structurally sound.

☛ That the premises be fit for the uses reasonably intended by the parties (for a residential apartment, this means that it is fit to live in)

☛ That the tenant not be subjected to conditions that are dangerous, hazardous, or detrimental to life, health, or safety

When something exists or happens that violates these requirements, it is called a *breach*. Breaches are often found by courts when there is an ongoing pattern of defects (a legal word for problems) or one very substantial defect. For example, a breach was found when a tenant was without hot water for eighteen consecutive days. *Romanov v. Heller*, 121 Misc.2d 469, N.Y.S.2d 876 (Civ.Ct., New York County, 1983). A breach did not occur when a tenant was without hot water for seven nonconsecutive days in one month. *Toomer v. Higgins*, 161 A.D.2d 347, 554 N.Y.S.2d 921 (1st Dept., 1990).

If a breach of the warranty is caused by something the tenant does, the landlord is not responsible (for example, if you break a window and it snows into your apartment, the landlord has not breached the warranty and is not responsible for the damage). Landlords are also not responsible for defects caused by strikes or other labor disputes.

If the warranty is breached, the tenant can sue and recover an amount equal to the rent minus the reasonable rent for the unit with the defect; for example: if your apartment has no heat for a month, you can sue the landlord for an amount equal to your rent (X) minus what the rent would be for an apartment with no heat (Y): X-Y= the amount for which you can sue. If a landlord fails to fix a defect that breaches the warranty, the tenant can do the repair himself or hire someone to do it and recover the cost of the repair from the landlord. However, landlords are not required to rebuild or make huge repairs from things such as fires, tornadoes, etc. If damage such as this occurs, the tenant has the option to terminate (or end) the lease without penalty. *Smith v. Kerr,* 108 N.Y. 31 (1888). If a breach by the landlord is malicious or intended, the tenant can recover punitive damages.

The following are cases that have examined certain types of breaches.

📖 Failure to comply with local housing codes can constitute a breach. *Park West Management Corp. v. Mitchell,* 47 N.Y.2d 316 (1979).

📖 Failure to maintain common areas. *Solow v. Wellner,* 154 Misc.2d 737, 595 N.Y.S.2d 619 (1st Dept., 1992)

📖 Failure to provide garbage and maintenance services. *Park West Management Corp. v. Mitchell,* 47 N.Y.2d 316, 418 N.Y.S.2d 310 (1979)

📖 Lack of heat and hot water. *Park West Management Corp. v. Mitchell,* 47 N.Y.2d 316, 418 N.Y.S.2d 310 (1979)

📖 Noise. *Justice Court Mutual Housing Cooperative, Inc. v. Sandow,* 50 Misc.2d 541, 270 N.Y.S.2d 829 (Sup.Ct., Queens County, 1966)

📖 Defective plumbing lines and fixtures. *Spatz v. Axelrod Management Co., Inc.,* 165 Misc.2d 759, 630 N.Y.S.2d 461 (City Ct., Yonkers, 1995)

📖 Lack of security. *Carp v. Marcus,* 112 A.D.2d 546, 491 N.Y.S.2d 484 (3d Dept., 1985)

📖 Vermin. *Town of Islip Community Development Agency v. Mulligan,* 130 Misc.2d 279, 496 N.Y.S.2d 195 (Dist.Ct., Suffolk County, 1985)

📖 Odor. *Keklass v. Saddy,* 88 Misc.2d 1042, 389 N.Y.S.2d 756 (Dist.Ct., 1974)

📖 Lack of building services. *111 East 88th Partners v. Simon,* 106 Misc.2d 693 (1980)

📖 Lack of ventilation. *Department of Housing Preservation and Development of the City of New York v. Sartor*, 109 A.D.2d 665 (1985)

📖 Lack of air conditioning. *Whitehouse Estates, Inc. v. Thomson*, 87 Misc.2d 813 (1976).

If the warranty of habitability is breached and you have to leave the premises, you can sue the landlord for the costs you incur, such as moving expenses and rent for a temporary place to live while repairs are being made. If your landlord suspends your lease during this period, and you do not pay him rent while repairs are being made, you will only be able to obtain the difference between the rent on your unit and the temporary rent, if it is higher.

LEAD

As discussed in chapter 5, your landlord is required to notify you if lead paint is present in your building. If your landlord does not notify you, he or she will be liable for any injury caused to you by the lead. In New York City, landlords are required to remove or cover the lead paint. New York State public health laws prohibit the application of lead paint on porches and indoor walls and surfaces. The law requires that tenants be notified about lead paint, if it is present, as well what can be done about it. Lead was a component that was commonly used in paint before its dangers were known. It is dangerous because it can cause lead poisoning which is particularly harmful to children because it can interfere with normal development. Do not assume that you and your children are safe just because the paint in your unit is not peeling. Lead dust particles can enter the air and be inhaled or get on children's hands and into their mouths. There is also the danger of lead poisoning in water from lead pipes and lead solder in the pipes.

Blood tests for lead poisoning are now routine for children who live in older buildings. Be sure to tell your pediatrician if you have been notified about lead in your building so that the proper precautions can be taken.

You can have special x-ray tests done to determine if, in fact, there is lead paint present in your unit. If you would like more information about the dangers of lead poisoning, contact the National Lead Information Center at 1-800-424-LEAD or http://www.nsc.org/ehc/lead.htm. The United States Department of Housing and Urban Development has a free pamphlet you can obtain, called *Guidelines for the Evaluation and Control of Lead-Based Paint Hazards in Housing*. Look in the government section of your phone book for your local HUD office.

CARBON MONOXIDE

Carbon monoxide is an invisible and odorless gas created by fuel burning engines, such as furnaces, automobiles, and gas appliances. The danger occurs when these engines are not properly vented or when something plugs the vent. Carbon monoxide is very deadly and kills quickly because victims are often unaware they are breathing it. Ask your landlord to install a carbon monoxide detector or install one yourself with his or her permission.

If you suspect carbon monoxide is present, or if your alarm goes off, get out of the building immediately and call 911. If the problem was caused by an appliance or furnace under the landlord's control, he is responsible for fixing the problem. If your own gas stove causes the problem, you would be responsible for fixing it.

Your local gas company can provide you with more information about the dangers of carbon monoxide.

ASBESTOS

Asbestos is a substance that was used in insulation, tiles, and other building materials before the danger of the substance was understood. If you live in a building built before 1981, the landlord must run tests prior to performing any work on the building, including even painting the walls. Asbestos, once it is airborne, can cause lung cancer. Any work that is done in an area that contains asbestos must be performed in a manner that encapsulates the fibers and keeps them from getting into the air.

If you live in a building that contains asbestos, don't panic. Unless the asbestos is breaking down and entering the air, there is no great danger. The landlord is not required to take any action if the asbestos is intact. If you suspect that the asbestos is breaking down and entering the air, get out and let your landlord know immediately. He or she is obligated to solve the problem.

Should work be done on asbestos areas in your building, you need to examine your risk. If work is being done two floors below in a hallway you never enter and the area is encapsulated so no fibers can escape, you are probably okay. If work is being done inside the ceiling of your unit, you might want to talk to the landlord about an Agreement Suspending Lease (form 29), which allows you to move out and put your lease on hold until the work is done and the danger has passed.

For more information about asbestos, contact the *Occupational Safety and Health Administration (OSHA)* at 202-219-8148 or http://www.osha.gov. They have free software available called the *OSHA Asbestos Adviser*.

RADON

Radon is a radioactive gas that is naturally occurring in areas where there is uranium soil or rock. Radon is not a problem unless it enters a building with poor ventilation. It can become trapped inside buildings that lack appropriate ventilation or are too tightly insulated. In these situations, radon can cause lung cancer. The risk is even higher if you smoke and live in a building with radon.

You can purchase a radon test kit, or ask your landlord to do so. If your tests find evidence of radon, show them to your landlord and request that he or she seal cracks in the foundation and install proper ventilation. In the meantime, you need to leave windows open to ensure that the radon can escape. If the levels are high, you need to move.

Contact the United States Environmental Protection Agency Radon Hotline at 1-800-767-7236 for more information. You can obtain a *Consumer's Guide to Radon Reduction* booklet for free from them.

UTILITIES

It is a class A misdemeanor for your landlord to terminate your utilities or disconnect pipes or wires. However, there are problems with utilities that can arise when you rent a unit.

SHARED METERS

Shared utility meters (that measure usage from more than one unit or one unit plus common areas) are illegal. If you have a shared meter, then your landlord is responsible for all charges on the meter. The landlord must switch the meter to his or her name or rewire/repipe to eliminate this problem from within the building. Contact your utility provider for assistance with this problem. You can also contact the New York Attorney General's office for help.

LANDLORD'S
FAILURE TO PAY

If the meter is in the landlord's name and he or she fails to pay the bill., you may find your utility being shut off. The utility company must give you written notice at least fifteen days before it will be turned off. Should the utility be turned off, you or other tenants can get it turned back on by paying the current charges (not including back charges) and deducting it from your rent. Do not switch the utility to your name if it is in your landlord's name because this will make you responsible for future bills.

There are many avenues you can pursue for assistance with utility problems. Always start with the utility company itself. The New York State Attorney General's office can be of assistance to you as well. In New York City, you could contact the New York City Heatline, the Central

Complaints Division of the New York City Department of Housing Preservation and Development or the New York City Bureau of Electrical Control. The Community Training and Resource Center in NEw York City (212-964-7200) can also be of help. Financial assistance with utility bills can be obtained from your local Social Services Department. A free booklet called *A Tenant's Guide to Getting and Keeping Gas and Electricity Service* can be obtained from Brooklyn Legal Services, 105 Court Street, Brooklyn, NY 11201 or online at http://www.tenantnet.com.

GETTING THINGS FIXED

Now that you have a better understanding of what maintenance your landlord is required to do, the next step is figuring out how to get it done! Your first step should always be to contact the landlord or building manager or superintendent if there is a problem. Do not be too quick to report your landlord for violations. Give your landlord a chance to make the repair. If he or she does not get the repair done in a timely manner, you should next check with your tenants' association (if your building has one). Your association can present your complaint to the landlord and assist you in making sure your complaint is taken seriously.

Send your landlord a letter (form 34) specifically listing the repairs that are needed and the dates you verbally discussed this. Explain the seriousness of the problem and the ways it has inconvenienced you and reduced the value of the unit. If you need a major repair, such as a complete replacement of all plumbing in your unit, explain to the landlord that the unit will not be habitable during the repair and complete an Agreement Suspending Lease (form 29) which will allow you to move out and stop paying rent unit the repair is made.

If you are getting nowhere with your landlord after trying these methods, or if your problem is an emergency and you have not received an immediate response from the landlord or building manager, you need to contact local agencies.

However, you need to think about your situation before taking steps that will involve such agencies. If you are behind on the rent or have breached the lease in some way, the landlord may just decide to evict you if you start making waves. Retaliatory eviction is illegal, but if you are not paying rent or have breached the lease, the landlord can evict you for those reasons. However, if there is a dangerous or uninhabitable condition present, you need to make sure it will be fixed, regardless of your situation.

If you are rent controlled or rent stabilized, your first call should be to the DHCR. If you have a problem that involves window guards or a situation that impacts your health, call the New York City Health Department or the health department in your county or city. For a problem like a gas leak or electrical danger, call the utility responsible. For problems that you believe are violations of your local building code, contact the local building inspector. In New York City, you should call the New York City Department of Housing Preservation and Development (HPD) at 212-960-4800. You could also call the New York City Building Department or the New York City Bureau of Electrical Control. You should only call these agencies when a real problem exists. If you call every time you are angry with your landlord, soon these agencies will come to know you and will not give your complaint priority.

If you have a serious problem in your building and nobody is listening to you, call a local news channel and ask to speak to their community complaints reporter. Many stations have a reporter who investigates problems and complaints in the area. Your city government may have a complaint line (check in the government pages of your phone book or call city hall and ask). If you are stumped about who to call, you can also call the New York General Services number (in the government pages of the phone book). This office can direct you to the appropriate agency. New York State also has a Department of Public Service which can be helpful. They have a consumer complaint line for utility problems (1-800-342-3377) and an emergency number (1-800-342-3355). If you are a senior citizen, your city or county may have a senior services department, sometimes also called an Office for the Aging.

TENANTS' RESPONSIBILITIES FOR MAINTENANCE

Tenants' duties are not set out in any statute and are usually specified in the lease. However, courts have found that tenants have a duty to make any repairs necessary to prevent further damage. For example, if your window breaks through no fault of your own, you should cover it to prevent water damage until the landlord can repair it. *Starpoli v. Starpoli*, 180 A.D.2d 727, 580 N.Y.S.2d 369 (2d Dept., 1992). The tenant who fails to do so may be liable for damage resulting from the failure to make a temporary repair (in the window example, if you don't cover it and it rains in and ruins the carpet, you would be responsible for replacing the carpet). The cost of such emergency repairs can be deducted from your rent. As with all repairs you make, keep your receipts! If you cause the original damage though, you are responsible for the cost of the repair.

A tenant is also expected to keep the premises in a reasonably safe condition. *Zito v. 241 Church Street Corp.*, 223 A.D.2d 353, 636 N.Y.S.2d 40 (1st Dept., 1996). This responsibility may make the tenant liable for a failure to notify the landlord of a condition that requires a repair (failing to tell the landlord about the broken window).

A tenant may install his or her own lock in addition to the landlord's locks, but it may not be more than three inches in circumference and the landlord must be provided with a key upon request (MDL 51-c).

Tenants are entitled to maintain a lobby attendant when one provided by the landlord is not on duty (MDL 50-c).

Tenants may contract for heating oil delivery if the landlord fails to supply sufficient fuel and may deduct the cost of the oil from the rent (MDL 302-c, MRL 305-c).

If damage results from the landlord's negligence and then you add to the damage yourself, you will be partly responsible for the result. For example, if the landlord doesn't repair a roof that is leaking and then you pull down part of the ceiling because you are tired of looking at the water stains, you are going to have to pay for a portion of the repairs.

REPAIRS BY TENANTS

If your landlord fails to make a necessary repair, even if you made a written request and he still has not done so, you may wish to make the repair and deduct its cost from your next rent payment. If you decide to do this, you would be wise to first send the landlord a letter stating that if the repair is not done by a certain date, you will make the repair and deduct it from your rent. However, should the landlord decide to sue you for failing to pay the full rent, you will need to be able to show the court evidence of the damage, the actual cost of the repair and the your notice to the landlord. If the judge disagrees with you or feels that the repair could have waited, you may be liable to the landlord.

IMPROVEMENTS BY TENANTS

It is often tempting to do things to improve your apartment. Generally, you need the landlord's permission to make any alterations to the premises. Any improvements you make become the property of the landlord. If you install a new faucet, it becomes part of the apartment and you cannot remove it and take it with you when you leave.

This rule applies to things that create structural changes. This would include things like the addition of shelves, light fixtures, carpeting, shower doors, etc. Something like a throw rug or hanging a painting are not considered structural changes. If there are improvements you want to make, you may want to offer to do the work if the landlord will buy the materials. Many tenants work out arrangements where the landlord pays for supplies and the tenant does the labor. This type of arrangement benefits both landlord and tenant.

For example, if the paint has some wear and tear but the landlord is not ready to pay for a repainting, you may be able to get the landlord to pay for the paint if you do the work. However, be sure the color is agreeable to the landlord. If you paint it a color few other tenants would like (red, purple, black, etc.) the cost of repainting may be deducted from your security deposit!

If you are able to reach this type of agreement with the landlord, make sure that you get the agreement in writing. Use the Agreement for Repairs by Tenant (form 30). Lofts are an exception to this. See Chapter 4 for more details.

IMPROVEMENTS FOR DISABLED ACCESS

If you are disabled, you can make certain improvements to the unit to make it more accessible for your personal use, as long as the changes will not make it unusable or a nuisance for future tenants or if you agree to put the unit back in its original condition before you move. If your landlord is resistant to the changes you are proposing, get a letter from your doctor stating why these changes are necessary for you to be able to function.

CABLE TELEVISION AND SATELLITE DISHES

If your unit is not wired for cable, you cannot install it without your landlord's permission because it is an alteration to the premises. If you have one cable company and want to switch to another, you cannot do so if it means the building will need to be rewired. Be aware that many cable companies provide cash incentives to landlords in order to wire a building. If you would like to get cable or to switch companies, find out what the company you are interested in can offer your landlord and then present this information to your landlord.

Satellite dishes are a different situation. The FCC has issued regulations that prohibit a landlord from interfering with a tenant's access to the airways. Because satellite TV travels over the airwaves, your landlord cannot prohibit you from installing a dish, as long as you do so on the unit you are renting and not on any public or common areas. You could install a dish on your balcony or window sill, but not on the front lawn of the building or on top of the common tenant garage.

Injuries on the Premises 8

Some people believe that any kind of injury that occurs on a rental property is the responsibility of the landlord, but this is not always the case. A tenant should be aware of the laws that spell out who is responsible for an injury and why.

Landlords' Liability

Liability is a word used by lawyers to mean that someone is responsible for something bad that happens to another person. If Bob punches Juan in the face and hurts him, Bob is liable for Juan's injury. Landlords are liable for injuries or damages caused by defects on the premises (things that are broken or unsafe) *only* when the landlord had a legal duty to make repairs and didn't. Such a duty may arise under the MDL, MRL, other laws and regulations, the Warranty of Habitability, or when the landlord was negligent.

NEGLIGENCE — Negligence is a complicated legal theory and occurs when a landlord violates a duty to keep the premises in a reasonably safe condition. The legal definition, broken into its main parts is as follows:

- ☞ a failure to exercise, or the breach of
- ☞ the degree of care

☞ that would be exercised by a reasonably prudent person

☞ under the circumstances

☞ which causes injury or damage

☞ that was reasonably foreseeable.

What this boils down to is that a landlord is liable for damage or injury caused by a defect that any reasonable person would know could cause damage or injury. This includes defects of which a landlord is unaware, but should know.

AREAS NOT UNDER THE LANDLORD'S CONTROL

A landlord is liable for injury or damage that occurs in areas not under his or her control (such as the inside of a tenant's unit) as follows:

☞ Where the landlord is negligent

☞ Where a danger exists that is, or should be, known to the landlord

☞ Where there is a defect in construction

☞ Where the condition of the premises violates a law or regulation

☞ Where the landlord is required under the lease to make repairs

☞ Where the landlord does or begins repairs

☞ Where the premises is a nuisance or could become one under the expected use of the premises

CASES WHERE THE LANDLORD WAS NOT LIABLE

These are examples of cases where a landlord was held not liable:

📖 Landlord was not liable when a tenant was injured after knocking boiling water off a hot plate. This injury was not a foreseeable result of not providing a stove. *Wells v. Finnegan*, 177 A.D.2d 893, 576 N.Y.S.2d 653 (3d Dept., 1991).

📖 Landlord who failed to provide adequate heat was not liable when a child fell into the bathtub that the tenant had filled with hot water to give off heat. This injury was not a foreseeable result of not providing heat. *Lam v. Neptune Assoc.*, 203 A.D.2d 334, 610 N.Y.S.2d 538 (2d Dept., 1994).

📖 Landlord was not liable when a child fell off a cliff on the property because there is no duty to fix natural, open conditions, even

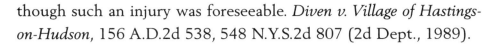

though such an injury was foreseeable. *Diven v. Village of Hastings-on-Hudson*, 156 A.D.2d 538, 548 N.Y.S.2d 807 (2d Dept., 1989).

📖 Landlord was not liable for injury when the lease made the tenant responsible for all repairs. Landlord did not reserve any control over the premises and thus the tenant was liable for the injury. *Fresina v. Nebush*, 209 A.D.2d 1004, 619 N.Y.S.2d 447 (4th Dept., 1994).

CASES WHERE LANDLORD WAS FOUND LIABLE

These are cases where a landlord was found to be liable:

📖 Landlord was liable when a child was injured falling on exposed metal from a broken window screen that the landlord should have repaired. *Contento v. Albany Medical Center Hospital*, 57 A.D.2d 691, 394 N.Y.S.2d 74 (3d Dept., 1977).

📖 Landlord was liable for a malfunctioning elevator, despite a contract for maintenance with an elevator repair company. The landlord's duty to keep the premises safe is nondelegable, meaning it can't be put off on someone else. *Camaj v. East 52nd Partners*, 215 A.D.2d 150, 626 N.Y.S.2d 110 (1st Dept., 1995).

📖 Landlord who had provided for a lobby attendant was liable for assault when the attendant was absent. When a landlord voluntarily provides a service, even if there is no obligation to do so, the tenant may rely on that service and hold the landlord liable if the service is discontinued. *Nallan v. Helmsley-Spear, Inc.*, 50 N.Y.2d 507, 429 N.Y.S.2d 606 (1980).

📖 Landlords can be liable to third party persons who are patrons or guests of the tenant because their presence is foreseeable. *Fitzsimmons v. State*, 34 N.Y.2d 739, 357 N.Y.S.2d 498 (1974).

WARRANTY OF HABITABILITY

Landlords are liable for injury or damage caused when the warranty of habitability is violated. The requirements of the warranty of habitability are explained in detail in chapter 7.

SEEKING COMPENSATION FOR YOUR INJURIES OR DAMAGES

If your landlord is responsible for damage to your property, you can bring a claim in your local housing court (see chapter 13 for more information). If you are injured due to your landlord's negligence or failure to make repairs, you can sue for your physical and emotional pain and suffering, your medical and psychiatric expenses, missed work, and permanent disabilities caused by the injury. Even if you are partially at fault for the injury (if you knew the landlord removed floorboards and covered the open area with a tarp and you stepped on it anyhow), you can still be compensated for the portion of your injuries and expenses that can be attributed to the landlord. Contact your local bar association for a referral to a good negligence lawyer. Remember, your landlord carries insurance to pay for these types of claims, so if you have been injured, you should not be afraid to make a claim.

In New York, a landlord can be held liable for criminal acts against a tenant if the landlord could have or should have foreseen a risk of harm. Past identical incidents are not necessary. The landlord, based upon all of the circumstances, must have had reason to anticipate the general type of crime, not its exact details.

    📖 Landlord was liable for the rape of a tenant because other rapes occurred in other buildings of a housing project, even though none had occurred in that building. *Jacqueline S. v. The City of New York*, 81 N.Y.2d 288, 598 N.Y.S.2d 160 (1993).

    📖 Landlord who failed to provide locks on outer doors was liable for a break-in. *Dawson v. New York City Housing Authority*, 203 A.D.2d 55, 610 N.Y.S.2d 28 (1st Dept., 1994).

    📖 When there was no prior evidence of criminal activity on the premises, a landlord was not liable for the stabbing of a tenant by an ex-lover. *Camacho v. Edelman*, 176 A.D.2d 453, 574 N.Y.S.2d 356 (1st Dept., 1991).

    📖 Landlord was not liable for injuries caused by arson when landlord was unaware the premises was being used for criminal activities or that there had been any threats of violence. *Rodriguez v. Mohr*, 174 A.D.2d 382, 571 N.Y.S.2d 221 (1st Dept., 1991).

Landlord Liability for Actions by Tenants

A landlord was liable to a tenant when a neighbor's (who was also a tenant) repeatedly overflowing sink (caused by the neighbor) flooded the first tenant's apartment and caused damage to personal belongings. The court found that the landlord should have evicted the tenant with the sink when the overflowing continued to happen and held the landlord liable for the damage caused. *Benitez v. Restifo*, N.Y.L.J. 3/27/96 p. 36, col. 3. City Ct., Westchester County, 1996.

Strict Liability

Landlords can also be held liable for things that are not their fault, this is called *strict liability*. It is not necessary that the landlord knew or should have known about the defect, nor is it necessary that the harm was foreseeable. The state legislature and the U.S. Congress have passed laws making landlords responsible for damage or injury caused by the following items:

- Improper operation of sprinklers and other fire prevention equipment (MRL 15, 52, 54, 58, 61; MDL 68, 284).

- Injuries to construction workers while they are working on the premises (Labor Law 240).

- Leakage of home heating oil and other petroleum products, including underground gas storage tanks on the premises. *Leone v. Leewood Service Station, Inc.*, 212 A.D.2d 669, 624 N.Y.S.2d 610 (2d Dept., 1995); *State v. N.Y.Cent. Mut. Fire Ins. Co.*, 147 A.D.2d 77, 542 N.Y.S.2d 402 (3d Dept., 1989).

- Injury or death of fire fighter or police officer in the line of duty on the premises as a result of violation of any statute or ordinance which causes the death or injury (GOL 11-106, GML 205-a, 205-e2).

☞ Failure to provide window guards in New York City (N.Y.C. Admin. Code 17-123).

☞ Environmental damage in violation of :

- Comprehensive Environmental Response, Compensation and Liability Act of 1980 (42 USCA 9607)

- Solid Waste Disposal Act (42 USCA 6973)

- Air Pollution Prevention and Control Act (42 USCA 7401)

- Water Pollution Control Act (33 USCA 1251)

TENANTS' LIABILITY

Tenants can also be liable for damage and injury caused by their own negligence. Reread the description of negligence at the beginning of this chapter. Basically, as a tenant, you want to keep your apartment free of problems that any reasonable person can see could cause injury. For example, you shouldn't leave eggs you dropped on the floor by your door, because someone could slip. You shouldn't let your bathtub overflow because it will damage the apartment and its contents below you. Essentially, you just need to use common sense as a tenant. You should report any needed repairs to the landlord because ignoring them could be negligence. Tenants can be held liable by their landlord, other tenants, or strangers.

LIABILITY FOR
WASTE

As a tenant, you can be held liable for damage you cause to the apartment and can be sued for the cost of repairing the damage. When you allow damage to happen, it is called *waste*. Waste can happen if you negligently or intentionally cause damage [*Granger University Ave. Corp. v. First State Ins. Co.*, 99 A.D.2d 1022, 473 N.Y.S.2d 813 (1st Dept., 1984)]. Waste has also been found when a tenant failed to board up a window and water damage resulted [*Staropoli v. Staropoli*, 180 A.D.2d 727, 580 N.Y.S.2d 369 (2d Dept., 1992)]. When a tenant makes alterations to the apartment without permission, it is another kind of waste [*Carter v. Helmsley-Spear Inc.*, 861 F.Supp. 303 (S.D.N.Y., 1994)]. Even though these alterations may seem beneficial to the landlord, they are an alteration to his property without permission.

PROTECTION
FROM LIABILITY

You should think of liability as a serious threat. If you ever were held liable, you could owe thousands or even millions of dollars. Take all necessary steps to be sure that your living environment is free of dangerous conditions. To protect yourself, consider purchasing a renter's insurance policy. This type of policy will not only insure your belongings (against theft, weather damage, etc.), but will also provide you with protection if you are ever sued for negligence occurring in your apartment. The cost is usually reasonable and well worth the protection.

CHANGES DURING THE LEASE PERIOD 9

ASSIGNMENTS

An *assignment* occurs when a tenant transfers all of his or her interest in a lease to someone else who takes over as the tenant. This new person becomes the new tenant and is responsible for rent and all the other obligations of the tenancy. The new tenant pays rent directly to the landlord and otherwise deals directly with the landlord; thus, the original tenant is no longer involved.

Unless the lease specifies otherwise, a tenant may not assign a lease without prior written consent from the landlord. The landlord may not withhold consent without cause (a good reason) [RPL 226-b(1)]. Use form 33 to formalize an assignment of a lease.

SUBLEASES

A *sublease* occurs when a tenant rents the apartment to a third person. The original tenant becomes a *sublessor* (which is like a landlord) and the third person becomes a *sublessee* (tenant). The sublessor still remains responsible to the landlord for rent and is still considered to be the tenant. The sublessee may pay rent to the sublessor (who then pays the rent to the landlord), or the sublessee may pay the landlord directly.

If the sublessee does not pay rent, the landlord can sue the sublessor for the money. *Gillette Bros. V. Aristocrat Restaurant*, 239 N.Y. 87 (1924).

A tenant is free to sublease the entire unit, or a portion of the unit. However, in a building with four or more units, the landlord's prior written consent is required. To obtain this consent, send the landlord form 12, by certified mail, return receipt requested (RPL § 226-b). The landlord may ask you for additional information within ten days after you mail it. The landlord has thirty days from the date of mailing to notify you of the decision. The landlord may not unreasonably withhold consent, but the landlord can withhold consent if it is reasonable to do so. For example, if you are seeking to sublease to a rock band who will use the unit as a practice studio each night from midnight to 3:00 A.M., it would be reasonable for the landlord to withhold consent. If consent is unreasonably withheld, the tenant may sublet without permission [RPL 226-b(2)]. If your landlord accepts rent from the sublessee, he waives the right to object to the subleasing arrangement. *Brentson Realty Corp. v. D'Urso Supermarkets, Inc.*, 182 A.D.2d 604, 582 N.Y.2d 216 (2d Dept., 1992).

Should you choose to sublease your unit, you should enter into a written agreement with your sublessee (form 16). Remember that when agreeing to sublease, you are ultimately the one responsible to the landlord for the rent and the condition of the unit. Select your sublessee as carefully as you would a roommate.

If you are rent stabilized, you cannot sublease for more than your rent plus ten percent. If you are subletting the unit furnished, you should increase the rent by no more than ten percent on account of the added value of the furnishings. Your landlord can add a sublet allowance charge to your rent, equal to the current vacancy allowance. You must maintain the unit as your primary residence and must intend to return after the sublet. Only you, as the original tenant, have the right to renew the lease. The sublessee does not take this from you. You may not sublease for more than two years in a four year period (RPL 226-b).

ROOMMATES

If you are the only person named in the lease, your immediate family (spouse and children) can live with you without making any special arrangements with the landlord. You can also choose to share the apartment with one other person and that person's dependent children. The number of people permitted in the apartment will be limited by your local overcrowding laws, which are part of the zoning ordinances.

If you choose to have a roommate, you will remain solely responsible to the landlord for the rent and for the condition of the unit. When you take in a roommate, you become a landlord to him or her and the roommate is your tenant. You have all the legal rights of a landlord and can evict the roommate, should it become necessary. See *Landlords' Rights and Duties in New York* by Brette McWhorter Sember and Mark Warda, published by Sourcebooks for forms and information about handling an eviction.

If you do decide to have a roommate, you must notify the landlord of the person's name within thirty days after the person moves in. Use the Notification of Roommate (form 13).

Before the roommate moves in, you should have a frank discussion about how you are going to share the same living space. You can collect a security deposit from the roommate. You need to reach an agreement as to how you are going to divide rent and utility fees. You should also have a clear understanding about which areas are shared and which are personal. Decide who is responsible for cleaning and how often this should occur. Talk about buying and sharing food, and when guests and overnight guests are welcome. Decide how much notice the roommate has to give before moving. Write all of your agreements down and sign them, using the Roommate Agreement (form 14). This will function as the roommate's lease.

If you are rent controlled or rent stabilized, read DHCR Fact Sheet #7 about adding a roommate.

CO-TENANTS   If you and one or more people decide to rent an apartment together and you all sign the lease, you are co-tenants. You are all responsible to the landlord. Make sure you choose co-tenants whom you can live with and trust. You may have an arrangement with your landlord where each of you writes a check for your own portion of the rent each month, or the landlord may request one check. Whatever your arrangement, you need to understand that if one co-tenant does not pay rent, the rest of you are liable to the landlord for it. If one of your co-tenants decides to move out before the lease is up, the rest of you are responsible for paying that person's share of the rent. Because all of you signed the lease together, you are all liable for the entire rent for the entire lease period. If everyone but you leaves, you are solely responsible.

Even though you have signed a lease together, you should still complete a Roommate Agreement (form 14), so that you can lay out on paper all of the terms about how you will live together.

Should you have a co-tenant who doesn't pay, you can all pressure him to pay up, but you can't evict him. Only the landlord can evict a tenant or a co-tenant. You should talk to the co-tenant and you should also talk to the landlord about the situation. If the landlord evicts one of you, he will probably evict all of you. You want to avoid this, so you should see what arrangements you can make with the landlord or the co-tenant to prevent this. You may find you want to pay the co-tenant to leave if there is no other way to get him or her out of the unit.

If a co-tenant moves out before the lease is up, the rest of you are going to be expected to pay the full amount of the rent. You can find another co-tenant and get the landlord's permission to amend the lease. Use the Lease Amendment (form 31) to include the new co-tenant in place of the old co-tenant. You could also assume the responsibility of paying all the rent and then you could rent the other co-tenant's space to a new roommate, to whom you will act as landlord.

When you replace a co-tenant, remember that the landlord is holding that person's portion of the security deposit. When the new co-tenant signs the lease, the landlord should repay the original co-tenant's security deposit and collect a security deposit from your new co-tenant.

When you have co-tenants, you all probably will pay a portion of the security deposit. However, the landlord can hold all of that money against damages even if the damages were created or caused by only one tenant.

LEASE SUCCESSION

In rent controlled and rent stabilized units, if the tenant dies, certain family members who live with the tenant have the right to take over the lease. Consult DHCR Fact Sheet #30 for details about who qualifies.

SALE OR FORECLOSURE OF THE PROPERTY

Your landlord has the right to sell the property you are leasing, but the new owner remains obligated by your lease. So, if your landlord sells your building, don't worry. You don't have to leave. The new owner cannot make any changes to your lease terms (unless your lease gave your original landlord the right to do so).

If your building is foreclosed on because your landlord failed to pay the mortgage, your lease will be terminated if you have been named in the court case. *United Security Corp. v. Suchman*, 307 N.Y. 48 (1954). However, you may be able to obtain a new lease from the mortgage holder or foreclosure purchaser. If foreclosure papers are delivered to you, read them carefully and let the party foreclosing know of your interest in signing a new lease. A foreclosure may also be an opportunity for you to buy the property.

CHANGES TO THE LEASE

Your landlord cannot require you to agree to changes to your lease. You are both obligated by the terms of the lease unless you both agree to a change. Should you choose to agree to a change, be sure to get it in writing. Use the Lease Amendment (form 31).

Problems During Your Tenancy 10

Landlord's Access to Your Unit

This is an area of frequent contention between landlords and tenants. Under New York law, your landlord may enter your apartment with reasonable notice only:

- ☛ when permitted by the lease, or
- ☛ to make repairs, or
- ☛ to show the premises for the purpose of renting or selling it.

No notice is necessary if there is an emergency or an emergency repair.

INSPECTIONS Your lease may give the landlord the right to make inspections of the unit during the rental period to make sure it is being kept in good condition. One or two inspections per year are reasonable. You should refuse if your landlord wants to inspect the unit more frequently.

A landlord who enters at other times is committing criminal trespass. Because your right to exclusive use and occupancy has been violated, you are entitled to monetary damages.

If your landlord is entering your unit other than as allowed above, you should mention that this is illegal under New York law and request that he or she stop. You should talk to other tenants to see if they have had the same experience. Send the landlord a letter detailing the dates illegal entry and request it stop. State that you will contact law enforcement if it continues. Keep a log or journal of the problems you are having and all the steps you take to get it to stop. The illegal entries reduced the value of the rental and you should be refunded the amount of the reduction in value. If the landlord continues to enter illegally, you should contact the DHCR if you are rent regulated or if not, the police. You can take the matter to small claims court and request an abatement (reduction) in rent you paid while this was occurring.

SEXUAL HARASSMENT

Certain types of sexual harassment can be a crime. Don't put up with it from your landlord! If your landlord is making unwelcome sexual advances to you (verbally, physically or otherwise) tell the landlord to stop. If it continues, send the landlord a letter stating that you want him or her to stop the sexual harassing behavior and that if it does not stop, you will contact the police. If the situation becomes intolerable for you, break the lease and move out. If the landlord should sue you for this, you can explain to the judge why you were forced to leave. Keep a journal or log of all inappropriate behavior by the landlord.

RETALIATORY CONDUCT BY THE LANDLORD

Landlords are prohibited from retaliating against tenants (RPL § 223-b). This means a landlord cannot retaliate against a tenant by:

- evicting the tenant,
- refusing to renew the lease, or
- substantially changing the terms of the tenancy (including raising the rent).

To decide if an act was retaliatory, a court looks at whether it was done *discriminatorily*, which means only to one or a few tenants. For example, the landlord can raise the rent for all tenants, but not for just the one tenant who has made a complaint.

RPL § 223-b specifically states that a landlord may not evict a tenant who:

☛ complains to a government agency in good faith about violations by the landlord;

☛ participates in a tenants' organization;

☛ complains to the landlord about maintenance or warranty of habitability problems; or

☛ takes actions to enforce the rights given by the lease.

If your landlord tries to evict you in order to retaliate against you, you can defend the case by stating it is a retaliatory eviction and giving evidence to support this. However, if you are being evicted for non-payment and it is true that you haven't paid, retaliation will not be accepted as a defense.

If your landlord is attempting to retaliatorily evict you, he or she can be subject to civil damages [RPL § 223-b(3)-(4)]. If you are in a rent regulated apartment, you should contact the DHCR if you believe the landlord is retaliating against you.

BAD CHECKS

If a tenant pays with a bad check, the landlord can collect double the amount of the check (up to $750) if the tenant didn't have an account at the bank. If the tenant did have an account, the landlord can collect twice the amount of the rent (up to $400). Notice must be sent by regular and certified mail [GOL § 11-104(8)]. There is also a criminal law that prohibits writing a bad check (Penal Law §§ 190.00 through 195.15). Making payment on the check within ten days may be a defense depending on the circumstances under which the check was written.

The important thing to know about bad checks is not to write them! It is better to pay your rent late than to attempt to pay it on time with a bad check. Many people who write bad checks do so with good intentions. They believe that they will have the money by the time the check clears. Don't write the check if you don't have the money in the bank.

DAMAGE TO THE PREMISES

If you damage the premises, the landlord can end the tenancy and can also get an injunction against you to prevent you from doing further damage. The landlord can then sue for the damage you have caused.

If you have damaged the premises, you can repair the damage yourself without involving the landlord. Otherwise, take photographs and document the extent of the damage to protect yourself against an exaggerated claim.

DEATH OF A TENANT

If a tenant dies during the term of a lease, the lease becomes part of his estate and the estate is liable for the rent due for the rest of the lease term. *MacDonald v. Rosenblum*, 150 Misc. 556, 269 N.Y.S. 562 (1934). However, a landlord may be willing to waive the rest of the lease if the decedent's belongings are removed from the premises so that the landlord can re-rent it.

DESTRUCTION OF THE PREMISES

If the premises is severely damaged or destroyed to the point where it is uninhabitable, and the tenant did not cause the damage, the tenant has the right to immediately terminate the lease (RPL 227).

📖 This right may be waived by a lease provision [*Johnson v. Oppenheim*, 55 N.Y. 28 (1873)].

VACATING EARLY

If you breach the lease by leaving the premises before the end of your lease, the landlord can:

- ☞ relieve you of your responsibility to pay any more rent (essentially let you off the hook and agree to terminate the lease early);

- ☞ hold you responsible for the rent you owe up to the end of the lease; or

- ☞ rent out the premises and hold you responsible for the amount you were supposed to pay, minus any rent the landlord was able to collect by re-renting the unit.

If a tenant vacates the premises before the expiration of the lease and the landlord enters and re-leases the premises without the tenant's permission, the landlord and is considered to have accepted the tenant's surrender. The tenant is no longer liable for rent. *Schnee v. Jonas Equities, Inc.*, 442 N.Y.S.2d 342 (1981)

📖 However, if a landlord enters to make repairs after the tenant vacates early, he is not considered to have taken possession and the tenant remains responsible for rent through the end of the lease. *Sammis v. Day*, 48 Misc. 327, 96 N.Y.S. 777 (County Ct., 1905)

Leaving before the end of your lease is a crap shoot. If you find yourself in a situation where you need to leave before the lease is up, you should talk to the landlord and explain your situation. Many landlords are willing to let you go as long as you give them reasonable notice. If you know someone who might be interested in renting the unit, let the landlord know and get that person in touch with the landlord. If you make it easy for the landlord to re-rent the unit, he or she may be more likely to let you go without a hassle.

BUYING OUT THE LEASE | If you want to leave early, but are concerned about your obligation under the lease, consider buying out the lease. Talk to the landlord and offer him or her an amount of money (less than the rent owed for the

tenants' rights in new york

rest of the lease) as a settlement. You pay the landlord this amount and he or she agrees to let you leave without being sued for breaching the lease. Get this agreement in writing, using the Lease Buy-Out Agreement (form 32).

SENIOR CITIZENS — A tenant who is sixty-two (or who has a spouse who is) can terminate a lease in order to enter a health or adult care facility or to enter subsidized housing. Thirty days notice is required with documentation from the facility (RPL § 227-a).

MILITARY SERVICE — Tenants may terminate a lease to serve in the military. Notice is required. Where rent is paid monthly, the lease terminates thirty days after the day the next payment is due. For all other leases, termination occurs on the last day of the next month after the notice is given (NY Military Law § 309-310).

PROBLEMS WITH OTHER TENANTS

You may encounter problems with other tenants. The tenant next door may play loud music all night. The tenant above you may practice tap dancing before the sun rises. The tenant across the hall may slide weird notes under your door. The first step you should take when you have a problem with another tenant is to talk to the person in a calm and friendly way. Explain what is bothering you and ask if the person can make some changes. The tenant honestly may not realize he or she is bothering you. If this does not work, send that tenant a letter asking him or her to stop the behavior.

If you can't seem to make any progress, or if you aren't comfortable talking to the person alone, ask some of the other tenants if they are having similar problems. Perhaps a group of you could calmly and politely speak to the offending tenant together. Go to the landlord if none of this works. Explain the problem and ask that the landlord speak to the offending tenant. The landlord has an obligation to keep the units safe and livable. A tenant who is a nuisance can make an apartment

82

unlivable. Follow up with the landlord as you would about a repair you want him to make.

If you feel you are in actual danger from another tenant, you need to first get yourself to a safe location. Next you need to contact the police and get a restraining order against this person. You should also let the landlord know about the severity of the problem so that he can evict the dangerous tenant.

Neighborhood Problems

If the area your building is in seems dangerous or unsafe, there are several things you can do. Form a tenant's association for your building. A tenant's association can take many steps to keep your building safe. Contact other tenant's associations on your block or in your general area. Propose forming a neighborhood organization. Talk to law enforcement about your concerns (don't call 911 if it is not an emergency; go to the precinct and ask to speak to someone about your concerns). Contact Safe Streets Now, a non-profit group that offers help to tenants who are trying to combat drugs and street crime, at 510-836-4622.

Talk to your landlord about the concerns tenants have and ask that additional safety improvements be made, such as automatic locks, a security guard, and lighting. Talk to neighborhood school administrators and area clergy about the dangers and ask for their help in making the area safe.

If all else fails and you feel you are in danger, talk to your landlord about getting out of your lease and move somewhere safer.

TENANT ORGANIZATION 11

Getting to know your fellow tenants may be one of the best investments you can make when you live in rental housing. Alone, you are but a small stone tumbling down a hillside, but united with other tenants, you can be a rock slide of change.

Not everyone needs a tenants' organization, but if you live in a large building where conditions are poor, it can make a huge difference. If talking to your landlord does not solve your problems, consider forming a tenants' organization.

FORMING A TENANT ORGANIZATION

Tenant organizations allow people who live in the same building to share information, discuss common concerns, and work together to make change. Anyone can form or join a tenant organization, and your landlord cannot evict anyone for doing so (RPL § 223-b). There are no requirements for how you form your organization. The best way is to start talking to other tenants and get to know them. Suggest forming a tenant organization and try to muster support. Distribute some fliers to people in your building or go door to door to tell people about an organizational meeting. Let the first meeting be informal. Get to know each other, talk about your concerns as tenants, and share any information available about the landlord or the conditions in the building.

TENANTS' FEARS

Some people are afraid to join a tenant organization because they fear the landlord will retaliate against them. As explained earlier, landlords may not retaliate against tenants for this (RPL § 223-b, 230). Explain to the other tenants that if you work as a group, the landlord is much more likely to take you seriously, listen to your concerns, and effect change. A tenant organization is like a labor union. Union leaders negotiate with employers on behalf of employees and are able to effect great change on their behalf. A tenant organization can do the same thing for people in your building.

ORGANIZING

Once some of the tenants have agreed that a tenants' organization is desirable, you need to decide how it will be run. Officers or board members can be elected, and negotiators selected. It would be wise to obtain a lawyer to advise your group on the law. Talk to other tenant organizations in other buildings to get information about how to be effective. If your landlord owns other buildings, find out if the tenants in those buildings have organized and make contact with them. Make a list of the greatest concerns brought up by tenants in your building and try to think of solutions, which may or may not involve the landlord.

NEGOTIATING

Once your group has decided what you are going to request from the landlord, you need to decide how to ask for it. You may first wish to circulate petitions among the tenants for signatures to show the landlord how much support there is for the requests. Next, your selected negotiators should request a meeting with the landlord at a neutral location. They should present the requests and attempt to convince the landlord that he or she should meet them. If you get nowhere after several meetings, you can be persuasive by reminding the landlord that building and health inspectors can become involved. Rent strikes (discussed later in this chapter) should be used as a final resort.

If your negotiations are not successful, you can pass out fliers, hang signs in the building's windows, and call press conferences to draw attention to your situation. If one of your complaints is building code violations, you can contact the local building inspector and request an inspection. This may light a fire under your landlord.

RENT STRIKES

A *rent strike* occurs when many or all of the tenants in a building withhold rent in order to compel the landlord to make repairs or provide services. Usually, the rent is collected and held by a tenants' organization. Landlords rely on rent, and withholding it can be a powerful way to convince them to take tenants' concerns seriously. However, it is important to realize that your landlord may not be financially able to make repairs if rent is withheld. A rent strike is a double edged sword. You must also be aware that nonpayment of rent is grounds for eviction. Rent strikes must involve many tenants to be effective, so that it is not feasible for a landlord to evict all of you.

A rent strike situation ends up in court if the tenants initiate an Article 7-A proceeding (based on Article 7-A of the RPAPL, see below) or if the landlord sues for nonpayment. Many rent strikes resolve themselves when the landlord makes the requested repairs or provides the requested services.

OBTAINING GOVERNMENT ASSISTANCE

If your landlord has not repaired violations that exist in your building and you live in New York City, you should contact the *Department of Housing Preservation and Development (HPD)*. If they find the violations are *rent-impairing* (are so bad that they would constitute a reason for lower rent), they will send the landlord a Notice of Violation. If the landlord fails to correct the violation within six months, he will not be permitted to recover rent for that time period (MDL § 302-a). In other locales, contact building inspectors.

RENT ABATEMENT

When a rent strike occurs, rent money is held until repairs are made. Once repairs have been made, the landlord is paid the rent money owed. Sometimes, a court will give the tenants an *abatement*, or reduction in the amount of rent owed, as compensation for putting up with the violations.

ARTICLE 7-A PROCEEDINGS

RPAPL § 7-A permits another kind of rent strike. In an Article 7-A proceeding, the rent of all of the tenants is deposited with the court, and a court-appointed administrator uses the rent money to make the repairs. To start an Article 7-A proceeding, the tenants must file a *petition* (form 36) and a *notice of petition* (form 35) with the landlord/tenant court in the county where the property is located. These forms can be obtained from the court. An attorney is recommended for an Article 7-A proceeding.

An Article 7-A proceeding may be commenced if there is a breach of the warranty of habitability (see chapter 7, for a full discussion of the warranty of habitability), which exposes tenants to conditions that are dangerous, hazardous, or detrimental to life, health, and safety [RPAPL § 770(1), RPL § 235-b]. An administrator can be appointed if there are deleterious conditions, such as:

📖 Lack of heat, running water, light electricity or adequate sewage disposal, *Lawrence v. Martin*, 131 Misc.2d 256, 499 N.Y.S.2d 835 (Civ.Ct., N.Y. County, 1986)

📖 Failure to make repairs cause by fire, *Oyola v. Combo Creditors*, 64 Misc.2d 727, 315 N.Y.S.2d 666 (Civ.Ct., N.Y. County, 1970)

📖 Exposed wiring and improper gas connections, *Maresca v. 167 Bleecker, Inc.*, 121 Misc.2d 846, 467 N.Y.S.2d 130 (Civ.Ct., N.Y. County, 1983)

or if there are multiple Housing Code violations.

One-third of the tenants in a building must agree to initiate an Article 7-A proceeding [RPAPL § 770(1)]. In New York City, the HPD can initiate this proceeding on behalf of the tenants [RPAPL § 770(1)].

To commence a case, the tenants, or HPD, must file a Notice of Petition and Petition which can be obtained from the court clerk's office. If you are outside New York City, your group will need to prepare both documents and have the Notice of Petition issued by the court clerk. Both documents must be served upon the landlord. The landlord may serve your group with an answer, either admitting or denying each of your claims. The court will ultimately decide whether or not an administrator will be appointed. Your tenant organization should employ an attorney to handle this type of matter.

END OF THE TENANCY 12

THE END OF YOUR TENANCY

A tenancy naturally ends when the lease expires unless you have made arrangements with the landlord to renew the lease or continue on a month-to-month basis. You must remove yourself and all of your belongings from the unit by midnight on the day the lease expires or the day it is terminated. The lease usually contains provisions about the condition in which the unit must be left. If nothing is stated, the tenant is responsible for removing her belongings and leaving the premises swept clean of debris. There is no requirement to thoroughly clean the unit, but it should not be left as a mess, otherwise the tenant will be responsible for the cost of cleaning.

You should not leave any property in the unit, even if you no longer want it. If you leave items behind, you may be held responsible for the cost of removal. If there are large items that you will need extra time to move, discuss this with your landlord.

Before you leave, you should contact all utilities and notify them of the date of your move so that your name can be removed from the account. You are not responsible for notifying them of the name of the new tenant or the date the new tenant will take over the unit.

It is always wise to confirm in writing that you are ending the tenancy and not renewing your lease. Send the landlord a letter stating this, requesting a date for a final inspection and giving your new address so you can receive your security deposit refund.

DAMAGE TO THE PREMISES

Before you leave, you should schedule a time for you and your landlord to walk through the premises together. This will allow both of you to discuss any damage. If you leave without doing this, it is much easier for a landlord to accuse you of damage you did not do. If you have done some damage to the premises (such as a hole in the wall), you should repair it before leaving if you can do so at a reasonable cost. Otherwise, the landlord might charge a much higher amount to fix it. When you leave the keys, you should give the landlord your new address and ask for your security deposit back, including interest that has accrued on it. If your landlord refuses to return your security deposit, contact your local small claims court for information about filing a lawsuit for its return.

If the landlord finds damage to the premises at the end of the tenancy, the expenses for repair can be deducted from the security deposit. If the damages exceed the amount of the security deposit, the landlord can sue in small claims court. See chapter 6 for more information on this issue.

HOLDING OVER

Holding over occurs when a tenant remains in the unit after the lease has expired or has been terminated. When a tenant holds over the landlord has three options:

1. Remove the tenant by instituting a *holdover proceeding* (see chapter 13). A tenant who holds over is liable for the reasonable value of the use and occupancy of the premises, and the landlord may

recover this and have the tenant evicted [RPAPL § 749(3)]. This means that if you stay after your lease is up, you will owe the landlord rent for the time you overstay until you leave or are evicted.

2. Collect double rent. If the tenant gave notice of his intent to vacate the premises, but then failed to do so, the landlord may collect double the rent normally due for the period of time the tenant remains (RPL 229). The landlord may evict the tenant as well.

3. Convert to a month-to-month tenancy. If a tenant holds over and the landlord accepts at least one rent payment after the expiration of the lease, the tenancy becomes a month-to-month tenancy. A month-to-month tenancy may be terminated upon thirty days notice. *Tubbs v. Hendrickson*, 88 Misc.2d 917, 390 N.Y.S.2d (1976); RPL §§ 232-a, 232-b.

Property left behind by a tenant may constitute a holding over if the amount and value of the property is very large. *Canfield v. Elmer E. Harris and Co.*, 222 A.D. 326, 225 N.Y.S. 709 (4th Dept., 1927).

If your lease will be up and you find you need to stay longer, discuss this with your landlord. You may be able to renew your lease or rent on a month-to-month basis.

TENANCIES WITH NO SPECIFIC TERM

Where the parties to a rental agreement (either written or oral) do not have an agreed length of the tenancy, either party may end it at any time by giving the *proper notice* (written statement notifying party of end of tenancy).

TENANCY AT WILL   A tenancy at will has either an indefinite term (e.g., as long as the tenant lives) or no term at all (such as until one of the parties decides to end it). It may be terminated by either party on thirty days written notice (RPL 228).

MONTH-TO-
MONTH TENANCY

A month-to-month tenancy is created when a tenant rents on a monthly basis or when a tenant with a term longer than one month holds over and the landlord accepts rent. The tenancy can be terminated as follows by either party:

☛ In New York City: with thirty days written notice (notice given on October 1 is sufficient to terminate the tenancy on October 31).

☛ Outside New York City: with one full calendar month written or oral notice (notice on July 31 terminates the tenancy on August 31; notice on August 1 does not terminate the tenancy until September 30). If the notice is written it can be served by mail.

A month to month tenancy continues until one of the parties terminates it by giving proper notice. The notice should be received by the other party by the deadline given above.

EARLY TERMINATION BY TENANT

When you leave the unit before the lease is over, you are responsible for rent through the end of the lease term. Leases may be ended early without responsibility for rent in the following circumstances:

☛ If the premises is damaged or destroyed and the tenant did not cause the damage, and if the premises is unfit for occupancy, the tenant may immediately vacate the premises and terminate the lease without penalty.

☛ If a landlord materially fails to comply with maintenance obligations or with the terms of the lease (for example by failing to provide essential services), the tenant can terminate the lease. This is also sometimes known as *constructive eviction* (the landlord's acts have essentially wrongfully evicted the tenant). The word *materially* means that the noncompliance must be in a fairly serious or important way. An example is when the warranty of habitability is breached.

If you fail to leave promptly in these circumstances, it may waive the right to terminate early (RPL § 227). If you pay rent after a violation by the landlord, you have waived the right to terminate the lease for that payment period. You can terminate the lease during the next payment period if the violation continues.

See chapter 10 for a discussion of the ability of senior citizens and military personnel to terminate leases early.

If you are terminating early, you should send a letter to your landlord saying so, giving the date you are leaving and giving your landlord your legal reasons for doing so. You should be sure that you have a valid reason under the law, or you may be sued for the rent for the entire remaining term of your lease. If you are not sure your reason for leaving would be legally valid, you should consult an attorney who specializes in landlord/tenant law.

EARLY TERMINATION BY LANDLORD

A landlord may terminate a tenancy early for only two reasons: (1) the tenant's nonpayment of rent; or (2) a breach of lease by the tenant. A tenant cannot be evicted until the tenancy is terminated.

The laws about terminating a tenancy are very strict and if a landlord does not follow them exactly, you may win the case and collect damages and attorney's fees.

NONPAYMENT OF RENT

Unlike when there is a breach of lease (see below), the landlord cannot terminate the tenancy himself. There is a procedure the landlord must follow in order to have the court terminate the tenancy. This procedure is described in detail in chapter 13. The landlord must first serve a Demand for Rent. If rent is not paid, the landlord must petition the court (see chapter 13) to have the tenancy terminated and the tenant evicted. A Demand for Rent must be used before any court can have jurisdiction over the case. There is no required form. A rent demand only need to include a good faith statement of the rent due, the period for which it is claimed, and a demand for the tenant to pay the rent due or leave. A nonpayment proceeding cannot be begun in court unless this notice is sent [RPAPL § 711(2)]. The rent demand must give the tenant at least three days to *cure* the nonpayment (pay what is owed). If the tenant fails to pay, the landlord can commence a nonpayment proceeding in court and recover the rent due and/or evict the tenant.

The Demand for Rent must be given personally to the tenant or affixed to the door or other place the tenant will easily see it.

If the tenant tries to pay the rent before the three days are up, the landlord must accept it. If the tenant attempts to pay after the three days are up, the landlord does not have to accept it (although he is free to accept it if he wishes). The landlord has the option of signing a written agreement allowing the tenant to remain and waiving his right to evict the tenant while the agreement is in effect [RPAPL § 711 (2)].

The Demand for Rent must be made after the rent becomes delinquent but before a nonpayment proceeding is commenced. *Meyers v. Knights of Pythias Bronx Temple Ass'n*, 194 App.Div. 405, 185 N.Y.S. 436 (1st Dept., 1920). If the rent demanded in the demand is paid and the tenant becomes delinquent for rent for another period, a new demand must be served. *Eichenblatt v. Shanghai Palace Restaurant*, N.Y.L.J. 4/15/77, p. 12, col., 3 (App. Term, 2d Dept.).

BREACH OF LEASE

If the lease provides, it may be canceled by the landlord if the tenant violates a substantial obligation of the lease. A substantial violation is:

- something defined in the lease as a violation, or
- a violation of the lease that would cause harm or injury to the landlord or the premises. *Park East Land Corp. v. Finkelstein*, 299 N.Y. 70 (1949).

Some examples of violations of substantial obligations include:

- Alterations to the premises. *Rumiche Corp. v. Eisenreich*, 40 N.Y.2d 174, 386 N.Y.S.2d 208 (1976)
- Subletting or assigning without permission (RPL § 226-a)

📖 Failure to provide a duplicate key. *Lavanant v. Lovelace*, 71 Misc.2d 974, 337 N.Y.S.2d 962 (1st Dept., 1973).

📖 Failure to pay rent. *National Shoes, Inc. v. Annex Camera*, 114 Misc.2d 751, 452 N.Y.S.2d 537 (Civ. Ct., N.Y. County, 1982)

📖 Failure to give a security deposit *Park Holding Co. v. Johnso*n, 106.

If the landlord accepts rent despite the fact that the tenant is not complying with some aspect of the lease, the landlord waives the right to evict the tenant for that noncompliance. *Silverstein v. Empire State Shoe Co.*, 20 A.D.2d 735, 246 N.Y.S.2d 832 (3d Dept., 1964). A lease provision stating that acceptance of rent with knowledge of a breach of the lease does not constitute a waiver of the breach has been upheld as enforceable. *Jefpaul Garage Corp. v. Presbyterian Hosp. In City of New York*, 61 N.Y.2d 442, 474 N.Y.S.2d 458.

Immoral or Illegal Use. RPAPL § 711 (5) allows a landlord to terminate a lease if the tenant uses the premises for prostitution, or for other illegal or immoral activities such as:

📖 Drug sales. *City of New York v. Wright*, 222 A.D.2d 374, 636 N.Y.S.2d 33 (1st Dept., 1995)

📖 Sex club. *31 West 21st Street Assoc. v. Evening of the Unusual*, 125 Misc.2d 661, 480 N.Y.S.2d 816 (Civ. Ct., N.Y. County, 1984)

📖 Illegal trade [RPL 231 (1)].

Nuisance or Objectionable Conduct. A tenancy may be terminated for creating a *nuisance*, which is defined as a continuous or pervasive condition which threatens the health, safety, or comfort of neighbors or other building occupants. *1021-27 Avenue St. John Housing Dev. Fund Corp. v. Hernandez*, 154 Misc.2d 141, 584 N.Y.S.2d 990 (Civ. Ct., Bronx County, 1992). *Objectionable conduct* includes things such as profanity, nudity, and other offensive acts which cause a nuisance. *Frank v. Park Summitt Realty Corp.*, 175 A.D.2d 33, 573 N.Y.S.2d 655 (1st Dept., 1991).

Rent Regulated Tenancies. Rent regulated tenancies may be terminated for other reasons, as discussed in chapter 4.

Termination Procedures for Breach of Lease. In order to terminate a lease for breach other than nonpayment of rent the landlord must first give the tenant a Notice of Default, and if the tenant does not cure (or fix) the default (the problem), then the landlord must give a Notice of Termination If the tenant fails to leave after the Notice of Termination, then a Ten-Day Notice to Quit must be given.

Notice of Default. The Notice of Default tells the tenant that the lease has been breached and must include:

☞ the nature (or description) of the violation;

☞ directions to cure the violation within a specific period; and

☞ the consequence of the failure to cure, which is the termination of the lease.

The Notice of Default gives the tenant a certain number of days to fix the violation or the landlord will take steps to terminate the tenancy. The number of days notice required is specified in the lease. Rent regulated tenancies require ten day notice.

If you receive one of these notices, you will need to either do what is required so that you are no longer in violation or deal with the possibility of termination. If you do nothing, you face the risk of eviction. If you believe that you have not violated the lease, then you can do nothing and present your innocence (with supporting evidence) as your defense in court. If you truly have not breached the lease, you should try to let your landlord know. It is simpler to have a talk with your landlord than go through a court case.

Notice of Termination. If the tenant fails to cure the violation, the landlord next must serve him or her with a Notice of Termination. This notice must be timely, definite, and unequivocal. *City of Buffalo Urban Renewal Agency v. Lane Bryant Queens, Inc.*, 90 A.D.2d 976, 456 N.Y.S.2d 568 (4th Dept., 1982). The Notice of Termination also may not include any conclusory, misleading or equivocal language. *Spencer v. Faulkner*, 65 Misc.2d 298, 317 N.Y.S.2d 374 (Civ. Ct., Kings County,

1971). All of this means that it has to be fairly clear. The Notice must state that the violation has continued and that the time to cure has expired. It must give facts that establish the breach. The Notice of Termination gives the tenant a certain number of days before the lease will be terminated. Regardless of whether the tenant vacates by that date, the lease is terminated on the date stated in the notice. If the tenant does not leave, a holdover proceeding (see chapter 13) can be commenced in court.

Number of Days Notice Required Before Termination

Tenancy at will (indefinite term): Thirty days

No Tenancy at all: Ten days

Rent Regulated : Ten days

Rent Control weekly tenant: Two days

New York City month to month tenancy: Thirty days

New York City Rent Stabilized violation of substantial obligation (including nuisance illegal occupancy, illegal/immoral use, illegal subletting): Seven days

New York City Rent Stabilized refusal to renew: Fifteen days

Outside New York City month to month tenancy: one calendar month

Outside New York City Rent Stabilized Refusal to renew: Fifteen days

Outside New York City Rent Stabilized Violation of substantial obligation: one month

If the unit is rent regulated, any notices that are served must also be filed with the DHCR. A Certificate of Eviction must be obtained from the DHCR before any tenancy can be terminated. If the unit is rent stabilized, the Default Notice and Termination Notice can be combined into one notice. When this is done, the tenant has ten days to cure from the date of service or the tenancy is terminated thirty days after the service.

Notice to Quit. After the Notice of Termination, the tenant must be served with a Ten Day Notice to Quit, which gives the tenant ten days to vacate the property. If the tenant does not, the landlord can begin a holdover proceeding in court (discussed in the next chapter) to have the tenant evicted.

EMPLOYMENT RENTALS

When occupancy is a benefit of or payment for employment (such as a building superintendent) there is no tenancy created and occupancy ends when employment ends. There are no notice requirements. Once the employment has ended, eviction procedures can be used by the landlord to remove the former employee [RPAPL § 713 (11)]. All of this would be spelled out on the employment contract. It is possible to agree that the tenancy can continue after the employment ends by signing a lease or agreeing to month-to-month tenancy.

OPTIONS TO CANCEL A LEASE

It is permissible for a lease to permit the landlord or tenant to cancel the lease for certain reasons, such as the sale of the property, alterations to the premises, upon the happening of an agreed upon event, or simply whenever either party wishes to do so.

   📖 A lease provision allowing termination of the lease by the landlord upon sale of the property is permissible. *Miller v Levi*, 44 N.Y. 489 (1871).

   📖 A landlord is not prevented from terminating a lease under a lease provision allowing termination even if the tenant has paid rent in advance. *In re Szpakowski*, 166 A.D. 578, 151 N.Y.S. 211 (4th Dept., 1915).

    📖 When exercising an option to terminate, a landlord must specifically state in the termination notice what clause in the lease is being invoked, or the option is not considered to be invoked. *Perrotta v. Western Regional Off-Track Betting Corp.*, 98 A.D.2d 1, 469 N.Y.S.2d 504 (4th Dept., 1983).

SPECIAL RULES FOR PUBLIC HOUSING

Public housing is governed by federal law. Most of the federal regulations governing public housing are contained in chapter 24 of the Code of Federal Regulations. If you live in public housing, you might want to get a copy of these regulations. Contact your local HUD office for free publications and assistance.

The most important rule regarding a public housing tenancy is that a tenant must be given fourteen days notice for non-payment of rent and the notice can be hand delivered or mailed [24 CFR 866.4(1),(2)]. The notice must tell the tenant of the right to a grievance procedure.

DEATH OF A TENANT

When a tenant dies, the tenancy does not end. The lease becomes part of the tenant's estate. The estate then becomes responsible for the rent (RPL § 236). If the unit is rent regulated, a relative who has been living there and who meets certain requirements may continue on as the tenant. See chapter 4 for more details.

EVICTIONS 13

In New York, there are two procedures that can be used by a landlord to evict a tenant. They are *holdover proceedings* and *nonpayment proceedings*. This chapter will discuss the procedures involved in both methods, as well as your possible defenses. The procedures involved in evictions are highly technical. Do not feel as if you must understand every step explained in this chapter. Use it for general knowledge now and for reference if you ever find yourself in this situation.

If you are in a situation where your landlord threatens you with eviction or actually serves you with papers, do not assume it is too late to do anything about the problem. Talk to your landlord. Apologize for any problems you have made and explain what you are willing to do to make it better (for example, pay the back rent due within a month or fix the windows you have broken). If there has been a misunderstanding (you paid the rent and the landlord forgot, or you had a brother visiting for two days and not a roommate you took without consent), explain it. If you can convince the landlord that you will not be a problem anymore, you might be able to get him or her to drop the eviction completely. You only have one shot at this, so if you mess up again, the landlord will surely want you out of the unit.

GETTING A LAWYER

If you find yourself in a situation where your landlord begins a holdover or nonpayment proceeding, you will need to proceed very carefully. You could potentially be liable for back rent, damages, and your landlord's attorney's fees. If your landlord has an attorney, you should have one too.

If you decide you want some legal assistance, you should first contact your local legal aid office to see if you qualify for free legal assistance. Some county or city bar associations also have volunteer groups of attorneys who may be able to help you. If your unit is rent regulated, you should call the DHCR for any information they can provide. If you do not qualify for free help, contact your local bar association or lawyer referral service and ask them for a referral to a lawyer who handles landlord/tenant cases. Ask your friends and family for referrals to lawyers they have used. If all else fails, call the New York State Bar Association Lawyer Referral Service (1-800-342-3661) for a referral to a lawyer who handles housing cases in your area.

SELF-HELP BY LANDLORD

Landlords are not permitted to evict tenants without going through the proper legal procedures. Landlords are not permitted to physically remove tenants or their property. Only a sheriff or marshall can evict a tenant, and only with a court order permitting the eviction.

Landlords are also not allowed to turn off utilities, change locks, remove appliances, or otherwise take steps to make the unit uninhabitable. If the landlord does so, he or she can be liable for breaching the warranty of habitability.

SURRENDER OR ABANDONMENT

If you wish to surrender your unit, you need to tell the landlord you are leaving or leave the keys. If you do not tell the landlord you are leaving, or leave the keys, you will continue to be liable for rent. If you have a lease, you will be liable for rent through the end of the lease even if you tell the landlord you are leaving unless you can work out an agreement with the landlord. A tenant who is absent for half of the rental term can be presumed to have abandoned the unit, unless the rent is kept current.

If you need to temporarily leave your unit for an extended period of time, be sure to tell the landlord you will be gone, and to keep your rent current so that you do not appear to have abandoned the unit. If it appears that you have abandoned the unit, your landlord can evict you and put all your possessions on the street even if you are not around to receive the court papers.

NONPAYMENT PROCEEDING

When a tenant has failed to pay rent, the landlord must make an oral demand or give a written Demand for Rent to the tenant telling the tenant to pay the rent within three days. After the demand has been made, if the tenant fails to pay within the three days, the landlord can serve and file a Notice of Petition and Petition for Nonpayment, which directs the tenant to appear in court. The judge can enter a judgment against the tenant for back rent, terminate the tenancy, and evict him or her. If the landlord seeks a judgment of possession in the Petition and it is granted by the court, the tenancy will be terminated by the court and the tenant can then be evicted. Note that this is different from a holdover proceeding where the landlord him or herself can terminate the tenancy. The landlord cannot terminate the tenancy him or herself using this method.

HOLDOVER PROCEEDINGS

A holdover proceeding is what a landlord uses to regain possession of a unit after the tenancy has been terminated by the landlord for breach of the lease and the tenant has not left. After the landlord has followed the procedures described in chapter 12 to terminate the tenancy, he or she can commence a holdover proceeding by filing a Notice of Petition and Petition with the court and having you served with it. In a holdover proceeding, the landlord is telling the court that the tenancy has ended and you have no right to remain, and is requesting that the court evict you.

COURTROOM PROCEDURES

After either a Demand for Rent (in a nonpayment proceeding) or a Default Notice and Notice of Termination (in a holdover proceeding) have been served, and the tenant has not remedied the problem in the allotted time period, the landlord must seek the assistance of the court to proceed any further. Landlord/tenant cases are called *summary proceedings* because they are meant to proceed more quickly than other civil cases. A summary proceeding is started when the tenant is served with a Notice of Petition and Petition.

All court papers (all papers starting with the Notice of Petition and Petition and anything that you receive after them) you receive from your landlord should have an index number on them. (The landlord purchases the number when filing the case.) This is your case's number and you must include it on any papers you file with the court. The papers you have received are not valid if your landlord did not obtain an index number. If you believe it may have been left off of your copy in error, you can check with the court clerk to determine if an index number was purchased.

Never ignore a paper that tells you to appear in court. If you cannot attend on the date in the papers, you should call the court and ask to have the date changed. If you simply don't show up, the judge could enter a judgment against you and issue a warrant for your eviction. To protect your rights, you must be at every appearance that is scheduled for your case. If you absolutely know that the landlord is dead wrong and has no evidence to back up his claim, you should go so that you can point this out to the judge.

NOTICE OF PETITION

The Notice of Petition is the form given to the tenant which gives information about who the parties are, which court is hearing the case, and when the parties must appear.

PETITION

The Petition gives specifics about the location of the rental property, what the problem is, what notices have been served, and if the property is rent regulated. The Petition must contain the following information for it to be valid:

- ☞ the identities of the Plaintiff (landlord) and Defendants (tenants and subtenants, if any)

- ☞ the date the lease began, date the lease expires, and date the parties signed the lease (if oral, the date they agreed)

- ☞ the full address, including the apartment or unit number of the rental premises

- ☞ the facts upon which the proceeding is based (the reason for the case)

- ☞ when any Demands for Rent, Default Notices or Termination Notices were served (a copy of the notice and the affidavit proving it was served on or given to the tenant called the *affidavit of service* should be attached to the Petition)

- ☞ whether the premises is a Multiple Dwelling and, if so, whether it is properly registered (a copy of the registration must be attached)

- ☞ whether the property is rent regulated and whether it is in compliance with the applicable laws

All petitions must be notarized.

SERVICE

The Notice of Petition and Petition may be served on (or personally given to) the tenant, or on someone of suitable age and discretion at the residence or place of work of the tenant and mailed (certified or registered mail and regular mail); or affixed in a conspicuous place and mailed (certified or registered mail and regular mail), known as "nail and mail." (This method may only be used if due diligence has been used to attempt the other two methods first.).

SUBMISSION TO
THE COURT

Once the papers have been served by the landlord, the copies must be filed with the clerk of the court. The Affidavit of Service (a document stating who served the tenant and when and how) must be filed as well. The papers must be filed five days before the court date or the case could be dismissed [RPAPL § 735(b)].

WAITING
PERIOD

The tenant, who is the defendant, can respond to the landlord's papers by filing an answer (see below). After the papers have been served, the defendant has five days to respond (in New York City nonpayment proceedings) or three days to respond (outside New York City in non-payment proceedings). In holdover proceedings, an answer must be received three days before the court date if the petition is served eight days before the court date, but only if the Petition requests an answer. If not, an answer may be made at the court appearance. The appropriate form of response is a form called an Answer; however, judges may be willing to consider other types of responses (such as a tenant speaking at the court appearance).

YOUR POSSIBLE DEFENSES

Before you can present any defense to the landlord's claims, you must deposit rent with the court (to pay for the unit while the case is pending—this is to ensure that the landlord gets paid even during a time period when you are naturally very upset with him or her). You also must file an answer before you will be allowed to bring up any defenses. Following is a list of possible defenses you could raise. The most obvious defense is that everything the landlord is claiming is simply untrue.

INCORRECT RENT AMOUNT	In a nonpayment proceeding, if the amount of overdue rent is stated in the Notice of Default is wrong, the case can be dismissed.
FICTITIOUS NAME NOT REGISTERED	If the landlord is operating under a fictitious name (business name) that is not registered with the county, the case will be held until the landlord properly registers the name.
CORPORATION DISSOLVED	A case may not be brought by a corporation that is not in good standing with the New York Department of State. If your landlord is a corporation, you can check if it is in good standing. Check your phone book for the number of the local Department of State office.
CORPORATION NOT REPRESENTED BY ATTORNEY	If your landlord is a corporation, an attorney must appear to represent the corporation in court. If you bring this up, the case may be delayed until the landlord hires an attorney.
WAIVER	If the landlord accepts rent after the three day period has expired, this is a waiver and the nonpayment proceeding will be dismissed. If a landlord accepts rent after a nonpayment suit is begun, he waives the right to continue the case. However, a new case can be begun. In a holdover proceeding, acceptance of rent after termination of the tenancy and before the commencement of the case waives the termination and reinstates the lease (RPL 232-c). Sending rent to a landlord's post office box does not constitute acceptance and there is no waiver.
JURISDICTION	The case must be held in the appropriate court. If it is not, this is a jurisdictional defect. For example, if a nonpayment case is filed in small claims court, this is the wrong court. The case must be filed in the court that handles landlord/tenant matters in that vicinity.
MISLEADING PETITION	If the Petition used by the landlord is misleading and looks like a court order of eviction, the case may be dismissed. *Chalfonte Realty Corp. v. Streater*, 142 Misc.2d 501, 537 N.Y.S.2d 980 (Civ. Ct., N.Y. County, 1989).
NO BUILDING REGISTRATION	If the landlord has failed to register the building as a multiple dwelling in New York City, the case may be dismissed (MDL 325). *Third Avenue Corp. v. Fifth Avenue Community Center of Harlem*, 164 Misc.2d 257, 623 N.Y.S.2d 1011 (Civ. Ct., N.Y. County, 1995).

MODIFICATION
OF THE LEASE

Even though most leases contain a clause prohibiting oral modification, if an oral modification is made for reduced rent, it is binding if the reduced rent has been accepted by the landlord. *Central Savings Bank v. Fashoda, Inc.*, 94 A.D.2d 927, 463 N.Y.S.2d 335 (3d Dept., 1983). This is a defense if you are sued for the difference between the original rent and the rent after the modification.

EVICTION

If the tenant has actually been ousted (forced to leave), it is a defense. Constructive eviction is also a defense.

LACHES

When the landlord waits too long to sue for back rent, the *doctrine of laches* prohibits recovery. Usually, it is a defense if a landlord waits more than three months to attempt to collect.

VIOLATIONS

Outside New York City, a tenant may raise violations by the landlord as a defense. In New York City it is not a defense, as the tenant can commence an HP (Housing Part) Proceeding (see below), seeking to have the court direct the landlord to make repairs (N.Y.C.Admin. Code 27-2001). Other municipalities have their own housing maintenance codes that can be enforced in similar ways.

UNCONSCIONABLE
RENT

If the rent that is being charged is wildly outrageous, this can be a defense if it is proven by showing rents that are much lower for identical or comparable units.

GRIEVANCE
PROCEDURE

In federally subsidized housing, the regulations require that tenants be given a grievance procedure in some evictions. Failure to receive this right can be a defense.

YOUR POSSIBLE COUNTERCLAIMS

If you have a claim against the landlord, you can make it in court by filing a *counterclaim* in your answer (see below) to the eviction. Filing a counterclaim usually makes the landlord more interested in settling the case and compromising.

AMOUNTS

Different courts in New York have different monetary limits. Check with your court for its limit. New York City Civil Court can only hear cases for amounts under $25,000. If you ask for damages greater than this, the case will be transferred to Supreme Court and take longer. If the tenant does seek damages over $25,000, an extra filing fee must be paid to transfer the case (CPLR Art. 81).

WARRANTY OF HABITABILITY

Counterclaims based on the warranty of habitability are permissible in nonpayment proceedings. *Century Apartments, Inc. v. Yalkowsky*, 106 Misc.2d 762, 435 N.Y.S.2d 627 (Civ. Ct., N.Y.County, 1980). Courts disagree as to whether this type of countersuit is allowed in a holdover proceeding.

RPAPL Article 7-A permits a minimum of one-third of the building's tenants to institute a suit against the landlord for the correction of dangerous conditions. Tenants pay the rent to the court and the court appoints an administrator who uses the funds to correct the condition. Get an attorney if you want to do this.

RENT OVERCHARGE

Rent regulated tenants in nonpayment proceedings may recover damages for rent overcharges [N.Y.C. Admin. Code 26-516, Unconsol. L. § 8632(a)(1)(f)].

RETALIATORY EVICTION

In holdover proceedings, damages may be sought for retaliatory eviction (RPL § 223-b).

CLASS ACTION AND RENT STRIKE

A *class action* suit is one in which a group of people who have been wronged in the same way by the same person put their claims together in the same lawsuit. Since the tenants' claims will probably all be different, a class action suit probably would not be feasible in most landlord/tenant cases. However, rent strikes are similar to class action suits. A rent strike occurs when the tenants in a building withhold rent to try to get the landlord to make repairs or fix a violation. MDL § 302-a authorizes this if there is a violation recognized by the Department of Housing Preservation and Development that has not been fixed in six months. A rent strike can be used as a defense when the tenants are sued for nonpayment and the individual tenants' cases are consolidated into a rent strike proceeding. This seems similar to a class action but it is not the same.

Generally, counterclaims that would delay the summary proceeding are severed into a separate case, especially those regarding negligence.

Your Answer

To respond to the landlord's claims, you need to file an Answer (form 18 for nonpayment proceedings or form 17 for holdover proceedings). In the answer, you list by paragraph numbers: (1) all the things in your landlord's Petition that you deny—this should include everything he has said that is untrue; (2) things that you admit, such as your name and the address of the rental unit; and (3) things you neither admit nor deny. This should include things that are true that hurt your case. You are not lying if you refuse to admit them.

Cross out any counterclaim on the form that you are not using (see the section earlier in this chapter about counterclaims). Attach the Verification (form 19) to your answer and every other form you complete and file with the court.

File the answer with the court and mail a copy of it to your landlord or to his attorney if he is represented.

Filing a Case in Housing Part (HP)

In New York City, you can bring a case on your own against a landlord who is not making repairs. The case is filed in Housing Part, the landlord/tenant court used there. You must complete an Order to Show Cause and Affidavit (form 37) and file it with the court and give a copy to the landlord. You list the repairs the landlord needs to make and indicate that you are asking that the court tell him or her to do them.

Court Appearances

If you fail to respond to the Petition and fail to appear in court, the judge can decide against you. It is important to always appear in court when there is a date scheduled. You can tell the judge at any time during the proceedings that you have decided you want an attorney.

If you do appear, you cannot present any defenses (see the section earlier in this chapter about defenses) to the case unless you have deposited rent with the court clerk for use and occupancy charges during the proceeding [RPAPL § 745 (2)(a)]. This means you have to give your rent to the court to hold while the case is in process. The court may waive this requirement if you can show a good reason. A tenant may still make a Motion to Dismiss (asking the court to dismiss the case because the Petition did not contain all it should) even if rent has not been deposited.

If the landlord does not appear at the first court appearance, tell the judge you are requesting a default judgment based on the landlord's non-appearance. This basically says that because the landlord didn't show up, you should win. If the judge reschedules the date, file a written Notice of Motion for Default Judgment (form 22) that you have mailed to the landlord. The written version of this is the same as the oral one. The landlord failed to appear; therefore, the tenant should win.

Trial

If a trial is held, you will need to provide proof that what the landlord claims is untrue and that what you claim is true. You may call witnesses, produce documents, and testify under oath. At a trial, the landlord will give his side first and call his witnesses. You may ask him or his witnesses questions. Then you may present your witnesses and your proof. After you have presented your side of the case, you may wish to make a Motion for Summary Judgment (form 21), which states that there is no triable issue of fact and that judgment should be awarded to you. This means that there isn't anything for the judge to decide. The landlord may make the same type of motion, asking that judgment be awarded to him or her. This motion is not usually successful, but it is worth a try!

You may also request that the court hold a hearing about the validity of service. If you were not served properly, then the case was not validly begun. However, it is likely the judge would give the landlord a second chance to serve the papers properly.

Note: Occasionally someone will write to us and say they followed the steps and advice in this book but that the judge allowed the landlord to have extra time or to use papers that were incorrect. Remember, most times a case will go smoothly, but judges do make mistakes. If your case gets complicated, you should hire an experienced landlord/tenant attorney.

COURTROOM
ETIQUETTE

Always appear in court when you are directed to do so. Be aware that you may have to have several court appearances before your case is concluded. Wait patiently and quietly until your case is called, then go to the front of the room. Sit at an empty table or stand in front of the judge's bench. Do not speak unless the judge or a bailiff speaks to you or you are questioned under oath. Think of the judge as the king of the courtroom and do not do anything to upset him. Keep all of your emotions under control. You want the judge to think you are reasonable person.

Always refer to the judge as "Your Honor." You should stand when speaking to the judge. Do not speak to the landlord unless he or she is testifying and you are questioning him or her, or if you are testifying and he or she questions you. Do not argue with the landlord. Refer to him or her as Mr. _____ or Ms. _____. Try not to become angry or upset in court as it makes it more difficult to get your facts across.

Never interrupt the judge. You may interrupt the landlord or other witnesses only to make an *objection*. An objection is when you suggest to the judge that whatever the landlord or his witness has said violates courtroom rules, for example, the information given is irrelevant. One rule that is often broken is called the *hearsay rule*. A person can only testify about something he or she learned about by seeing or hearing it themselves and not about something which someone else told them. You can testify that you saw the landlord disconnect the pipe bringing water to your apartment. You cannot testify that your neighbor told you he saw the landlord do it, your neighbor would have to come in and testify to what he saw or did not see. In a landlord/tenant case where the parties are not represented by attorneys, objections are not usually necessary, but if you know enough about evidence to not look foolish, and the landlord is using bad evidence, you might try objecting. To make an objection say "Objection" and explain to what it is you are objecting.

COURT PERSONNEL

Remember that court personnel are overworked and that they deal with people who are upset all day! Be very nice to them. If you have questions about scheduling or need to change the date of a court appearance, call and speak to the judge's secretary. You will never see her in person as she works in the judge's office which is off-limits to the public. If you have questions about papers filed by you or the landlord, speak to the court clerk. If you are in the courthouse and are confused about where you should be, ask any security guard or bailiff.

MEDIATION

In some areas, mediation services are recommended or required by the court before a trial can be held. In mediation, the parties are encouraged to try to resolve their differences in a way that will benefit them both. A *mediator* is a neutral person, not involved in your case, who tries to help you reach a mutually agreeable solution. If your case is sent to mediation, be sure to attend the session and remain calm throughout it. It is to your benefit to honestly make an effort to compromise. It will save you a lot of time and possibly a lot of money. If you do reach an agreement, be sure that it is formalized into a written document called a *stipulation*.

STIPULATION

A *stipulation* is a written agreement that settles your case. It may be made orally on the record in court or may be hand written or typed. Forms to write the stipulation on are available from the court. Several types of stipulations are included at the back of this book as forms 24, 25, 26, and 27 to use in different situations.

You would use a stipulation if you and your landlord were able to agree on a compromise. For example, you might agree to pay past due rent and late fees, and the landlord would agree to fix the broken stove. Or you would agree to move out immediately and the landlord would agree to release you from the future rent under the lease. A stipulation can include just about anything to which you and the landlord agree.

A stipulation may state that the parties will return to court if there is a default, that a money judgment is due, that possession is given to the landlord, and that a warrant of eviction is stayed. It may provide that a stayed warrant (see below) of eviction be issued upon default. When a stipulation is made, it cannot be appealed by either party.

WARRANT OF EVICTION

If you have won your case, the court may ask you to prepare the Judgment (form 23) (in New York City, the court will prepare it) and submit it for the judge's signature. If you have lost, and if possession has been awarded to the landlord, the court will issue a *Warrant of Eviction*. The warrant cancels the lease (if not already terminated by the landlord) and allows a law enforcement officer to take back possession for the land-lord, which means removing you and your belongings from the property.

The law enforcement agent first serves the tenant with a seventy-two hour Notice of Eviction. After the time expires, the law enforcement agent will evict the tenant. Different counties have different procedures for the removal of the tenant's possessions.

STAYING THE EVICTION

Any time before a Warrant of Eviction is issued, the tenant may pay the rent due plus interest and costs by depositing it with the court clerk, thus preventing (or staying) the warrant from being issued [RPAPL § 751 (1)]. The tenant may also submit an *undertaking* (which is like a bond) with the court securing that the amount due will be paid in ten days and preventing the issue of the warrant. Once a warrant is issued, the eviction cannot be stopped except for very good reason. For example:

 Tenant was wrongfully denied welfare, causing rent arrears. Tenant became employed after the judgment and could pay the amount due. Good cause was found and the warrant vacated. *Anthony Associated v. Montgomery*, 149 Misc.2d 731, 567 N.Y.S.2d 200 (Civ. Ct., Bronx County, 1991).

 Tenant filed for bankruptcy after warrant was issued. This was not good cause and the warrant was stayed. *Radol v. Centeno*, 165 Misc.2d 448, 627 N.Y.S.2d 887 (Civ. Ct., Queens County, 1995).

In New York City, a warrant must be stayed for ten days when the case was based on a breach of the lease [RPAPL § 753(4)]. This gives the tenant another chance to cure. A warrant in New York City may be stayed for up to six months if the tenant cannot find a new place to live that is comparable after making reasonable efforts or when extreme hardship would result to the tenant if the stay were not granted [RPAPL § 753(1)]. This does not apply when the premises is going to be demolished [RPAPL § 753(3)]. Outside New York City, the warrant may be stayed for up to four months for this reason.

YELLOWSTONE INJUNCTIONS

A tenant can seek an injunction, called a *Yellowstone Injunction*, that freezes the parties in their current positions so that the tenant may have extra time to cure. *First National Stores v. Yellowstone Shopping Center*, 21 N.Y.2d 630, 290 N.Y.S.2d 721 (1968). The request for this injunction must be made before the time to cure expires. It cannot be used in a nonpayment proceeding. If you wish to seek a Yellowstone Injunction, you will need an attorney to assist you.

MONEY DAMAGES AND BACK RENT

LANDLORD'S CLAIM FOR BACK RENT

When a landlord institutes a nonpayment proceeding, the Petition includes a claim for back rent. In a holdover proceeding, the landlord can also include a claim for back rent if he chooses. A landlord can instead choose to file a claim for back rent in small claims court. To defend against a claim for back rent, show receipts or canceled checks. If you do not have these, you could try to use ATM withdrawal receipts in the amount of the rent if you paid in cash.

LANDLORD'S CLAIM FOR DAMAGES

When a landlord decides to pursue a claim for damages, he can include a claim for it in the Petition or can bring a small claims action against you. To defend against this, you will need to prove you did not cause the damage (for example, show photos taken of the damage when you moved into the unit, or show the inspection checklist which you and the landlord initialed.) The landlord is not entitled to damages from normal wear and tear. The cost of repairs may be deducted from the security deposit. If the deposit is not large enough, the landlord would include it in the Petition or in a small claims case.

AMOUNT OF CLAIM   At the time this book was written, in New York City Civil Court, the limit on claims is $25,000. Different courts have different money limits. Check with your court.

If the landlord took possession of the unit for his own benefit, the tenant will only be liable for rent up until he vacates the premises. The landlord is entitled to sue for rent up to the end of the lease if he takes possession for the benefit of the tenant.

The landlord is entitled to interest on the rent from the day it is due until the date of judgment. If you win a counterclaim against the landlord, you are also entitled to collect interest. Check with your court for the current legal rate of interest.

LIENS   When a tenant gives a notice to quit and then holds over, the landlord can collect double the rent for as long as the tenant remains (RPL § 229). A landlord may make a claim against the tenant for other losses related to the damage or breach.

A money judgment can become a lien against any real estate owned by the tenant (or the landlord if the judgment is against him or her). This lien is in effect for up to ten years in any county in which a certified copy of the judgment and copy of transcript is recorded in the county clerk's office in that county.

SATISFACTION OF JUDGMENT   After you have paid your landlord what the court has ordered in the judgment, you want to make sure that the landlord files a Satisfaction of Judgment in the clerk's office. This will end your obligation and show you have paid what you owe.

Likewise, if you win a money judgment against your landlord, you must file a Satisfaction of Judgment if the landlord pays you in full.

MOTION FOR REHEARING

The first way to try to get a decision changed is to ask the judge to hear the case again. If important new evidence has been discovered or an important court case was overlooked by the judge, this may work. Where there has been a jury trial, the motion is called a Motion for New Trial.

YOUR APPEAL

If the judge has made a mistake in interpreting the law, or if she ignored a law, then you can appeal to a higher court. This is done by serving a copy of the Notice of Appeal on the other party and filing a copy with the court clerk within thirty days of the judgment. After filing this notice, the appeal must be completed, or perfected. This means that papers showing your argument must be filed. You need an attorney to handle the appeal. Each court has its own time requirements for perfection.

You have thirty days from the date the judgment is entered in which to file the Notice of Appeal (form 20), but since the Warrant of Eviction only gives you twenty-four hours to vacate the premise, you need to act immediately. The eviction is generally not halted by the filing of a Notice of Appeal. If a tenant wants to appeal a money judgment, he must obtain a *stay* from either the trial or appellate court to prevent the enforcement of the judgment. If the tenant files an undertaking (a bond), the tenant is entitled to an automatic stay of a money judgment [CPLR § 5519(a)(2)]. Other stays may be granted if money is deposited into court, if payment is made for the use and occupancy during the period of the appeal, or if there is good faith prosecution of the appeal.

Appeals from county court are usually made to the Appellate Term of Supreme Court. Rulings by the Appellate Term can be appealed to the Appellate Division and then to the Court of Appeals. Appeals can stretch out for over a year and are very costly. If you choose to appeal you will need an attorney.

An appeal does not give you the opportunity to have your case heard a second time. The purpose of an appeal is to have a higher court review possible mistakes made by the court which heard your case.

If you were evicted by a warrant and you win your appeal, the eviction itself cannot be reversed, but you might be entitled to damages, such as your moving expenses since the appellate court decided you should never have been evicted in the first place. *Uffman v. Myle*, 181 A.D. 944, 168 N.Y.S. 483 (2d Dept. 1917).

ORDER TO
SHOW CAUSE

You may seek to have a judge sign an Order to Show Cause (form 37), staying the judgment. Should you have new evidence or an important reason the judge did not consider, you could file an Order to Show Cause. This type of motion is rarely successful since judges tend to stick by their decisions. Use form 37, which contains the Order to Show Cause and an Affidavit. Take the Order to the court clerk and ask to have the judge sign it. An appearance will be scheduled so you can explain to the judge what this concerns. Attach your Affidavit to the Order to Show Cause. This is your written explanation of why you are asking the court to do this. Attach any documents or evidence that supports your argument. The landlord may respond with a motion to vacate the stay and cancel the order to show cause under CPLR § 5704(b). This means he can ask the court to lift the stay and let the judgment be enforced.

BANKRUPTCY

If you file for bankruptcy, all legal actions against you must stop (called a stay). This is automatic the instant you file a bankruptcy petition (11 USC § 362). No formal notice to anyone is necessary. Anyone who attempts to seize your property, impose a lien, or use your security deposit for unpaid rent can be held in contempt in federal court.

The bankruptcy stay remains in effect until the debtor is discharged, the case is dismissed, the property is abandoned or surrendered, or the bankruptcy judge lifts the stay.

Your landlord can ask the bankruptcy court for the right to continue the eviction by filing a motion to lift the stay.

LANDLORD'S APPEAL

If your landlord loses the case, he or she can appeal. However, you would most likely be allowed to remain in the unit during the course of the appeal. If your landlord appeals, you need an attorney.

SELF-SERVICE STORAGE 14

Self-service storage spaces are a convenient way to store belongings; however, you must be sure not to fall too far behind on payments because the landlord can have your stored items sold to pay for overdue rent.

A written agreement is required for self-service storage space. The agreement must contain the names and addresses of the parties, the address of the storage facility, a description of the property being stored, a statement of limitation of damages and the charges applicable. It must also contain the following notice:

> "Notice: The monthly occupancy charge and other charges stated in this agreement are the actual charges you must pay."

This notice has been required because some storage space owners in the past have tried to confuse tenants about what their actual fees are. Be sure to read the entire agreement and understand any late fees for which you could be responsible.

The owner of the facility has a lien on all of the property kept in the facility, no matter who owns it (so if you store your mother's china in your storage space, the owner has a lien on that). A lien is security interest in favor of the landlord, which gives him a right to sell the property if you do not pay him what you owe him. This lien is superior to most other liens or security interests. If the charges are not paid, the landlord may sell the property in a public or private block or parcel sale. When the property is sold, the costs of the sale are subtracted from what the property is sold for and then the landlord deducts what you owe him. If the items to be sold are large, such as cars or machinery, any prior liens on these items would take priority over the landlord's lien. If any funds remain after the sale, they are yours. To stop the sale anytime before it occurs, pay the amount due. The owner of the facility must return any goods stored (if the charges are paid) upon request.

Any violation of the provisions of this law by the landlord can result in civil penalties of up to $1,000 per violation or three times the value of the goods stored plus attorney's fees.

If there is any balance remaining after the sale and its expenses are deducted and after the landlord deducts her amount due, a notice must be sent to the tenant at the last known address and to any other lienholder. Either may claim the balance within five years of the date of the sale. If the money is not claimed within five years, it must be turned over to the municipality in which the storage facility is located.

Notice must be given to the tenant of the sale. The notice must include:

- ☛ An itemized statement of the amount due

- ☛ A description of the property to be sold (which should be the same as the description in the occupancy agreement)

- ☛ The nature of the sale

- ☛ A demand for payment with a due date no sooner than 10 days after the notice is received

- ☛ A conspicuous statement that unless the charges are paid by that date that the goods will be sold

- ☛ The time and place of the sale

- ☛ That the tenant (or anyone else with a claim to the property) is entitled to bring a proceeding within ten days of receiving the notice to dispute the sale

The notice must be personally delivered or sent by registered or certified mail with return receipt requested to the tenant's last known address.

If you encounter any problems with your self-service storage space that cannot be resolved, contact the New York State Attorney General's office.

MOBILE HOME OWNERS' RIGHTS 15

New York law refers to mobile homes as *manufactured homes*. Most people own their own mobile homes and are tenants in a mobile home park where they rent a lot. New York has carefully revised its laws to provide a lot of protection to mobile home tenants. Real Property Law § 233 governs manufactured homes and is often called the Mobile Home Owner's Bill of Rights.

The New York State Department of Housing and Community Renewal (DHCR) regulates mobile home parks (see chapter 4 for information on how to contact this agency). Park owners are required to file a yearly registration with the DHCR. The New York State Attorney General's office (1-800-771-7755) makes itself available for mediating tenants' disputes with mobile home park owners. They also have a free pamphlet available, *Manufactured Home Tenants' Rights*.

Detailed explanations of mobile home laws are beyond the scope of this book; however, the law is similar to landlord/tenant laws described elsewhere in this book. If you find yourself in a situation where you cannot resolve a problem with you landlord, you should read RPL § 233 closely and consult an experienced attorney if you cannot handle the problem on your own. You would be wise to speak with other tenants in your park or in other parks and share information.

A brief summary of some of the important parts of the law is as follows:

☛ The law applies to parks of three lots or more

☛ The law does not require any certain lease form for mobile home parks; beware of landlords who tell you must sign a specific lease form because it is required by law

☛ Roommates are permitted as long as the landlord is notified within thirty days

☛ The park owner may issue rules and regulations (they must not be unreasonable or arbitrary) and they must be posted and given to all tenants

☛ Fees may be charged for rent, utilities, facilities and services that are available to tenants; "entrance fees" for moving into the park or additional fees for each member of your family are not permitted

☛ If you have no lease, fees may be increased only with ninety days written notice; if you have a lease the terms of the lease will govern this

☛ The landlord cannot require you to buy the mobile home or any equipment from her

☛ You may sell your mobile home within the park if you give the landlord twenty days written notice and you may sell it to anyone you choose. The landlord may reserve the right in your rental agreement to approve the purchaser, but may not unreasonably deny the approval

☛ You have the right to sublease if you obtain the written consent of the landlord. The landlord cannot unreasonably withhold this consent

☛ Eviction is governed by RPL § 233(d) and is allowed only for the following reasons:

  • holding over

  • nonpayment of rent

  • violation of the law by the tenant that affects the safety and welfare of other tenants

- violation of park rules and regulations by the tenant that continues after notice of violation
- park owner proposes a change in the use of the park by written notice; eviction can occur
- six months after the notice or at the end of the lease, whichever is later

☛ A warrant of eviction will be issued after ninety days, or after thirty days if the tenant is endangering the safety of other tenants or there is nonpayment

☛ Landlord cannot charge extra if you install gas or electric appliances

☛ When you enter the park you must be offered at least a one year lease; current tenants must be offered a one or two year renewal lease

☛ The warranty of habitability applies (the landlord warrants that the lots and all common areas and roads are fit for habitation and that no dangerous condition exists)

☛ The landlord cannot retaliate against the tenant; if this occurs, attorney fees can be recovered from the landlord

☛ Rent and fees charged must be reasonable

☛ The landlord cannot restrict occupancy

☛ The landlord may enter a rented mobile home if notice if given but may not enter a mobile home you except in emergencies when notice is not required

☛ The landlord must designate an agent in the park to ensure an emergency response for matters affecting the health, safety and well-being of the tenants

☛ The landlord may be charged up to $1,500 in fines for each violation of this law and may also be civilly liable to the tenants

APPENDIX A
NEW YORK STATUTES

This appendix includes the following New York Statutes:

The Multiple Dwelling Law and Multiple Residence Law are too long to include in this book. You can make copies at your local library or download them from the Internet at the following site: http://assembly.state.ny.us/cgi-bin/claws.

Note: Keep in mind that these laws are occasionally amended by the legislature. You should check periodically for changes.

REAL PROPERTY ACTIONS & PROCEEDINGS LAW

ARTICLE 7

SUMMARY PROCEEDING TO RECOVER
POSSESSION OF REAL PROPERTY

Sec. 701.   Jurisdiction; courts; venue.

1. A special proceeding to recover real property may be maintained in a county court, the court of a police justice of the village, a justice court, a court of civil jurisdiction in a city, or a district court.

2. The place of trial of the special proceeding shall be within the jurisdictional area of the court in which the real property or a portion thereof is situated; except that where the property is located in an incorporated village which includes parts of two or more towns the proceeding may be tried by a justice of the peace of any such town who keeps an office in the village.

Sec. 711.   Grounds where landlord-tenant relationship exists. A tenant shall include an occupant of one or more rooms in a rooming house or a resident, not including a transient occupant, of one or more rooms in a hotel who has been in possession for thirty consecutive days or longer; he shall not be removed from possession except in a special proceeding. A special proceeding may be maintained under this article upon the following grounds:

1. The tenant continues in possession of any portion of the premises after the expiration of his term, without the permission of the landlord or, in a case where a new lessee is entitled to possession, without the permission of the new lessee. Acceptance of rent after commencement of the special proceeding upon this ground shall not terminate such proceeding nor effect any award of possession to the landlord or to the new lessee, as the case may be. A proceeding seeking to recover possession of real property by reason of the termination of the term fixed in the lease pursuant to a provision contained therein giving the landlord the right to terminate the time fixed for occupancy under such agreement if he deem the tenant objectionable, shall not be maintainable unless the landlord shall by competent evidence establish to the satisfaction of the court that the tenant is objectionable.

2. The tenant has defaulted in the payment of rent, pursuant to the agreement under which the premises are held, and a demand of the rent has been made, or at least three days' notice in writing requiring, in the alternative, the payment of the rent, or the possession of the premises, has been served upon him as prescribed in section 735. The landlord may waive his right to proceed upon this ground only by an express consent in writing to permit the tenant to continue in possession, which consent shall be revocable at will, in which event the landlord shall be deemed to have waived his right to summary dispossess for nonpayment of rent accruing during the time said consent remains unrevoked. Any person succeeding to the landlord's interest in the premises may proceed under this subdivision for rent due his predecessor in interest if he has a right thereto. Where a tenant dies during the term of the lease and rent due has not been paid and no representative or person has taken possession of the premises and no administrator or executor has been appointed, the proceeding may be commenced after three months from the date of death of the tenant by joining the surviving spouse or if there is none, then one of the surviving issue or if there is none, then any one of the distributees.

3. The tenant, in a city defaults in the payment, for sixty days after the same shall be payable, of any taxes or assessments levied on the premises which he has agreed in writing to pay pursuant to the agreement under which the premises are held, and a demand for payment has been made, or at least three days' notice in writing, requiring in the alternative the payment thereof and of any interest and penalty thereon, or the possession of the premises, has been served upon him, as prescribed in section 735. An acceptance of any rent shall not be construed as a waiver of the agreement to pay taxes or assessments.

4. The tenant, under a lease for a term of three years or less, has during the term taken the benefit of an insolvency statute or has been adjudicated a bankrupt.

5. The premises, or any part thereof, are used or occupied as a bawdy-house, or house or place of assignation for lewd persons, or for purposes of prostitution, or for any illegal trade or manufacture, or other illegal business.

6. The tenant, in a city having a population of one million or more, removes the batteries or otherwise disconnects or makes inoperable an installed smoke or fire detector which the tenant has not requested be moved from its location so as not to interfere with the reasonable use of kitchen facilities provided that the court, upon complaint thereof, has previously issued an order of violation of the provisions heretofore stated and, subsequent to the thirtieth day after service of such order upon the tenant, an official inspection report by the appropriate department of housing preservation and development is presented, in writing, indicating non-compliance herewith; provided further, that the tenant shall have the additional ten day period to cure such violation in accordance with the provisions of subdivision four of section seven hundred fifty-three of this chapter.

Sec. 713. Grounds where no landlord-tenant relationship exists. A special proceeding may be maintained under this article after a ten-day notice to quit has been served upon the respondent in the manner prescribed in section 735, upon the following grounds:

1. The property has been sold by virtue of an execution against him or a person under whom he claims and a title under the sale has been perfected.

2. He occupies or holds the property under an agreement with the owner to occupy and cultivate it upon shares or for a share of the crops and the time fixed in the agreement for his occupancy has expired.

3. He or the person to whom he has succeeded has intruded into or squatted upon the property without the permission of the person entitled to possession and the occupancy has continued without permission or permission has been revoked and notice of the revocation given to the person to be removed.

4. The property has been sold for unpaid taxes and a tax deed has been executed and delivered to the purchaser and he or any subsequent grantee, distributee or devisee claiming title through such purchaser has complied with all provisions of law precedent to the right to possession and the time of redemption by the former owner or occupant has expired.

5. The property has been sold in foreclosure and either the deed delivered pursuant to such sale, or a copy of such deed, certified as provided in the civil practice law and rules, has been exhibited to him.

6. He is the tenant of a life tenant of the property, holding over and continuing in possession of the property after the termination of the estate of such life tenant without the permission of the person entitled to possession of the property upon termination of the life estate.

7. He is a licensee of the person entitled to possession of the property at the time of the license, and (a) his license has expired, or (b) his license has been revoked by the licensor, or (c) the licensor is no longer entitled to possession of the property; provided, however, that a mortgagee or vendee in possession shall not be deemed to be a licensee within the meaning of this subdivision.

8. The owner of real property, being in possession of all or a part thereof, and having voluntarily conveyed title to the same to a purchaser for value, remains in possession without permission of the purchaser.

9. A vendee under a contract of sale, the performance of which is to be completed within ninety days after its execution, being in possession of all or a part thereof, and having defaulted in the performance of the terms of the contract of sale, remains in possession without permission of the vendor.

10. The person in possession has entered the property or remains in possession by force or unlawful means and he or his predecessor in interest was not in quiet possession for three years before the time of the forcible or unlawful entry or detainer and the petitioner was peaceably in actual possession at the time of the forcible or unlawful entry or in constructive possession at the time of the forcible or unlawful detainer; no notice to quit shall be required in order to maintain a proceeding under this subdivision.

11. The person in possession entered into possession as an incident to employment by petitioner, and the time agreed upon for such possession has expired or, if no such time was agreed upon, the employment has been terminated; no notice to quit shall be required in order to maintain the proceeding under this subdivision.

Sec. 713-a. Special proceeding for termination of adult home and residence for adults admission agreements. A special proceeding to terminate the admission agreement of a resident of an adult home or residence for adults and discharge a resident therefrom may be maintained in a court of competent jurisdiction pursuant to the provisions of section four hundred sixty-one-h of the social services law and nothing contained in such section shall be construed to create a relationship of landlord and tenant between the operator of an adult home or residence for adults and a resident thereof.

Sec. 715. Grounds and procedure where use or occupancy is illegal.

1. An owner or tenant, including a tenant of one or more rooms of an apartment house, tenement house or multiple dwelling, of any premises within two hundred feet from other demised real property used or occupied in whole or in part as a bawdy-house, or house or place of assignation for lewd persons, or for purposes of prostitution, or for any illegal trade, business or manufacture, or any domestic corporation organized for the suppression of vice, subject to or which submits to visitation by the state department of social services and possesses a certificate from such department of such fact and of conformity with regulations of the department, or any duly authorized enforcement agency of the state or of a subdivision thereof, under a duty to enforce the provisions of the penal law or of any state or local law, ordinance, code, rule or regulation relating to buildings, may serve personally upon the owner or landlord of the premises so used or occupied, or upon his agent, a written notice requiring the owner or landlord to make an application for the removal of the person so using or occupying the same. If the owner or landlord or his agent does not make such application within five days thereafter; or, having made it, does not in good faith diligently prosecute it, the person, corporation or enforcement agency giving the notice may bring a proceeding under this article for such removal as though the petitioner were the owner or landlord of the premises, and shall have precedence over any similar proceeding thereafter brought by such owner or landlord or to one theretofore brought by him and not prosecuted diligently and in good faith. Proof of the ill repute of the demised premises or of the inmates thereof or of those resorting thereto shall constitute presumptive evidence of the unlawful use of the demised premises required to be stated in the petition for removal. Both the person in possession of the property and the owner or landlord shall be made respondents in the proceeding.

2. For purposes of this section, two or more convictions of any person or persons had, within a period of one year, for any of the offenses described in section 230.00, 230.05, 230.20, 230.25, 230.30 or 230.40 of the penal law arising out of conduct engaged in at the same real property consisting of a dwelling as that term is defined in subdivision four of section four of the multiple dwelling law shall be presumptive evidence of conduct constituting use of the premises for purposes of prostitution.

3. For the purposes of this section, two or more convictions of any person or persons had, within a period of one year, for any of the offenses described in section 225.00, 225.05, 225.10, 225.15, 225.20, 225.30, 225.32, 225.35 or 225.40 of the penal law, arising out of conduct engaged in at the same premises consisting of a dwelling as that term is defined in subdivision four of section four of the multiple dwelling law shall be presumptive evidence of unlawful use of such premises and of the owner's knowledge of the same.

4. A court granting a petition pursuant to this section may, in addition to any other order provided by law, make an order imposing and requiring the payment by the respondent of a civil penalty not exceeding five thousand dollars to the municipality in which the subject premises is located and, the payment of reasonable attorneys fees and the costs of the proceeding to the petitioner. In any such case multiple respondents shall be jointly and severally liable for any payment so ordered and the amounts of such payments shall constitute a lien upon the subject realty.

5. For the purposes of a proceeding under this section, an enforcement agency of the state or of a subdivision thereof, which may commence a proceeding under this section, may subpoena witnesses, compel their attendance, examine them under oath before himself or a court and require that any books, records, documents or papers relevant or material to the inquiry be turned over to him for inspection, examination or audit, pursuant to the civil practice law and rules. If a person subpoenaed to attend upon such inquiry fails to obey the command of a subpoena without reasonable cause, or if a person in attendance upon such inquiry shall, without reasonable cause, refuse to be sworn or to be examined or to answer a question or to produce a book or paper, when ordered to do so by the officer conducting such inquiry, he shall be guilty of a class B misdemeanor.

Sec. 721. Person who may maintain proceeding.
The proceeding may be brought by:

1. The landlord or lessor.

2. The reversioner or remainderman next entitled to possession of the property upon the termination of

the estate of a life tenant, where a tenant of such life tenant holds over.

3. The purchaser upon the execution or foreclosure sale, or the purchaser on a tax sale to whom a deed has been executed and delivered or any subsequent grantee, distributee or devisee claiming title through such purchaser.

4. The person forcibly put out or kept out.

5. The person with whom, as owner, the agreement was made, or the owner of the property occupied under an agreement to cultivate the property upon shares or for a share of the crops.

6. The person lawfully entitled to the possession of property intruded into or squatted upon.

7. The person entitled to possession of the property occupied by a licensee who may be dispossessed.

8. The person, corporation or law enforcement agency authorized by this article to proceed to remove persons using or occupying premises for illegal purposes.

9. The receiver of a landlord, purchaser or other person so entitled to apply, when authorized by the court.

10. The lessee of the premises, entitled to possession.

11. Not-for-profit corporations, and tenant associations authorized in writing by the commissioner of the department of the city of New York charged with enforcement of the housing maintenance code of such city to manage residential real property owned by such city.

Sec. 731. Commencement; notice of petition.

1. The special proceeding prescribed by this article shall be commenced by petition and a notice of petition. A notice of petition may be issued only by an attorney, judge or the clerk of the court; it may not be issued by a party prosecuting the proceeding in person.

2. Except as provided in section 732, relating to a proceeding for non-payment of rent, the notice of petition shall specify the time and place of the hearing on the petition and state that if respondent shall fail at such time to interpose and establish any defense that he may have, he may be precluded from asserting such defense or the claim on which it is based in any other proceeding or action.

Sec. 732. Special provisions applicable in non-payment proceeding if the rules so provide. If the appropriate appellate division shall so provide in the rules of a particular court, this section shall be applicable in such court in a proceeding brought on the ground that the respondent has defaulted in the payment of rent; in such event, all other provisions of this article shall remain applicable in such proceeding, except to the extent inconsistent with the provisions of this section.

1. The notice of petition shall be returnable before the clerk, and shall be made returnable within five days after its service.

2. If the respondent answers, the clerk shall fix a date for trial or hearing not less than three nor more than eight days after joinder of issue, and shall immediately notify by mail the parties or their attorneys of such date. If the determination be for the petitioner, the issuance of a warrant shall not be stayed for more than five days from such determination.

3. If the respondent fails to answer within five days from the date of service, as shown by the affidavit or certificate of service of the notice of petition and petition, the judge shall render judgment in favor of the petitioner and may stay the issuance of the warrant for a period of not to exceed ten days from the date of service.

4. The notice of petition shall advise the respondent of the requirements of subdivisions 1, 2 and 3, above.

Sec. 733. Time of service; order to show cause.

1. Except as provided in section 732, relating to a proceeding for non-payment of rent, the notice of petition and petition shall be served at least five and not more than twelve days before the time at which the petition is noticed to be heard.

2. The court may grant an order to show cause to be served in lieu of a notice of petition. If the special proceeding is based upon the ground specified in subdivision 1 of section 711, and the order to show cause is sought on the day of the expiration of the lease or the next day thereafter, it may be served at a time specified therein which shall be at least two hours before the hour at which the petition is to be heard.

Sec. 734. Notice of petition; service on the Westchester county department of social services. In the county of Westchester, if the local legislative body has, by local law, opted to require such notice, service of a copy of the notice of petition and petition in any proceeding commenced against a residential tenant in accordance with the provisions of this article shall be served upon the county commissioner of social services. Such service shall be made by certified mail, return receipt requested, directed to an address set forth in the local law, or pursuant to the provisions of the civil practice law and rules. Such service shall be made at least five days before the return date set in the notice of petition. Proof of such service shall be filed with the court. Failure to serve the commissioner shall not be a jurisdictional defect and shall not be a defense to a proceeding brought pursuant to the provisions of this article.

Sec. 735.   Manner of service; filing; when service complete.

1. Service of the notice of petition and petition shall be made by personally delivering them to the respondent; or by delivering to and leaving personally with a person of suitable age and discretion who resides or is employed at the property sought to be recovered, a copy of the notice of petition and petition, if upon reasonable application admittance can be obtained and such person found who will receive it; or if admittance cannot be obtained and such person found, by affixing a copy of the notice and petition upon a conspicuous part of the property sought to be recovered or placing a copy under the entrance door of such premises; and in addition, within one day after such delivering to such suitable person or such affixing or placement, by mailing to the respondent both by registered or certified mail and by regular first class mail;

   (a) if a natural person, as follows: at the property sought to be recovered, and if such property is not the place of residence of such person and if the petitioner shall have written information of the residence address of such person, at the last residence address as to which the petitioner has such information, or if the petitioner shall have no such information, but shall have written information of the place of business or employment of such person, to the last business or employment address as to which the petitioner has such information; and

   (b) if a corporation, joint-stock or other unincorporated association, as follows: at the property sought to be recovered, and if the principal office or principal place of business of such corporation, joint stock or other unincorporated association is not located on the property sought to be recovered, and if the petitioner shall have written information of the principal office or principal place of business within the state, at the last place as to which petitioner has such information, or if the petitioner shall have no such information but shall have written information of any office or place of business within the state, to any such place as to which the petitioner has such information. Allegations as to such information as may affect the mailing address shall be set forth either in the petition, or in a separate affidavit and filed as part of the proof of service.

2. The notice of petition, or order to show cause, and petition together with proof of service thereof shall be filed with the court or clerk thereof within three days after;

   (a) personal delivery to respondent, when service has been made by that means, and such service shall be complete immediately upon such personal delivery; or

   (b) mailing to respondent, when service is made by the alternatives above provided, and such service shall be complete upon the filing of proof of service.

Sec. 741.   Contents of petition.

The petition shall be verified by the person authorized by section seven hundred twenty-one to maintain the proceeding; or by a legal representative, attorney or agent of such person pursuant to subdivision (d) of section thirty hundred twenty of the civil practice law and rules. An attorney of such person may verify the petition in information and belief notwithstanding the fact that such person is in the county where the attorney has his office. Every petition shall:

1. State the interest of the petitioner in the premises from which removal is sought.

2. State the respondent's interest in the premises and his relationship to petitioner with regard thereto.

3. Describe the premises from which removal is sought.

4. State the facts upon which the special proceeding is based.

5. State the relief sought. The relief may include a judgment for rent due, and for a period of occupancy during which no rent is due, for the fair value of use and occupancy of the premises if the notice of petition contains a notice that a demand for such a judgment has been made.

Sec. 743.   Answer.

Except as provided in section 732, relating to a proceeding for non-payment of rent, at the time when the petition is to be heard the respondent, or any person in possession or claiming possession of the premises, may answer, orally or in writing. If the answer is oral the substance thereof shall be indorsed upon the petition. If the notice of petition was served at least eight days before the time at which it was noticed to be heard and it so demands, the answer shall be made at least three days before the time the petition is noticed to be heard and, if in writing, it shall be served within such time; whereupon any reply shall be served at least one day before such time. The answer may contain any legal or equitable defense, or counterclaim. The court may render affirmative judgment for the amount found due on the counterclaim.

Sec. 745.   Trial.

1. Where triable issues of fact are raised, they shall be tried by the court unless, at the time the petition is noticed to be heard, a party demands a trial by jury, in which case trial shall be by jury. At the time when issue is joined the court, in its discretion at the request of either party and upon proof to its satisfaction by affidavit or orally that an adjournment

is necessary to enable the applicant to procure his necessary witnesses, or by consent of all the parties who appear, may adjourn the trial of the issue, but not more than ten days, except by consent of all parties.

2. In the city of New York:

(a) In a summary proceeding upon the second request by the tenant for an adjournment, the court shall direct that the tenant post all sums as they become due for future rent and use and occupancy, which may be established without the use of expert testimony, unless waived by the court for good cause shown. Two adjournments shall not include an adjournment requested by a tenant unrepresented by counsel for the purpose of securing counsel made on the initial return date of the proceeding. Such future rent and use and occupancy sums shall be deposited with the clerk of the court or paid to such other person or entity, including the petitioner, as the court shall direct or shall be expended for such emergency repairs as the court shall approve.

(b) In any adjournment of a summary proceeding, other than on consent or at the request of the petitioner, the court shall at the petitioner's request state on the record why for good cause shown it is not directing the tenant to pay or post all sums demanded pursuant to a lease or rental agreement in the proceeding as rent and use and occupancy.

(c) The provisions of this subdivision shall not apply if the housing accommodation in question or the public areas pertaining thereto are charged with immediately hazardous violations of record as defined by the New York city housing maintenance code.

(d) The court may dismiss any summary proceeding without prejudice and with costs to the respondent by reason of excessive adjournments requested by the petitioner.

(e) The provisions of this subdivision shall not be construed as to deprive a tenant of a trial of any summary proceeding.

Sec. 747.   Judgment.

1. The court shall direct that a final judgment be entered determining the rights of the parties. The judgment shall award to the successful party the costs of the special proceeding.

2. The judgment shall not bar an action to recover the possession of real property. The judgment shall not bar an action, proceeding or counterclaim, commenced or interposed within sixty days of entry of the judgment, for affirmative equitable relief which was not sought by counterclaim in the proceeding because of the limited jurisdiction of the court.

3. If the proceeding is founded upon an allegation of forcible entry or forcible holding out the court may award to the successful party a fixed sum as costs, not exceeding fifty dollars, in addition to his disbursements.

4. The judgment, including such money as it may award for rent or otherwise, may be docketed in such books as the court maintains for recording the steps in a summary proceeding; unless a rule of the court, or the court by order in a given case, otherwise provides, such judgment need not be recorded or docketed in the books, if separately maintained, in which are docketed money judgments in an action.

Sec. 749.   Warrant.

1. Upon rendering a final judgment for petitioner, the court shall issue a warrant directed to the sheriff of the county or to any constable or marshal of the city in which the property, or a portion thereof, is situated, or, if it is not situated in a city, to any constable of any town in the county, describing the property, and commanding the officer to remove all persons, and, except where the case is within section 715, to put the petitioner into full possession.

2. The officer to whom the warrant is directed and delivered shall give at least seventy-two hours notice, in writing and in the manner prescribed in this article for the service of a notice of petition, to the person or persons to be evicted or dispossessed and shall execute the warrant between the hours of sunrise and sunset.

3. The issuing of a warrant for the removal of a tenant cancels the agreement under which the person removed held the premises, and annuls the relation of landlord and tenant, but nothing contained herein shall deprive the court of the power to vacate such warrant for good cause shown prior to the execution thereof. Petitioner may recover by action any sum of money which was payable at the time when the special proceeding was commenced and the reasonable value of the use and occupation to the time when the warrant was issued, for any period of time with respect to which the agreement does not make any provision for payment of rent.

Sec. 751.   Stay upon paying rent or giving undertaking; discretionary stay outside city of New York.

The respondent may, at any time before a warrant is issued, stay the issuing thereof and also stay an execution to collect the costs, as follows:

1. Where the lessee or tenant holds over after a default in the payment of rent, or of taxes or assessments, he may effect a stay by depositing the amount of the rent due or of such taxes or assessments, and interest and penalty, if any thereon due, and the costs of the special proceeding, with the clerk of the court, or

where the office of clerk is not provided for, with the court, who shall thereupon, upon demand, pay the amount deposited to the petitioner or his duly authorized agent; or by delivering to the court or clerk his undertaking to the petitioner in such sum as the court approves to the effect that he will pay the rent, or such taxes or assessments, and interest and penalty and costs within ten days, at the expiration of which time a warrant may issue, unless he produces to the court satisfactory evidence of the payment.

2. Where the lessee or tenant has taken the benefit of an insolvency statute or has been adjudicated a bankrupt, he may effect a stay by paying the costs of the special proceeding and by delivering to the court or clerk his undertaking to the petitioner in such a sum as the court approves to the effect that he will pay the rent of the premises as it has become or thereafter becomes due.

3. Where he continues in possession of real property which has been sold by virtue of an execution against his property, he may effect a stay by paying the costs of the special proceeding, and delivering to the court or clerk an affidavit that he claims the possession of the property by virtue of a right or title acquired after the sale or as guardian or trustee for another; together with his undertaking to the petitioner in such a sum as the court approves to the effect that he will pay any costs and damages which may be recovered against him in an action to recover the property brought against him by the petitioner within six months thereafter; and that he will not commit any waste upon or injury to the property during his occupation thereof.

Sec. 753. Stay where tenant holds over in premises occupied for dwelling purposes in city of New York.

1. In a proceeding to recover the possession of premises in the city of New York occupied for dwelling purposes, other than a room or rooms in an hotel, lodging house, or rooming house, upon the ground that the occupant is holding over and continuing in possession of the premises after the expiration of his term and without the permission of the landlord, or, in a case where a new lessee is entitled to possession, without the permission of the new lessee, the court, on application of the occupant, may stay the issuance of a warrant and also stay any execution to collect the costs of the proceeding for a period of not more than six months, if it appears that the premises are used for dwelling purposes; that the application is made in good faith; that the applicant cannot within the neighborhood secure suitable premises similar to those occupied

by him and that he made due and reasonable efforts to secure such other premises, or that by reason of other facts it would occasion extreme hardship to him or his family if the stay were not granted.

2. Such stay shall be granted and continue effective only upon the condition that the person against whom the judgment is entered shall make a deposit in court of the entire amount, or such installments thereof from time to time as the court may direct, for the occupation of the premises for the period of the stay, at the rate for which he was liable as rent for the month immediately prior to the expiration of his term or tenancy, plus such additional amount, if any, as the court may determine to be the difference between such rent and the reasonable rent or value of the use and occupation of the premises; such deposit shall also include all rent unpaid by the occupant prior to the period of the stay. The amount of such deposit shall be determined by the court upon the application for the stay and such determination shall be final and conclusive in respect to the amount of such deposit, and the amount thereof shall be paid into court, in such manner and in such installments, if any, as the court may direct. A separate account shall be kept of the amount to the credit of each proceeding, and all such payments shall be deposited in a bank or trust company and shall be subject to the check of the clerk of the court, if there be one, or otherwise of the court. The clerk of the court, if there be one, and otherwise the court shall pay to the landlord or his duly authorized agent, the amount of such deposit in accordance with the terms of the stay or the further order of the court.

3. The provisions of this section shall not apply to a proceeding where the petitioner shows to the satisfaction of the court that he desires in good faith to recover the premises for the purpose of demolishing same with the intention of constructing a new building, plans for which new building shall have been duly filed and approved by the proper authority; nor shall it apply to a proceeding to recover possession upon the ground that an occupant is holding over and is objectionable if the landlord shall establish to the satisfaction of the court that such occupant is objectionable.

4. In the event that such proceeding is based upon a claim that the tenant or lessee has breached a provision of the lease, the court shall grant a ten day stay of issuance of the warrant, during which time the respondent may correct such breach.

5. Any provision of a lease or other agreement whereby a lessee or tenant waives any provision of this section shall be deemed against public policy and void.

Sec. 755. Stay of proceeding or action for rent upon failure to make repairs.

1. (a) Upon proper proof that a notice or order to remove or cease a nuisance or a violation or to make necessary and proper repairs has been made by the municipal department charged with the enforcement of the multiple dwelling law, the multiple residence law, or any other applicable local housing code, or officer or officers thereof charged with the supervision of such matters, if the condition against which such notice or order is directed is, in the opinion of the court, such as to constructively evict the tenant from a portion of the premises occupied by him, or is, or is likely to become, dangerous to life, health, or safety, the court before which the case is pending may stay proceedings to dispossess the tenant for non-payment of rent or any action for rent or rental value. In any such proceeding, on the question of fact, as to the condition of the dwelling the landlord or petitioner shall have the burden of disproving the condition of the dwelling as such condition is described in the notice or order.

   (b) Upon proper proof of the existence of a condition that is in the opinion of the court, such as to constructively evict the tenant from a portion of the premises occupied by him, or is or is, likely to become, dangerous to life, health, or safety, the court before which the case is pending may stay proceedings to dispossess the tenant for non-payment of rent, or any action for rent or rental value.

   (c) The court shall in no case grant a stay where it appears that the condition against which the notice or order is directed has been created by the wilful or negligent act of the tenant or his agent. Such stay shall continue in force, until an order shall be made by the court vacating it, but no order vacating such stay shall be made, except upon three days' notice of hearing to the tenant, or respondent, or his attorney, and proof that such notice or order has been complied with.

2. The tenant or respondent shall not be entitled to the stay unless he shall deposit with the clerk of the court the rent then due, which shall, for the purposes of this section, be deemed the same as the tenant was liable for during the preceding month or such as is reserved as the monthly rent in the agreement under which he obtained possession of the premises. The stay may be vacated upon three days' notice upon failure to deposit with the clerk the rent within five days after it is due, during the pendency of the proceeding or action.

3. During the continuance of the stay, the court may direct, in its discretion, upon three days notice to all parties, the release to a contractor or materialman of all or such part of the moneys on deposit as shall be sufficient to pay bills properly presented by such contractor or materialman for the maintenance of and necessary repairs to the building (including but not limited to payments for fuel, electricity, gas, janitorial services and repairs necessary to remove violations), upon a showing by the tenant that the landlord is not meeting his legal obligations therefor or direct such release to a municipal department to pay bills and expenses for such maintenance and repairs upon a showing that the landlord did not meet his legal obligation to provide such maintenance or perform repairs and that the department incurred expenses therefor. Upon the entry of an order vacating the stay the remaining money deposited shall be paid to the plaintiff or landlord or his duly authorized agent.

4. Neither party shall be entitled to any costs in any proceeding or action wherein the stay shall be granted except that costs may be awarded against the tenant or defendant in the discretion of the court in the event the condition complained of shall be found to be due to the wilful act of the tenant or defendant, such costs, however, not to exceed the sum of twenty-five dollars.

Sec. 756. Stay of summary proceedings or actions for rent under certain conditions.
In the event that utilities are discontinued in any part of a multiple dwelling because of the failure of the landlord or other person having control of said multiple dwelling to pay for utilities for which he may have contracted, any proceeding to dispossess a tenant from said building or an action against any tenant of said building for rent shall be stayed until such time as the landlord or person having control of said multiple dwelling pays the amount owing for said utilities and until such time as the utilities are restored to working order.

Sec. 761. Redemption by lessee.
Where the special proceeding is founded upon an allegation that a lessee holds over after a default in the payment of rent, and the unexpired term of the lease under which the premises are held exceeds five years at the time when the warrant is issued the lessee, his executor, administrator or assignee, at any time within one year after the execution of the warrant, unless by the terms of the lease such lessee shall have waived his right to redeem, or such lessee, executor, administrator or assignee shall have subsequently waived the right to redeem by a written instrument filed and recorded in the office in which the lease is recorded, or if not so recorded, in the office in which deeds are required to be recorded of

the county in which the leased premises are located, may pay or tender to the petitioner, his heir, executor, administrator or assignee, or if, within five days before the expiration of the year he cannot be found with reasonable diligence within the city or town wherein the property or a portion thereof is situated, then to the court which issued the warrant, all rent in arrears at the time of the payment or tender with interest thereupon and the costs and charges incurred by the petitioner. Thereupon the person making the payment or tender shall be entitled to the possession of the demised premises under the lease and may hold and enjoy the same according to the terms of the original demise, except as otherwise prescribed in section 765.

Sec. 763.   Redemption by creditor of lessee. In a case specified in section 761, a judgment creditor of the lessee whose judgment was docketed in the county before the precept was issued, or a mortgagee of the lease whose mortgage was duly recorded in the county before the precept was issued, unless by the terms of the lease the lessee shall have waived his right to redeem, or such lessee, or his executor, administrator or assignee shall have subsequently waived the right to redeem by a written instrument filed and recorded in the office in which the lease is recorded, or if not so recorded, in the office in which deeds are required to be recorded of the county in which the leased premises are located, before such judgment was docketed or such mortgage recorded, or such judgment creditor or mortgagee himself shall have waived in writing his right to redeem, may at any time before the expiration of one year after the execution of the warrant, unless a redemption has been made as prescribed in section 761, file with the court which issued the warrant a notice specifying his interest and the sum due to him, describing the premises, and stating that it is his intention to redeem as prescribed in this section. If a redemption is not made by the lessee, his executor, administrator or assignee within a year after the execution of the warrant, the person so filing a notice, or, if two or more persons have filed such notices the one who holds the first lien, at any time before two o'clock of the day, not a Sunday or a public holiday, next succeeding the last day of the year, may redeem for his own benefit in like manner as the lessee, his executor, administrator or assignee might have so redeemed. Where two or more judgment creditors or mortgagees have filed such notices, the holder of the second lien may so redeem at any time before two o'clock of the day, not a Sunday or a public holiday, next succeeding that in which the holder of the first lien might have redeemed; and the holder of the third and each subsequent lien may redeem in like manner at any time before two o'clock of the day, not a Sunday or a public holiday, next succeeding that in which his predecessor might have redeemed. But a second or subsequent redemption is not valid unless the person redeeming pays or tenders to each of his predecessors who has redeemed the sum paid by him to redeem and also the sum due upon his judgment or mortgage; or deposits those sums with the court for the benefit of his predecessor or predecessors.

Sec. 765.   Effect of redemption upon lease. Where a redemption is made, as prescribed in this article, the rights of the person redeeming are subject to a lease, if any, executed by the petitioner since the warrant was issued, so far that the new lessee, his assigns, undertenants, or other representatives, upon complying with the terms of the lease, may hold the premises so leased until twelve o'clock, noon, of the first day of May next succeeding the redemption. And in all other respects, the person so redeeming, his assigns and representatives succeed to all the rights and liabilities of the petitioner under such a lease.

Sec. 767.   Order of redemption; liability of persons redeeming. The person redeeming, as prescribed in this article or the owner of the property so redeemed, may present to the court which issued the warrant a petition setting forth the facts of the redemption and praying for an order establishing the rights and liabilities of the parties upon the redemption, whereupon the court must make an order requiring the other party to the redemption to show cause at a time and place therein specified why the prayer of the petition should not be granted. The order to show cause must be made returnable not less than two nor more than ten days after it is granted; and it must be served at least two days before it is returnable. Upon the return thereof, the court must hear the allegations and proofs of the parties and must make such a judgment as justice requires. The costs and expenses must be paid by the petitioner. The judgment, or a certified copy thereof, may be recorded in like manner as a deed. A person, other than the lessee, who redeems as prescribed in this article succeeds to all the duties and liabilities of the lessee accruing after the redemption as if he was named as lessee in the lease.

GENERAL OBLIGATIONS LAW

ARTICLE 7
SECURITY DEPOSIT LAW

Sec. 7-101. Money deposited or advanced for use or rental of personal property; waiver void.

1. Whenever money shall be deposited or advanced on a contract for the use or rental of personal property as security for performance of the contract or to be applied to payments upon such contract when due, such money, with interest accruing thereon, if any, until repaid or so applied, shall continue to be the money of the person making such deposit or advance and shall be a trust fund in the possession of the person with whom such deposit or advance shall be made and shall be deposited in a bank or trust company and shall not be mingled with other funds or become an asset of such trustee.

2. Any provision of a contract whereby a person who has deposited or advanced money on a contract for the use or rental of personal property as security for the performance of the contract waives any provision of this section is absolutely void.

3. This section shall not be applicable to any deposit or advance of money made in connection with the borrowing of securities for any lawful purpose.

Sec. 7-103. Money deposited or advanced for use or rental of real property; waiver void; administration expenses.

1. Whenever money shall be deposited or advanced on a contract or license agreement for the use or rental of real property as security for performance of the contract or agreement or to be applied to payments upon such contract or agreement when due, such money, with interest accruing thereon, if any, until repaid or so applied, shall continue to be the money of the person making such deposit or advance and shall be held in trust by the person with whom such deposit or advance shall be made and shall not be mingled with the personal moneys or become an asset of the person receiving the same, but may be disposed of as provided in section 7-105 of this chapter.

2. Whenever the person receiving money so deposited or advanced shall deposit such money in a banking organization, such person shall thereupon notify in writing each of the persons making such security deposit or advance, giving the name and address of the banking organization in which the deposit of security money is made, and the amount of such deposit. Deposits in a banking organization pursuant to the provisions of this subdivision shall be made in a banking organization having a place of business within the state. If the person depositing such security money in a banking organization shall deposit same in an interest bearing account, he shall be entitled to receive, as administration expenses, a sum equivalent to one per cent per annum upon the security money so deposited, which shall be in lieu of all other administrative and custodial expenses. The balance of the interest paid by the banking organization shall be the money of the person making the deposit or advance and shall either be held in trust by the person with whom such deposit or advance shall be made, until repaid or applied for the use or rental of the leased premises, or annually paid to the person making the deposit of security money.

2-a. Whenever the money so deposited or advanced is for the rental of property containing six or more family dwelling units, the person receiving such money shall, subject to the provisions of this section, deposit it in an interest bearing account in a banking organization within the state which account shall earn interest at a rate which shall be the prevailing rate earned by other such deposits made with banking organizations in such area.

2-b. In the event that a lease terminates other than at the time that a banking organization in such area regularly pays interest, the person depositing such security money shall pay over to his tenant such interest as he is able to collect at the date of such lease termination.

3. Any provision of such a contract or agreement whereby a person who so deposits or advances money waives any provision of this section is absolutely void.

4. The term "real property" as used in this section is co-extensive in meaning with lands, tenements and hereditaments.

Sec. 7-105. Landlord failing to turn over deposits made by tenants or licensees and to notify tenants or licensees thereof in certain cases.

1. Any person, firm or corporation and the employers, officers or agents thereof, whether the owner or lessee of the property leased, who or which has or hereafter shall have received from a tenant or licensee a sum of money or any other thing of value as a deposit or advance of rental as security for the full performance by such tenant or licensee of the terms of his lease or license agreement, or who or which has or shall have received the same from a former owner or lessee, shall, upon conveying such property or assigning his or its lease to another, or upon the judicial appointment and qualifying of a

receiver in an action to foreclose a mortgage or other lien of record affecting the property leased, or upon the conveyance of such property to another person, firm or corporation by a referee in an action to foreclose a mortgage or other lien of record affecting the property leased if a receiver shall not have been appointed and qualified in such action, at the time of the delivery of the deed or instrument or assignment or within five days thereafter, or within five days after the receiver shall have qualified, deal with the security deposit as follows:

Turn over to his or its grantee or assignee, or to the receiver in the foreclosure action, or to the purchaser at the foreclosure sale if a receiver shall not have been appointed and qualified the sum so deposited, and notify the tenant or licensee by registered or certified mail of such turning over and the name and address of such grantee, assignee, purchaser or receiver.

2. Any owner or lessee turning over to his or its grantee, assignee, to a purchaser of the leased premises at a foreclosure sale, or to the receiver in the foreclosure action the amount of such security deposit is hereby relieved of and from liability to the tenant or licensee for the repayment thereof; and the transferee of such security deposit is hereby made responsible for the return thereof to the tenant or licensee, unless he or it shall thereafter and before the expiration of the term of the tenant's lease or licensee's agreement, transfer such security deposit to another, pursuant to subdivision one hereof and give the requisite notice in connection therewith as provided thereby. A receiver shall hold the security subject to such disposition thereof as shall be provided in an order of the court to be made and entered in the foreclosure action. The provisions of this section shall not apply if the agreement between the landlord and tenant or licensee is inconsistent herewith.

3. Any failure to comply with this section is a misdemeanor.

Sec. 7-106. Money deposited or advanced for certain installations; waiver void.

1. Whenever any non-public moneys shall be deposited or advanced by the owner of an occupied residential dwelling on a contract for the installation of a private connection to a public sewer line as security for payments or to be applied to payments upon such contract when due, such money, with interest accruing thereon, if any, until repaid or so applied, shall continue to be the money of the person making such deposit or advance and shall be a trust fund in the possession of the person with whom such deposit or advance shall be made and shall be deposited in a bank, trust company, savings bank, savings and loan association, federal savings and loan

association or federal mutual savings bank and shall not be mingled with other funds or become an asset of such trustee.

2. Any provision of a contract whereby a person who has deposited or advanced money on a contract for the installation of a private connection to a public sewer line as security for payments or to be applied to payments upon such contract when due waives any provision of this section is absolutely void.

Sec. 7-107. Liability of a grantee or assignee for deposits made by tenants upon conveyance of rent stabilized dwelling units.

1. This section shall apply only to dwelling units subject to the New York city rent stabilization law of nineteen hundred sixty-nine or the emergency tenant protection act of nineteen seventy-four.

2. (a) Any grantee or assignee of any dwelling unit referred to in subdivision one of this section shall be liable to a tenant for any sum of money or any other thing of value deposited as security for the full performance by such tenant of the terms of his lease, plus any accrued interest, if his or its predecessor in interest was liable for such funds. Such liability shall attach whether or not the successor in interest has, upon the conveyance of such dwelling unit, received the sum as deposited.

   (b) The liability of a receiver for payment of any security deposit plus accrued interest pursuant to this subdivision shall be limited to the amount of such deposit actually turned over to him or it pursuant to subdivision one of section 7-105 of this chapter and to the operating income in excess of expenses generated during his or its period of receivership.

3. Any agreement by a lessee or tenant of a dwelling unit waiving or modifying his rights as set forth in this section shall be void.

Sec. 7-108. Liability of a grantee or assignee for deposits made by tenants upon conveyance of non-rent stabilized dwelling units.

1. This section shall apply to all dwelling units with written leases in residential premises containing six or more dwelling units and to all dwelling units subject to the city rent and rehabilitation law or the emergency housing rent control law, unless such dwelling unit is specifically referred to in section 7-107 of this chapter.

2. (a) In circumstances where any sum of money or any other thing of value deposited as security for the full performance by a tenant of the terms of his lease is not turned over to a successor in interest pursuant to section 7-105 of this chapter, the grantee or assignee of the leased premises

shall also be liable to such tenant, upon conveyance of such leased premises, for the repayment of any such security deposit, plus accrued interest, as to which such grantee or assignee has actual knowledge.

(b) For purposes of this section, a grantee or assignee of the leased premises shall be deemed to have actual knowledge of any security deposit which is

(i) deposited at any time during the six months immediately prior to closing or other transfer of title in any banking organization pursuant to subdivision two-a of section 7-103 of this chapter, or

(ii) acknowledged in any lease in effect at the time of closing or other transfer of title, or

(iii) supported by documentary evidence provided by the tenant or lessee as set forth in paragraph (c) of this subdivision.

(c) With respect to any leased premises for which there is no record of security deposit pursuant to subparagraph (i) or (ii) of paragraph (b) of this subdivision, the grantee or assignee of the leased premises shall be obligated to notify the tenant thereof in writing no later than thirty days following the closing or other transfer of title to the fact that there is no record of a security deposit for said leased premises and that unless the tenant within thirty days after receiving notice provides him or it with documentary evidence of deposit, the tenant shall have no further recourse against him or it for said security deposit. For purposes of this subdivision, "documentary evidence" shall be limited to any cancelled check drawn to the order of, a receipt from, or a lease signed by any predecessor in interest, if such predecessor's interest in the leased premises existed on or after the effective date of this section. Except as otherwise provided by subparagraphs (i) and (ii) of paragraph (b) of this subdivision the grantee or assignee of the leased premises shall not be charged with actual knowledge of the security deposit where the tenant fails within the thirty-day period to provide said documentary evidence. Where the grantee or assignee of the leased premises fails to notify the tenant as specified in this paragraph within thirty days following the closing or other transfer of title, the tenant shall be entitled to produce documentary evidence at any time.

(d) The grantee or assignee of the leased premises shall have the right to demand that the grantor or assignor thereof establish an escrow account equal to one month's rent for any leased premises for which there is no record of a security deposit pursuant to paragraph (b) of this subdivision to be used for the purpose of holding harmless the grantee or assignee in any case where, at a date subsequent to the closing or other transfer of title, the tenant gives notice pursuant to paragraph (c) of this subdivision.

(e) The liability of a receiver for payment of any security deposit plus accrued interest pursuant to this subdivision shall be limited to the amount of such deposit actually turned over to him or it pursuant to subdivision one of section 7-105 of this chapter and to the operating income in excess of expenses generated during his or its period of receivership.

3. Any agreement by a lessee or tenant of a dwelling waiving or modifying his rights as set forth in this section shall be absolutely void.

Sec. 7-109. Commencement of a proceeding or action by the attorney general to compel compliance. If it appears to the attorney general that any person, association, or corporation has violated or is violating any of the provisions of title one of this article, an action or proceeding may be instituted by the attorney general in the name of the people of the state of New York to compel compliance with such provisions and enjoin any violation or threatened violation thereof.

NEW YORK STATE CONSOLIDATED LAWS
REAL PROPERTY

ARTICLE 7
LANDLORD AND TENANT

Sec. 220. Action for use and occupation. The landlord may recover a reasonable compensation for the use and occupation of real property, by any person, under an agreement, not made by deed; and a parol lease or other agreement may be used as evidence of the amount to which he is entitled.

Sec. 221. Rent due on life leases recoverable. Rent due on a lease for life or lives is recoverable by action, as well after as before the death of the person on whose life the rent depends, and in the same manner as rent due on a lease for years.

Sec. 222. When rent is apportionable. Where a tenant for life, who shall have demised the real property, dies before the first rent day, or between two rent days, his executor or administrator may recover the proportion of rent which accrued to him before his death.

Sec. 223. Rights where property or lease is transferred. The grantee of leased real property, or of a reversion thereof, or of any rent, the devisee or assignee of the lessor of such a lease, or the heir or personal representative of either of them, has the same remedies, by entry, action or otherwise, for the nonperformance of any agreement contained in the assigned lease for the recovery of rent, for the doing of any waste, or for other cause of forfeiture as his grantor or lessor had, or would have had, if the reversion had remained in him. A lessee of real property, his assignee or personal representative, has the same remedy against the lessor, his grantee or assignee, or the representative of either, for the breach of an agreement contained in the lease, that the lessee might have had against his immediate lessor, except a covenant against incumbrances or relating to the title or possession of the premises leased. This section applies as well to a grant or lease in fee, reserving rent, as to a lease for life or for years; but not to a deed of conveyance in fee, made before the ninth day of April, eighteen hundred and five, or after the fourteenth day of April, eighteen hundred and sixty.

Sec. 223-a. Remedies of lessee when possession is not delivered. In the absence of an express provision to the contrary, there shall be implied in every lease of real property a condition that the lessor will deliver possession at the beginning of the term. In the event of breach of such implied condition the lessee shall have the right to rescind the lease and to recover the consideration paid. Such right shall not be deemed inconsistent with any right of action he may have to recover damages.

Sec. 223-b. Retaliation by landlord against tenant.

1. No landlord of premises or units to which this section is applicable shall serve a notice to quit upon any tenant or commence any action to recover real property or summary proceeding to recover possession of real property in retaliation for:

   a. A good faith complaint, by or in behalf of the tenant, to a governmental authority of the landlord's alleged violation of any health or safety law, regulation, code, or ordinance, or any law or regulation which has as its objective the regulation of premises used for dwelling purposes or which pertains to the offense of rent gouging in the third, second or first degree; or

   b. Actions taken in good faith, by or in behalf of the tenant, to secure or enforce any rights under the lease or rental agreement, under section two hundred thirty-five-b of this chapter, or under any other law of the state of New York, or of its governmental subdivisions, or of the United

States which has as its objective the regulation of premises used for dwelling purposes or which pertains to the offense of rent gouging in the third, second or first degree; or

c. The tenant's participation in the activities of a tenant's organization.

2. No landlord or premises or units to which this section is applicable shall substantially alter the terms of the tenancy in retaliation for any actions set forth in paragraphs a, b, and c of subdivision one of this section. Substantial alteration shall include, but is not limited to, the refusal to continue a tenancy of the tenant or, upon expiration of the tenant's lease, to renew the lease or offer a new lease; provided, however, that a landlord shall not be required under this section to offer a new lease or a lease renewal for a term greater than one year and after such extension of a tenancy for one year shall not be required to further extend or continue such tenancy.

3. A landlord shall be subject to a civil action for damages and other appropriate relief, including injunctive and other equitable remedies, as may be determined by a court of competent jurisdiction in any case in which the landlord has violated the provisions of this section.

4. In any action to recover real property or summary proceeding to recover possession of real property, judgment shall be entered for the tenant if the court finds that the landlord is acting in retaliation for any action set forth in paragraphs a, b, and c of subdivision one of this section and further finds that the landlord would not otherwise have commenced such action or proceeding. Retaliation shall be asserted as an affirmative defense in such action or proceeding. The tenant shall not be relieved of the obligation to pay any rent for which he is otherwise liable.

5. In an action or proceeding instituted against a tenant of premises or a unit to which this section is applicable, a rebuttable presumption that the landlord is acting in retaliation shall be created if the tenant establishes that the landlord served a notice to quit, or instituted an action or proceeding to recover possession, or attempted to substantially alter the terms of the tenancy, within six months after:

a. A good faith complaint was made, by or in behalf of the tenant, to a governmental authority of the landlord's violation of any health or safety law, regulation, code, or ordinance, or any law or regulation which has as its objective the regulation of premises used for dwelling purposes or which pertains to the offense of rent gouging in the third, second or first degree; or

b. The tenant in good faith commenced an action or proceeding in a court or administrative body of competent jurisdiction to secure or enforce against the landlord or his agents any rights under the lease or rental agreement, under section two hundred thirty-five-b of this chapter, or under any other law of the state of New York, or of its governmental subdivisions, or of the United States which has as its objective the regulation of premises used for dwelling purposes or which pertains to the offense of rent gouging in the third, second or first degree.

c. Judgment under subdivision three or four of this section was entered for the tenant in a previous action between the parties; or an inspection was made, an order was entered, or other action was taken as a result of a complaint or act described in paragraph a or b of this subdivision.

But the presumption shall not apply in an action or proceeding based on the violation by the tenant of the terms and conditions of the lease or rental agreement, including nonpayment of the agreed-upon rent.

The effect of the presumption shall be to require the landlord to provide a credible explanation of a non-retaliatory motive for his acts. Such an explanation shall overcome and remove the presumption unless the tenant disproves it by a preponderance of the evidence.

6. This section shall apply to all rental residential premises except owner-occupied dwellings with less than four units. However, its provisions shall not be given effect in any case in which it is established that the condition from which the complaint or action arose was caused by the tenant, a member of the tenant's household, or a guest of the tenant. Nor shall it apply in a case where a tenancy was terminated pursuant to the terms of a lease as a result of a bona fide transfer of ownership.

Sec. 224. Attornment by tenant. The attornment of a tenant to a stranger is absolutely void and does not in any way affect the possession of the landlord unless made either:

1. With the consent of the landlord; or,

2. Pursuant to or in consequence of a judgment, order, or decree of a court of competent jurisdiction; or

3. To a purchaser at foreclosure sale.

Sec. 225. Notice of action adverse to possession of tenant. Where a process or summons in an action to recover the real property occupied by him, or the possession thereof, is served upon a tenant, he must forthwith give notice thereof to his landlord; otherwise he forfeits the value of three years' rent of such property, to the landlord or other person of whom he holds.

Sec. 226. Effect of renewal on sub-lease. The surrender of an under-lease is not requisite to the validity of the surrender of the original lease, where a new lease is given by the chief landlord. Such a surrender and renewal do not impair any right or interest of the chief landlord, his lessee or the holder of an under-lease, under the original lease; including the chief landlord's remedy by entry, for the rent or duties secured by the new lease, not exceeding the rent and duties reserved in the original lease surrendered.

Sec. 226-a. Effect of new lease on tenant's right to remove fixtures or improvements. Unless otherwise expressly agreed, where a tenant has a right to remove fixtures or improvements, such right shall not be lost or impaired by reason of his acceptance of a new lease of the same premises without any surrender of possession between terms.

Sec. 226-b. Right to sublease or assign.

1. Unless a greater right to assign is conferred by the lease, a tenant renting a residence may not assign his lease without the written consent of the owner, which consent may be unconditionally withheld without cause provided that the owner shall release the tenant from the lease upon request of the tenant upon thirty days notice if the owner unreasonably withholds consent which release shall be the sole remedy of the tenant. If the owner reasonably withholds consent, there shall be no assignment and the tenant shall not be released from the lease.

2. (a) A tenant renting a residence pursuant to an existing lease in a dwelling having four or more residential units shall have the right to sublease his premises subject to the written consent of the landlord in advance of the subletting. Such consent shall not be unreasonably withheld.

    (b) The tenant shall inform the landlord of his intent to sublease by mailing a notice of such intent by certified mail, return receipt requested. Such request shall be accompanied by the following information: (i) the term of the sublease, (ii) the name of the proposed sublessee, (iii) the business and permanent home address of the proposed sublessee, (iv) the tenant's reason for subletting, (v) the tenant's address for the term of the sublease, (vi) the written consent of any co-tenant or guarantor of the lease, and (vii) a copy of the proposed sublease, to which a copy of the tenant's lease shall be attached if available, acknowledged by the tenant and proposed subtenant as being a true copy of such sublease.

    (c) Within ten days after the mailing of such request, the landlord may ask the tenant for additional information as will enable the landlord to determine if rejection of such request shall be unreasonable. Any such request for additional information shall not be unduly burdensome. Within thirty days after the mailing of the request for consent, or of the additional information reasonably asked for by the landlord, whichever is later, the landlord shall send a notice to the tenant of his consent or, if he does not consent, his reasons therefor. Landlord's failure to send such a notice shall be deemed to be a consent to the proposed subletting. If the landlord consents, the premises may be sublet in accordance with the request, but the tenant thereunder, shall nevertheless remain liable for the performance of tenant's obligations under said lease. If the landlord reasonably withholds consent, there shall be no subletting and the tenant shall not be released from the lease. If the landlord unreasonably withholds consent, the tenant may sublet in accordance with the request and may recover the costs of the proceeding and attorneys fees if it is found that the owner acted in bad faith by withholding consent.

3. The provisions of this section shall apply to leases entered into or renewed before or after the effective date of this section, however they shall not apply to public housing and other units for which there are constitutional or statutory criteria covering admission thereto nor to a proprietary lease, viz.: a lease to, or held by, a tenant entitled thereto by reason of ownership of stock in a corporate owner of premises which operates the same on a cooperative basis.

4. With respect to units covered by the emergency tenant protection act of nineteen seventy-four or the rent stabilization law of nineteen hundred sixty-nine the exercise of the rights granted by this section shall be subject to the applicable provisions of such laws. Nothing contained in this section two hundred twenty-six-b shall be deemed to affect the rights, if any, of any tenant subject to title Y of chapter 51 of the administrative code of the city of New York or the emergency housing rent control law.

5. Any sublet or assignment which does not comply with the provisions of this section shall constitute a substantial breach of lease or tenancy.

6. Any provision of a lease or rental agreement purporting to waive a provision of this section is null and void.

7. The provisions of this section except for items in paragraph (b) of subdivision two of this section not

previously required, shall apply to all actions and proceedings pending on the effective date of this section.

8. Nothing contained in this section shall be deemed to prevent or limit the right of a tenant to sell improvements to a unit pursuant to article seven-C of the multiple dwelling law.

Sec. 227. When tenant may surrender premises.

Where any building, which is leased or occupied, is destroyed or so injured by the elements, or any other cause as to be untenantable, and unfit for occupancy, and no express agreement to the contrary has been made in writing, the lessee or occupant may, if the destruction or injury occurred without his or her fault or neglect, quit and surrender possession of the leasehold premises, and of the land so leased or occupied; and he or she is not liable to pay to the lessor or owner, rent for the time subsequent to the surrender. Any rent paid in advance or which may have accrued by the terms of a lease or any other hiring shall be adjusted to the date of such surrender.

Sec. 227-a. Termination of residential lease by senior citizens entering certain health care facilities, adult care facilities or housing projects.

1. In any lease or rental agreement covering premises occupied for dwelling purposes in which a lessee or tenant has attained the age of sixty-two years or older, or will attain such age during the term of such lease or rental agreement or a husband or wife of such a person residing with him or her, there shall be implied a covenant by the lessor or owner to permit such lessee or tenant who is notified of his or her opportunity to commence occupancy in an adult care facility (as defined in subdivision twenty-one of section two of the social services law) except for a shelter for adults (as defined in subdivision twenty-three of section two of such law), a residential health care facility (as defined in section two thousand eight hundred one of the public health law), or a housing unit which receives substantial assistance of grants, loans or subsidies from any federal, state or local agency or instrumentality, or any not-for-profit philanthropic organization one of whose primary purposes is providing low or moderate income housing, or in less expensive premises in a housing project or complex erected for the specific purpose of housing senior citizens, to terminate such lease or rental agreement and quit and surrender possession of the leasehold premises, and of the land so leased or occupied; and to release the lessee or tenant from any liability to pay to the lessor or owner, rent or other payments in lieu of rent for the time subsequent to the date of termination of such lease in accordance with subdivision two of this section; and to adjust to the date of surrender any rent or other payments made in

advance or which have accrued by the terms of such lease or rental agreement.

2. Any lease or rental agreement covered by subdivision one of this section may be terminated by notice in writing delivered to the lessor or owner or to the lessor's or owner's agent by a lessee or tenant. Such termination shall be effective no earlier than thirty days after the date on which the next rental payment subsequent to the date when such notice is delivered is due and payable. Such notice shall be accompanied by a documentation of admission or pending admission to a facility set forth in subdivision one of this section. Such notice shall be deemed delivered five days after mailing.

3. Any person who shall knowingly seize, hold, or detain the personal effects, clothing, furniture or other property of any person who has lawfully terminated a lease or rental agreement covered by this section or the spouse or dependent of any such person, or in any manner interferes with the removal of such property from the premises covered by such lease or rental agreement, for the purpose of subjecting or attempting to subject any of such property to a purported claim for rent accruing subsequent to the date of termination of such lease or rental agreement, or attempts so to do, shall be guilty of a misdemeanor and shall be punished by imprisonment not to exceed one year or by fine not to exceed one thousand dollars, or by both such fine and imprisonment.

3-a. Each owner or lessor of a facility or unit into which a lessee or tenant is entitled to move after quitting and surrendering as provided for herein shall in writing, upon an application, notify prospective tenants of the provision of this section. Such notice shall include, in plain and simple English, in conspicuous print of at least eighteen point type, an explanation of a tenants right to terminate the existing lease and all other applicable requirements and duties relating thereto. Such notice shall read as follows:

NOTICE TO SENIOR CITIZENS:
RESIDENTIAL LEASE TERMINATION

SECTION 227-a OF THE REAL PROPERTY LAW OF THE STATE OF NEW YORK ALLOWS FOR THE TERMINATION OF A RESIDENTIAL LEASE BY SENIOR CITIZENS ENTERING CERTAIN HEALTH CARE FACILITIES, ADULT CARE FACILITIES OR HOUSING PROJECTS.

Who is eligible?

Any lessee or tenant who is age sixty-two years or older, or who will attain such age during the term of the lease or rental agreement, or a spouse of such person residing with him or her.

What kind of facilities does this law apply to?

This law will apply if the senior citizen is relocating to:

A. An adult care facility;

B. A residential health care facility;

C. Subsidized low income housing; or

D. Senior citizen housing.

What are the responsibilities of the rental property owner?

When the tenant gives notice of his or her opportunity to move into one of the above facilities the landlord must allow:

A. for the termination of the lease or rental agreement, and

B. the release of the tenant from any liability to pay rent or other payments in lieu of rent from the termination of the lease in accordance with section 227-a of the real property law, to the time of the original termination date, and

C. to adjust any payments made in advance or payments which have accrued by the terms of such lease or rental agreement.

How do you terminate the lease?

If the tenant can move into one of the specified facilities, he or she must terminate the lease or agreement in writing no earlier than thirty days after the date on which the next rental payment (after the notice is delivered) is due and payable. The notice is deemed delivered five days after being mailed. The written notice must include documentation of admission or pending admission to one of the above mentioned facilities.

For example: Mail the notice: May 5th
Notice received: May 10th
Next rental payment due: June 1st
Termination effective: July 1st

Will the landlord face penalties if he or she does not comply?

Yes, according to section 227-a of the real property law, if anyone interferes with the removal of your property from the premises they will be guilty of a misdemeanor and will be either imprisoned for up to one year or fined up to $1000.00 or both.

4. Any agreement by a lessee or tenant of premises occupied for dwelling purposes waiving or modifying his or her rights as set forth in this section shall be void as contrary to public policy.

Sec. 228. Termination of tenancies at will or by sufferance, by notice. A tenancy at will or by sufferance, however created, may be terminated by a written notice of not less than thirty days given in behalf of the landlord, to the tenant, requiring him to remove from the premises; which notice must be served, either by delivering to the tenant or to a person of suitable age and discretion, residing upon the premises, or if neither the tenant nor such a person can be found, by affixing it upon a conspicuous part of the premises, where it may be conveniently read. At the expiration of thirty days after the service of such notice, the landlord may re-enter, maintain an action to recover possession, or proceed, in the manner prescribed by law, to remove the tenant, without further or other notice to quit.

Sec. 229. Liability of tenant holding over after giving notice of intention to quit. If a tenant gives notice of his intention to quit the premises held by him, and does not accordingly deliver up the possession thereof, at the time specified in such notice, he or his personal representatives must, so long as he continue in possession, pay to the landlord, his heirs or assigns, double the rent which he should otherwise have paid, to be recovered at the same time, and in the same manner, as the single rent.

Sec. 230. Right of tenants to form, join or participate in tenants' groups.

1. No landlord shall interfere with the right of a tenant to form, join or participate in the lawful activities of any group, committee or other organization formed to protect the rights of tenants; nor shall any landlord harass, punish, penalize, diminish, or withhold any right, benefit or privilege of a tenant under his tenancy for exercising such right.

2. Tenants' groups, committees or other tenants' organizations shall have the right to meet without being required to pay a fee in any location on the premises including a community or social room where use is normally subject to a fee which is devoted to the common use of all tenants in a peaceful manner, at reasonable hours and without obstructing access to the premises or facilities. No landlord shall deny such right.

Sec. 231. Lease, when void; liability of landlord where premises are occupied for unlawful purpose.

1. Whenever the lessee or occupant other than the owner of any building or premises, shall use or occupy the same, or any part thereof, for any illegal trade, manufacture or other business, the lease or agreement for the letting or occupancy of such building or premises, or any part thereof shall thereupon become void, and the landlord of such lessee or occupant may enter upon the premises so let or occupied.

2. The owner of real property, knowingly leasing or giving possession of the same to be used or occupied, wholly or partly, for any unlawful trade, manufacture or business, or knowingly permitting the

same to be so used, is liable severally, and also jointly with one or more of the tenants or occupants thereof, for any damage resulting from such unlawful use, occupancy, trade, manufacture or business.

3. For the purposes of this section, two or more convictions of any person or persons had, within a period of one year, for any of the offenses described in section 230.00, 230.05, 230.20, 230.25, 230.30, or 230.40 of the penal law arising out of conduct engaged in at the same premises consisting of a dwelling as that term is defined in subdivision four of section four of the multiple dwelling law shall be presumptive evidence of unlawful use of such premises and of the owners knowledge of the same.

4. Any lease or agreement hereafter executed for the letting or occupancy of real property or any portion thereof, to be used by the lessee as a residence, which contains therein a provision pledging personal property exempt by law from levy and sale by virtue of an execution, as security for the payment of rent due or to become due thereunder, is void as to such provision.

5. For the purposes of this section, two or more convictions of any person or persons had, within a period of one year, for any of the offenses described in section 225.00, 225.05, 225.10, 225.15, 225.20, 225.30, 225.32, 225.35 or 225.40 of the penal law, arising out of conduct engaged in at the same premises consisting of a dwelling as that term is defined in subdivision four of section four of the multiple dwelling law shall be presumptive evidence of unlawful use of such premises and of the owner's knowledge of the same.

6. The attorney general may commence an action or proceeding in the supreme court to enjoin the continued unlawful trade, manufacture or business in such premises.

7. Any owner or tenant, including a tenant of one or more rooms of an apartment house, tenement house or multiple dwelling of any premises within two hundred feet of the demised real property, may commence an action or proceeding in supreme court to enjoin the continued unlawful trade, manufacture or other business in such premises.

Sec. 232.   Duration of certain agreements in New York. An agreement for the occupation of real estate in the city of New York, which shall not particularly specify the duration of the occupation, shall be deemed to continue until the first day of October next after the possession commences under the agreement.

Sec. 232-a. Notice to terminate monthly tenancy or tenancy from month to month in the city of New York. No monthly tenant, or tenant from month to month, shall

hereafter be removed from any lands or buildings in the city of New York on the grounds of holding over his term unless at least thirty days before the expiration of the term the landlord or his agent serve upon the tenant, in the same manner in which a notice of petition in summary proceedings is now allowed to be served by law, a notice in writing to the effect that the landlord elects to terminate the tenancy and that unless the tenant removes from such premises on the day on which his term expires the landlord will commence summary proceedings under the statute to remove such tenant therefrom.

Sec. 232-b. Notification to terminate monthly tenancy or tenancy from month to month outside the city of New York. A monthly tenancy or tenancy from month to month of any lands or buildings located outside of the city of New York may be terminated by the landlord or the tenant upon his notifying the other at least one month before the expiration of the term of his election to terminate; provided, however, that no notification shall be necessary to terminate a tenancy for a definite term.

Sec. 232-c. Holding over by a tenant after expiration of a term longer than one month; effect of acceptance of rent. Where a tenant whose term is longer than one month holds over after the expiration of such term, such holding over shall not give to the landlord the option to hold the tenant for a new term solely by virtue of the tenant's holding over. In the case of such a holding over by the tenant, the landlord may proceed, in any manner permitted by law, to remove the tenant, or, if the landlord shall accept rent for any period subsequent to the expiration of such term, then, unless an agreement either express or implied is made providing otherwise, the tenancy created by the acceptance of such rent shall be a tenancy from month to month commencing on the first day after the expiration of such term.

Sec. 233.   Manufactured home parks; duties, responsibilities.

a. Wherever used in this section:

1. The term "manufactured home tenant" means one who rents space in a manufactured home park from a manufactured home park owner or operator for the purpose of parking his manufactured home or one who rents a manufactured home in a manufactured home park from a manufactured home park owner or operator.

2. The term "manufactured home owner" means one who holds title to a manufactured home.

3. The term "manufactured home park" means a contiguous parcel of privately owned land which is used for the accommodation of three or more manufactured homes occupied for year-round living.

4. The term "manufactured home" means a structure, transportable in one or more sections, which in the traveling mode, is eight body feet or more in width or forty body feet or more in length, or, when erected on site, is three hundred twenty or more square feet, and which is built on a permanent chassis and designed to be used as a dwelling with or without a permanent foundation when connected to the required utilities, and includes the plumbing, heating, air-conditioning, and electrical systems contained therein; except that such term shall include a "mobile home" as defined in paragraph five, and shall include a structure which meets all the requirements of this subdivision except the size requirements and with respect to which the manufacturer voluntarily files a certification required by the secretary of housing and urban development.

5. The term "mobile home" means a moveable or portable unit, manufactured prior to January first, nineteen hundred seventy-six, designed and constructed to be towed on its own chassis, comprised of frame and wheels, connected to utilities, and designed and constructed without a permanent foundation for year-round living. A unit may contain parts that may be folded, collapsed or telescoped when being towed and expanded later to provide additional cubic capacity as well as two or more separately towable components designed to be joined into one integral unit capable of being again separated into the components for repeated towing. "Mobile home" shall mean units designed to be used exclusively for residential purposes, excluding travel trailers.

b. A manufactured home park owner or operator may not evict a manufactured home tenant other than for the following reasons:

1. The manufactured home tenant continues in possession of any portion of the premises after the expiration of his term without the permission of the manufactured home park owner or operator.

2. The manufactured home tenant has defaulted in the payment of rent, pursuant to the agreement under which the premises are held, and a demand of the rent with at least thirty days notice in writing has been served upon him as prescribed in section seven hundred thirty-five of the real property actions and proceedings law. Upon the acceptance of such delinquent rent together with allowable costs, an action instituted for nonpayment of rent shall be terminated. Any person succeeding to the manufactured home park owner or operator's interest in the premises may proceed under this subdivision for rent due his predecessor in interest if he has a right thereto.

3. The premises, or any part thereof, are used or occupied as a bawdy-house, or house or place of assignation for lewd purposes or for purposes of prostitution, or for any illegal trade or business.

4. The manufactured home tenant is in violation of some federal, state or local law or ordinance which may be deemed detrimental to the safety and welfare of the other persons residing in the manufactured home park.

5. The manufactured home tenant or anyone occupying the manufactured home is in violation of any lease term or rule or regulation established by the manufactured home park owner or operator pursuant to this section, and has continued in violation for more than ten days after the manufactured home park owner or operator has given written notice of such violation to the manufactured home tenant setting forth the lease term or rule or regulation violated and directing that the manufactured home tenant correct or cease violation of such lease term or rule or regulation within ten days from the receipt of said notice. Upon the expiration of such period should the violation continue or should the manufactured home tenant or anyone occupying the manufactured home be deemed a persistent violator of the lease term or rules and regulations, the park owner or operator may serve written notice upon the manufactured home tenant directing that he vacate the premises within thirty days of the receipt of said notice.

6. The manufactured home park owner or operator proposes a change in the use of the land comprising the manufactured home park, or a portion thereof, on which the manufactured home is located, from manufactured home lot rentals to some other use, provided the manufactured home owner is given written notice of the proposed change of use and the manufactured home owner's need to secure other accommodations. Whenever a manufactured home park owner or operator gives a notice of proposed change of use to any manufactured home owner, the manufactured home park owner or operator shall, at the same time, give notice of the proposed change of use to all other manufactured home owners in the manufactured home park who will be required to secure other accommodations as a result of such proposed change of use. Eviction proceedings based on a change in use shall not be commenced prior to six months from the service of notice of proposed

change in use or the end of the lease term, whichever is later. Such notice shall be served in the manner prescribed in section seven hundred thirty-five of the real property actions and proceedings law or by certified mail, return receipt requested.

c. If the manufactured home park owner or operator does not have one of the above grounds available, the manufactured home tenant may raise the same by affirmative defense to an action for eviction.

d. The proceedings to evict shall be governed by the procedures set forth in article seven of the real property actions and proceedings law, except for the provisions of subdivision two of section seven hundred forty-nine of the real property actions and proceedings law which shall be superseded by the provisions of this subdivision.

1. The officer to whom the warrant is directed and delivered shall give at least ninety days notice, in writing and in the manner prescribed in article seven of the real property actions and proceedings law for the service of notice of petition, to the person or persons to be evicted or dispossessed and shall execute the warrant between the hours of sunrise and sunset.

2. The court may order that such warrant be directed and delivered with only thirty days written notice to the person or persons to be evicted or dispossessed if the conditions upon which the eviction is founded pose an imminent threat to the health, safety, or welfare of the other manufactured home tenants in the manufactured home park.

3. The court shall order that such warrant be directed and delivered with thirty days written notice to the person or persons to be evicted or dispossessed if the condition upon which the eviction is founded is that such person is in default in the payment of rent.

4. Notwithstanding the provisions of paragraphs one and two of this subdivision, nor of any other general, special or local law, rule or regulation to the contrary, the officer to whom the warrant is directed and delivered shall give seventy-two hours written notice to the person or persons to be evicted or dispossessed, if such person or persons rents a manufactured home in a manufactured home park from a manufactured home park owner or operator and such officer shall execute such warrant between the hours of sunrise and sunset.

e. Leases.

1. The manufactured home park owner or operator shall offer every manufactured home tenant prior to occupancy, the opportunity to sign a lease for a minimum of one year, which offer shall be made in writing.

2. (i) On or before, as appropriate, (a) the first day of October of each calendar year with respect to a manufactured home owner then in good standing who is not currently a party to a written lease with a manufactured home park owner or operator or (b) the ninetieth day next preceding the expiration date of any existing written lease between a manufactured home owner then in good standing and a manufactured home park owner or operator, the manufactured home park owner or operator shall submit to each such manufactured home owner a written offer to lease for a term of at least twelve months from the commencement date thereof unless the manufactured home park owner or operator has previously furnished the manufactured home owner with written notification of a proposed change of use pursuant to paragraph six of subdivision b of this section. Any such offer shall include a copy of the proposed lease containing such terms and conditions, including provisions for rent and other charges, as the manufactured home park owner shall deem appropriate; provided such terms and conditions are consistent with all rules and regulations promulgated by the manufactured home park operator prior to the date of the offer and are not otherwise prohibited or limited by applicable law. Such offer shall also contain a statement advising the manufactured home owner that if he or she fails to execute and return the lease to the manufactured home park owner or operator within thirty days after submission of such lease, the manufactured home owner shall be deemed to have declined the offer of a lease and shall not have any right to a lease from the manufactured home park owner or operator for the next succeeding twelve months.

(ii) For purposes of this paragraph, a manufactured home owner shall be deemed in good standing if he or she is not in default in the payment of more than one month's rent to the manufactured home park owner, and is not in violation of paragraph three, four or five of subdivision b of this section. No manufactured home park owner or operator shall refuse to provide a written offer to lease based on a default of rent payments or a violation of paragraph three, four or five of subdivision b of this section unless, at least thirty days prior to the last date on which the owner or operator would otherwise be required to provide such written offer to lease, the owner or operator notifies the manufactured home owner, in writing, of the default in rent or the specific grounds constituting the violation and such grounds continues up and until the fifth calendar day immediately preceding the last date on which the written offer would otherwise be required to be made.

(iii) For purposes of this paragraph, the commencement date of any lease offered by the manufactured home park owner to the manufactured home owner shall be the ninetieth day after the date upon which the manufactured home park owner shall have provided the offer required pursuant to this paragraph; provided, however, that no such lease shall be effective if, on such commencement date, the manufactured home owner is in default of more than one month's rent. In the event the manufactured home owner shall have failed to execute and return said lease to the manufactured home park owner or operator within thirty days after it is submitted to the manufactured home owner as required by subparagraph (i) of this paragraph the manufactured home owner shall be deemed to have declined to enter said lease.

3. No lease provision shall be inconsistent with any rule or regulation in effect at the commencement of the lease.

f. Rules and regulations.

1. A manufactured home park owner or operator may promulgate rules and regulations governing the rental or occupancy of a manufactured home lot provided such rules and regulations shall not be unreasonable, arbitrary or capricious. A copy of all rules and regulations shall be delivered by the manufactured home park owner or operator to all manufactured home tenants at the commencement of occupancy. A copy of the rules and regulations shall be posted in a conspicuous place upon the manufactured home park grounds.

2. If a rule or regulation is not applied uniformly to all manufactured home tenants of the manufactured home park there shall be a rebuttable presumption that such rule or regulation is unreasonable, arbitrary and capricious, provided, however, that an inconsistency between a rule or regulation and a lease term contained in a lease signed before

the date the rule or regulation is effective shall not raise a rebuttable presumption that such rule is unreasonable, arbitrary or capricious.

3. Any rule or regulation which does not conform to the requirements of this section or which has not been supplied or posted as required by paragraph one of this subdivision shall be unenforceable and may be raised by the manufactured home tenant as an affirmative defense in any action to evict on the basis of a violation of such rule or regulation.

4. No rules or regulations may be changed by the manufactured home park owner or operator without specifying the date of implementation of said changed rules and regulations, which date shall be no fewer than thirty days after written notice to all tenants.

g. 1. No tenant shall be charged a fee for other than rent, utilities and charges for facilities and services available to the tenant. All fees, charges or assessments must be reasonably related to services actually rendered.

2. A manufactured home park owner or operator shall be required to fully disclose in writing all fees, charges, assessments, including rental fees, rules and regulations prior to a manufactured home tenant assuming occupancy in the manufactured home park.

3. No fees, charges, assessments or rental fees may be increased by manufactured home park owner or operator without specifying the date of implementation of said fees, charges, assessments or rental fees which date shall be no less than ninety days after written notice to all manufactured home tenants. Failure on the part of the manufactured home park owner or operator to fully disclose all fees, charges or assessments shall prevent the manufactured home park owner or operator from collecting said fees, charges or assessments, and refusal by the manufactured home tenant to pay any undisclosed charges shall not be used by the manufactured home park owner or operator as a cause for eviction in any court of law.

4. (a) Whenever money shall be deposited or advanced on a contract or license agreement for the use or rental of premises and the manufactured home, if rented, in a manufactured home park as security for performance of the contract or agreement or to be applied to payments upon such contract or agreement when due, such money with interest accruing thereon, if any, until repaid or so applied, shall continue to be the money

of the person making such deposit or advance and shall be a trust fund in the possession of the person with whom such deposit or advance shall be made and shall not be mingled with other funds or become an asset of the park owner, operator or his agent.

(b) Whenever the person receiving money so deposited or advanced shall deposit such money in a banking organization, such person shall thereupon notify in writing each of the persons making such security deposit or advance, giving the name and address of the banking organization in which the deposit of security money is made, and the amount of such deposit. Deposits in a banking organization pursuant to the provisions of this subdivision shall be made in a banking organization having a place of business within the state. If the person depositing such security money in a banking organization shall deposit same in an interest bearing account, he shall be entitled to receive, as administration expenses, a sum equivalent to one percent per annum upon the security money so deposited, which shall be in lieu of all other administrative and custodial expenses. The balances of the interest paid by the banking organization shall be the money of the person making the deposit or advance and shall either be held in trust by the person with whom such deposit or advance shall be made, until repaid or applied for the use or rental of the leased premises, or annually paid to the person making the deposit of security money.

(c) Whenever the money so deposited or advanced is for the rental of a manufactured home park lot on property on which are located six or more manufactured home park lots, the person receiving such money shall, subject to the provisions of this section, deposit it in an interest bearing account in a banking organization within the state which account shall earn interest at a rate which shall be the prevailing rate earned by other such deposits made with the banking organizations in such area.

(d) In the event that a lease terminates other than at the time that a banking organization in such area regularly pays interest, the person depositing such security money shall pay over to his manufactured home tenant such interest as he is able to collect at the date of such lease termination.

(e) Any provision of such a contract or agreement whereby a person who so deposits or advances money waives any provision of this subdivision is void.

h. No manufactured home park owner shall:

1. Require a manufactured home tenant therein to purchase from said manufactured home park owner or operator skirting or equipment for tying down manufactured homes, or any other equipment. However, the manufactured home park owner or operator may determine by rule or regulation the style or quality of such equipment to be purchased by the manufactured home tenant from the vendor of the manufactured home tenant's choosing, providing such equipment is readily available.

2. Charge any manufactured home tenant who chooses to install an electric or gas appliance in his manufactured home an additional fee solely on the basis of such installation unless such installation is performed by the manufactured home park owner or operator at the request of the manufactured home tenant, nor shall the manufactured home park owner or operator restrict the installation, service or maintenance of any such appliance, restrict the ingress or egress of repairers to enter the manufactured home park for the purpose of installation, service or maintenance of any such appliance, or restrict the making of any interior improvement in such manufactured home, so long as such an installation or improvement is in compliance with applicable building codes and other provisions of law and further provided that adequate utilities are available for such installation or improvement.

3. Require, by contract, rule, regulation or otherwise, a manufactured home dweller to purchase from the manufactured home park owner or any person acting directly or indirectly on behalf of the park owner, commodities or services incidental to placement or rental within such park; nor shall the park owner restrict access to the manufactured home park to any person employed, retained or requested by the manufactured home dweller to provide such commodity or service, unless the manufactured home park owner establishes that such requirement or restriction is necessary to protect the property of such park owner from substantial harm or impairment.

4. Require a manufactured home owner or a prospective manufactured home owner to purchase his or her manufactured home from the manufactured home park owner or operator, or from any person or persons designated by the manufactured home

park owner or operator. Nothing herein shall be construed to prevent a manufactured home park owner or operator from requiring that any new manufactured home to be installed in his or her manufactured home park comply with the rules and regulations of said manufactured home park or conform to the physical facilities then existing for installation of a manufactured home in said manufactured home park.

i. 1. No manufactured home park owner or operator shall deny any manufactured home tenant the right to sell his manufactured home within the manufactured home park provided the manufactured home tenant shall give to the manufactured home park owner or operator twenty days' written notice of his intention to sell, provided that if the manufactured home owner is deceased no such notice shall be required from the administrator or executor of the home owner's estate, and provided further that no manufactured home park owner or operator shall restrict access to the manufactured home park to any potential purchaser or representatives of any seller unless the manufactured home park owner establishes that such restriction is necessary to protect the property of such park owner or operator from substantial harm or impairment. No manufactured home park owner or operator shall require the manufactured home owner or subsequent purchaser to remove the manufactured home from the manufactured home park solely on the basis of the sale thereof. The manufactured home park owner or operator may reserve the right to approve the purchaser of said manufactured home as a manufactured home tenant for the remainder of the seller's or deceased tenant's term but such permission may not be unreasonably withheld. If the manufactured home park owner or operator unreasonably withholds his permission or unreasonably restricts access to the manufactured home park, the manufactured home tenant or the executor or administrator of a deceased tenant's estate may recover the costs of the proceedings and attorneys' fees if it is found that the manufactured home park owner or operator acted in bad faith by withholding permission or restricting access.

2. The manufactured home park owner or operator shall not exact a commission or fee with respect to the price realized by the seller unless the manufactured home park owner or operator has acted as agent for the manufactured home owner in the sale pursuant to a written contract.

3. If the ownership or management rejects a purchaser as a prospective tenant, the selling tenant must be informed in writing of the reasons therefor.

j. The owner or operator of a manufactured home park may enter a manufactured home owner's manufactured home without the prior consent of the occupant only in case of emergency. The owner or operator of a manufactured home park may enter a manufactured home tenant's manufactured home during reasonable hours on reasonable notice.

k. The owner or operator shall provide reasonable notice where practicable to all manufactured home tenants who would be affected by any planned disruption of necessary services caused by the owner, operator or his agent.

l. The park owner shall designate an agent on the premises or in close proximity to the manufactured home park to insure the availability of emergency response actions in matters affecting the health, safety, well-being and welfare of manufactured home tenants in the park. The designated agent's name, address and telephone number shall be posted in a conspicuous location in the park, given in writing to each tenant and registered with appropriate county law enforcement and health officials and local fire officials.

m. Warranty of habitability, maintenance, disruption of services. In every written or oral lease or rental agreement entered into by a manufactured home tenant, the manufactured home park owner or operator shall be deemed to covenant and warrant that the premises so leased or rented and the manufactured home if rented and all areas used in connection therewith in common with other manufactured home tenants or residents including all roads within the manufactured home park are fit for human habitation and for the uses reasonably intended by the parties and that the occupants of such premises and such manufactured homes if rented shall not be subjected to any conditions which would be dangerous, hazardous or detrimental to their life, health or safety. When any such condition has been caused by the misconduct of the manufactured home tenant or lessee or persons under his direction or control, it shall not constitute a breach of such covenants and warranties. The rights and obligations of the manufactured home park owner or operator and the manufactured home tenant shall be governed by the provisions of this subdivision and subdivisions two and three of section two hundred thirty-five-b of this article.

n. 1. No manufactured home park owner or operator shall serve a notice to quit upon any manufactured home tenant or commence any action to recover real property or summary proceeding to recover possession of real property in retaliation for:

(a) A good faith complaint, by or in behalf of the tenant, to a governmental authority of the manufactured home park owner's or operator's alleged violation of any health or safety law, regulation, code, or ordinance, or any law or regulation which has as its objective the regulation of premises used for dwelling purposes; or

(b) Actions taken in good faith, by or in behalf of the manufactured home tenant, to secure or enforce any rights under the lease or rental agreement, under subdivision m of this section and subdivisions two and three of section two hundred thirty-five-b of this article, or under any other local law, law of the state of New York, or of its governmental subdivisions, or of the United States which has as its objective the regulation of premises used for dwelling purposes; or

(c) The manufactured home tenant's participation in the activities of a tenant's organization.

2. No manufactured home park owner or operator shall substantially alter the terms of the tenancy in retaliation for any actions set forth in subparagraphs (a), (b), and (c) of paragraph one of this subdivision. Substantial alteration shall include, but is not limited to, the refusal to continue a tenancy of the manufactured home tenant or, upon expiration of the manufactured home owner's lease, to renew the lease or offer a new lease; provided, however, that a manufactured home park owner or operator shall not be required under this subdivision to offer a manufactured home owner a new lease or a lease renewal for a term greater than one year.

3. This subdivision shall apply to all manufactured home parks with four or more manufactured homes. However, its provisions shall not be given effect in any case in which it is established that the condition from which the complaint or action arose was caused by the manufactured home tenant, a member of the manufactured home tenant's household, or a guest of the manufactured home tenant. Nor shall it apply in a case where a tenancy was terminated pursuant to the terms of a lease as a result of a bona fide transfer of ownership. The rights and obligations of the manufactured home park owner or operator and the manufactured home tenant shall be governed by the provisions of this subdivision and subdivisions three, four and five of section two hundred twenty-three-b of this article.

o. Whenever a lease shall provide that in any action or summary proceeding the manufactured home park owner or operator may recover attorney's fees and/or expenses incurred as the result of the failure of the tenant to perform any covenant or agreement contained in such lease, or that amounts paid by the manufactured home park owner or operator therefor shall be paid by the tenant as additional rent, there shall be implied in such lease a covenant by the manufactured home park owner or operator, to pay to the tenant the reasonable attorney's fees and/or expenses incurred by the tenant to the same extent as is provided in section two hundred thirty-four of this article which section shall apply in its entirety.

p. Any manufactured home park owner or operator who has agreed to provide hot or cold water, heat, light, power, or any other service or facility to any occupant of the manufactured home park who willfully or intentionally without just cause fails to furnish such water, heat, light, power, or other service or facility, or who interferes with the quiet enjoyment of the leased premises, is guilty of a violation.

q. Upon receipt of rent, fees, charges or other assessments, in the form of cash or any instrument other than the personal check of the tenant, it shall be the duty of the manufactured home park owner or operator to provide the payor with a written receipt containing the following:

1. the date;

2. the amount;

3. the identity of the premises and the period for which paid;

4. the signature and title of the person receiving rent.

r. Limitation on late charges. A late charge on any rental payment by a manufactured home owner which has become due and remains unpaid shall not exceed and shall be enforced to the extent of five percent of such delinquent payment; provided, however, that no charge shall be imposed on any rental payment by a manufactured home owner received within ten days after the due date. In the absence of a specific provision in the lease or the manufactured home park's rules and regulations, no late charge on any delinquent rental payment shall be assessed or collected.

s. It shall be a violation for a manufactured home park owner, operator or his agent to restrict occupancy of a manufactured home or manufactured home park lot intended for residential purposes by express lease terms or otherwise, to a manufactured home tenant or tenants or to such tenants and immediate family. Any such restriction in a lease or rental agreement entered into or renewed before or after the effective date of this subdivision shall be unenforceable as against public policy. The rights and obligations of a manufactured home park owner or operator and the manufactured home tenant shall be governed by the provisions of this subdivision and subdivisions one, three, four, five, six, seven, eight and nine of section two hundred thirty-five-f of this article.

t. 1. Unless a greater right to assign is conferred by the lease, a manufactured home tenant may not assign his lease without the written consent of the manufactured home park owner or operator, which consent may be unconditionally withheld without cause provided that the manufactured home park owner or operator shall release the manufactured home tenant from the lease upon request of the mobile home tenant upon thirty days notice if the manufactured home park owner or operator unreasonably withholds consent which release shall be the sole remedy of the tenant. If the owner reasonably withholds consent, there shall be no assignment and the manufactured home tenant shall not be released from the lease.

2. (a) A manufactured home tenant renting space or a manufactured home in a manufactured home park with four or more manufactured homes pursuant to an existing lease shall have a right to sublease his premises subject to the written consent of the park owner in advance of the subletting. Such consent shall not be unreasonably withheld.

(b) The manufactured home tenant shall inform the manufactured home park owner or operator of his intent to sublease by mailing a notice of such intent by certified mail, return receipt requested. Such request shall be accompanied by the following information: (i) the term of the sublease, (ii) the name of the proposed sublessee, (iii) the business and permanent home address of the proposed sublessee, (iv) the tenant's reason for subletting, (v) the tenant's address for the term of the sublease, (vi) the written consent of any co-tenant or guarantor of the lease, and (vii) a copy of the proposed sublease, to which a copy of the manufactured home tenant's lease shall be attached if available, acknowledged by the manufactured home tenant and proposed subtenant as being a true copy of such sublease.

(c) Within ten days after the mailing of such request, the manufactured home park owner or operator may ask the manufactured home tenant for additional information as will enable the manufactured home park owner or operator to determine if rejection of such request shall be unreasonable. Any such request for additional information shall not be unduly burdensome. Within thirty days after the mailing of the request for consent, or of the additional information reasonably asked for by the manufactured home park owner or operator, whichever is later, the manufactured home park owner or operator shall send a notice to the manufactured home tenant of his consent or, if he does not consent, his reasons therefor. Manufactured home park owner's or operator's failure to send such a notice shall be deemed to be a consent to the proposed subletting. If the manufactured home park owner or operator consents, the premises may be sublet in accordance with the request, but the manufactured home tenant thereunder, shall nevertheless remain liable for the performance of manufactured home tenant's obligations under said lease. If the manufactured home park owner or operator reasonably withholds consent, there shall be no subletting and the manufactured home tenant shall not be released from the lease. If the manufactured home park owner or operator unreasonably withholds consent, the manufactured home tenant may sublet in accordance with the request and may recover the costs of the proceeding and attorneys fees if it is found that the manufactured home park owner or operator acted in bad faith by withholding consent. The rights and obligations of the manufactured home park owner or operator and the manufactured home tenant shall be governed by the provisions of this subdivision and subdivisions three, five, six, seven and eight of section two hundred twenty-six-b of this article.

u. In the event of a breach by a manufactured home park owner or operator of any of the requirements of this section, the manufactured home tenant may commence an action for damages actually incurred as a result of such breach, or in an action or summary proceeding commenced by such manufactured home park owner or operator, may counterclaim for damages occasioned by such breach.

v. On and after April first, nineteen hundred eighty-nine, the commissioner of housing and community renewal shall have the power and duty to enforce and ensure compliance with the provisions of this section. However, the commissioner shall not have the power or duty to enforce manufactured home park rules and regulations established under subdivision f of this section. On or before January first, nineteen hundred eighty-nine, each manufactured home park owner or operator shall file a registration statement with the commissioner and shall thereafter file an annual registration statement on or before January first of each succeeding year. The commissioner, by regulation, shall provide that such registration statement shall include only the names of all persons owning an interest in the park, the names of all tenants of the park, all services provided by the park owner to the tenants and a copy of all current manufactured home park rules and regulations. Whenever there shall be a violation of this section, an application may be made by the commissioner of housing and community renewal in the name of the people of the state of New York to a court or justice having jurisdiction by a special proceeding to issue an injunction, and upon notice to the defendant of not less than five days, to enjoin and restrain the continuance of such violation; and if it shall appear to the satisfaction of the court or justice that the defendant has, in fact, violated this section, an injunction may be issued by such court or justice, enjoining and restraining any further violation and with respect to this subdivision, directing the filing of a registration statement. In any such proceeding, the court may make allowances to the commissioner of housing and community renewal of a sum not exceeding two thousand dollars against each defendant, and direct restitution. Whenever the court shall determine that a violation of this section has occurred, the court may impose a civil penalty of not more than one thousand five hundred dollars for each violation. Such penalty shall be deposited in the manufactured home cooperative fund, created pursuant to section fifty-nine-h of the private housing finance law. In connection with any such proposed application, the commissioner of housing and community renewal is authorized to take proof and make a determination of the relevant facts and to issue subpoenas in accordance with the civil practice law and rules. The provisions of this subdivision shall not impair the rights granted under subdivision u of this section.

w. Real property tax payments.

1. A manufactured home park owner, operator or the agent of such owner or operator shall reduce the annual rent paid by a manufactured home tenant for use of the land upon which such manufactured home sits in an amount equal to the total of the real property taxes actually paid by such manufactured home tenant for such manufactured home plus the amount by which the taxes on such manufactured home were reduced as a result of the partial real property tax exemption granted to the manufactured home tenant pursuant to article four of the real property tax law, provided such manufactured home tenant:

   (a) owns a manufactured home which is separately assessed, subject to the provisions of paragraph two of this subdivision;

   (b) is entitled to and actually receives a partial real property tax exemption pursuant to article four of the real property tax law; and

   (c) pays the real property taxes due on such home.

2. In the case of a manufactured home which is not separately assessed, but which is entitled to and actually receives the school tax relief (STAR) exemption authorized by section four hundred twenty-five of the real property tax law, the tenant of such manufactured home shall be entitled to a rent reduction pursuant to this subdivision to the same extent as a tenant of a manufactured home which satisfies the criteria set forth in paragraph one of this subdivision. Such rent reduction shall be equal to the amount by which the taxes on such manufactured home were reduced as a result of such exemption.

3. A manufactured home park owner or operator providing a reduction in rent as required by paragraph one or two of this subdivision may retain, in consideration for record keeping expenses, two percent of the amount of such reduction.

4. The failure of a manufactured home park owner or operator to comply with the provisions of this subdivision shall be a violation punishable by a fine not to exceed five hundred dollars for each violation.

Sec. 234. Tenants' right to recover attorneys' fees in actions or summary proceedings arising out of leases of residential property. Whenever a lease of residential property shall provide that in any action or summary proceeding the landlord may recover attorneys' fees and/or expenses incurred as the result of the failure of the tenant to perform any covenant or agreement contained in such lease, or that amounts paid by the landlord therefor shall be paid by the tenant as additional rent, there shall be implied in such lease a covenant by the landlord to pay to the tenant the reasonable attorneys' fees and/or expenses incurred by the tenant as the result of the failure of the landlord to perform any covenant or agreement on its part to be performed under the lease or in the successful defense of any action or summary proceeding commenced by the landlord against the tenant arising out of the lease, and an agreement that such fees and expenses may be recovered as provided by law in an action commenced against the landlord or by way of counterclaim in any action or summary proceeding commenced by the landlord against the tenant. Any waiver of this section shall be void as against public policy.

Sec. 235. Wilful violations.

1. Any lessor, agent, manager, superintendent or janitor of any building, or part thereof, the lease or rental agreement whereof by its terms, expressed or implied, requires the furnishing of hot or cold water, heat, light, power, elevator service, telephone service or any other service or facility to any occupant of said building, who wilfully or intentionally fails to furnish such water, heat, light, power, elevator service, telephone service or other service or facility at any time when the same are necessary to the proper or customary use of such building, or part thereof, or any lessor, agent, manager, superintendent or janitor who wilfully and intentionally interferes with the quiet enjoyment of the leased premises by such occupant, is guilty of a violation.

2. Any lessor, agent, manager, superintendent or janitor of any building, or part thereof, who wilfully or intentionally acts to prevent or obstruct the delivery of fuel oil ordered in compliance with either section three hundred two-c of the multiple dwelling law or section three hundred five-c of the multiple residence law or the refiring of an oil burner after such a delivery shall be guilty of a violation.

Sec. 235-a. Tenant right to offset payments and entitlement to damages in certain cases.

1. In any case in which a tenant shall lawfully make a payment to a utility company pursuant to the provisions of sections thirty-three, thirty-four and one hundred sixteen of the public service law, such payment shall be deductible from any future payment of rent.

2. Any owner (as defined in the multiple dwelling law or multiple residence law) of a multiple dwelling responsible for the payment of charges for gas, electric, steam or water service who causes the discontinuance of that service by failure or refusal to pay the charges for past service shall be liable for compensatory and punitive damages to any tenant whose utility service is so discontinued.

3. Nothing contained in this section and no payment made pursuant to this section shall be deemed to discharge the liability of a renter with an interest in real property pursuant to subdivision two of section three hundred four of the real property tax law from taxes levied on such interest. *(Effective pending ruling by Commissioner of Internal Revenue.)

Sec. 235-b. Warranty of habitability.

1. In every written or oral lease or rental agreement for residential premises the landlord or lessor shall be deemed to covenant and warrant that the premises so leased or rented and all areas used in connection therewith in common with other tenants or residents are fit for human habitation and for the uses reasonably intended by the parties and that the occupants of such premises shall not be subjected to any conditions which would be dangerous, hazardous or detrimental to their life, health or safety. When any such condition has been caused by the misconduct of the tenant or lessee or persons under his direction or control, it shall not constitute a breach of such covenants and warranties.

2. Any agreement by a lessee or tenant of a dwelling waiving or modifying his rights as set forth in this section shall be void as contrary to public policy.

3. In determining the amount of damages sustained by a tenant as a result of a breach of the warranty set forth in the section, the court;

   (a) need not require any expert testimony; and

   (b) shall, to the extent the warranty is breached or cannot be cured by reason of a strike or other labor dispute which is not caused primarily by the individual landlord or lessor and such damages are attributable to such strike, exclude recovery to such extent, except to the extent of the net savings, if any, to the landlord or lessor by reason of such strike or labor dispute allocable to the tenant's premises, provided, however, that the landlord or lesser has made a good faith attempt, where practicable, to cure the breach.

   (c) where the premises is subject to regulation pursuant to the local emergency housing rent control law, the emergency tenant protection act of nineteen seventy-four, the rent stabilization law of nineteen hundred sixty-nine or the city rent and rehabilitation law, reduce the amount awarded hereunder by the total amount of any rent reduction ordered by the state division of housing and community renewal pursuant to such laws or act, awarded to the tenant, from the effective date of such rent reduction order, that relates to one or more matters for which relief is awarded hereunder.

Sec. 235-c. Unconscionable lease or clause.

1. If the court as a matter of law finds a lease or any clause of the lease to have been unconscionable at the time it was made the court may refuse to enforce the lease, or it may enforce the remainder of the lease without the unconscionable clause, or it may so limit the application of any unconscionable clause as to avoid any unconscionable result.

2. When it is claimed or appears to the court that a lease or any clause thereof may be unconscionable the parties shall be afforded a reasonable opportunity to present evidence as to its setting, purpose and effect to aid the court in making the determination.

Sec. 235-d. Harassment.

1. Notwithstanding any other provision of law, within a city having a population of one million or more, it shall be unlawful and shall constitute harassment for any landlord of a building which at any time was occupied for manufacturing or warehouse purposes, or other person acting on his behalf, to engage in any course of conduct, including, but not limited to intentional interruption or discontinuance or willful failure to restore services customarily provided or required by written lease or other rental agreement, which interferes with or disturbs the comfort, repose, peace or,quiet of a tenant in the tenant's use or occupancy of rental space if such conduct is intended to cause the tenant (i) to vacate a building or part thereof; or (ii) to surrender or waive any rights of such tenant under the tenant's written lease or other rental agreement.

2. The lawful termination of a tenancy or lawful refusal to renew or extend a written lease or other rental agreement shall not constitute harassment for purposes of this section.

3. As used in this section the term "tenant" means only a person or business occupying or residing at the premises pursuant to a written lease or other rental agreement, if such premises are located in a building which at any time was occupied for manufacturing or warehouse purposes and a certificate of occupancy for residential use of such building is not in effect at the time of the last alleged acts or incidents upon which the harassment claim is based.

4. A tenant may apply to the supreme court for an order enjoining acts or practices which constitute harassment under subdivision one of this section; and upon sufficient showing, the supreme court may issue a temporary or permanent injunction, restraining order or other order, all of which may, as the court determines in the exercise of its sound discretion, be granted without bond. In the event the court issues a preliminary injunction it shall make provision for an expeditious trial of the underlying action.

5. The powers and remedies set forth in this section shall be in addition to all other powers and remedies in relation to harassment including the award of damages. Nothing contained herein shall be construed to amend, repeal, modify or affect any existing local law or ordinance, or provision of the charter or administrative code of the city of New York, or to limit or restrict the power of the city to amend or modify any existing local law, ordinance or provision of the charter or administrative code, or to restrict or limit any power otherwise conferred by law with respect to harassment.

6. Any agreement by a tenant in a written lease or other rental agreement waiving or modifying his rights as set forth in this section shall be void as contrary to public policy.

Sec. 235-e. Duty of landlord to provide written receipt.

(a) Upon the receipt of rent for residential premises in the form of cash or any instrument other than the personal check of the tenant, it shall be the duty of the landlord to provide the payor with a written receipt containing the following:
   1. The date;
   2. The amount;
   3. The identity of the premises and period for which paid; and
   4. The signature and title of the person receiving the rent.

(b) Where a tenant, in writing, requests that a landlord provide a receipt for rent paid by personal check, it shall be the duty of the landlord to provide the payor with the receipt described in subdivision (a) of this section for each such request made in writing.

Sec. 235-f. Unlawful restrictions on occupancy.

1. As used in this section, the terms:
   (a) "Tenant" means a person occupying or entitled to occupy a residential rental premises who is either a party to the lease or rental agreement for such premises or is a statutory tenant pursuant to the emergency housing rent control law or the city rent and rehabilitation law or article seven-c of the multiple dwelling law.
   (b) "Occupant" means a person, other than a tenant or a member of a tenant's immediate family, occupying a premises with the consent of the tenant or tenants.

2. It shall be unlawful for a landlord to restrict occupancy of residential premises, by express lease terms or otherwise, to a tenant or tenants or to such tenants and immediate family. Any such restriction in a lease or rental agreement entered into or renewed before or after the effective date of this section shall be unenforceable as against public policy.

3. Any lease or rental agreement for residential premises entered into by one tenant shall be construed to permit occupancy by the tenant, immediate family of the tenant, one additional occupant, and dependent children of the occupant provided that the tenant or the tenant's spouse occupies the premises as his primary residence.

4. Any lease or rental agreement for residential premises entered into by two or more tenants shall be construed to permit occupancy by tenants, immediate family of tenants, occupants and dependent children of occupants; provided that the total number of tenants and occupants, excluding occupants' dependent children, does not exceed the number of tenants specified in the current lease or rental agreement, and that at

least one tenant or a tenants' spouse occupies the premises as his primary residence.

5. The tenant shall inform the landlord of the name of any occupant within thirty days following the commencement of occupancy by such person or within thirty days following a request by the landlord.

6. No occupant nor occupant's dependent child shall, without express written permission of the landlord, acquire any right to continued occupancy in the event that the tenant vacates the premises or acquire any other rights of tenancy; provided that nothing in this section shall be construed to reduce or impair any right or remedy otherwise available to any person residing in any housing accommodation on the effective date of this section which accrued prior to such date.

7. Any provision of a lease or rental agreement purporting to waive a provision of this section is null and void.

8. Nothing in this section shall be construed as invalidating or impairing the operation of, or the right of a landlord to restrict occupancy in order to comply with federal, state or local laws, regulations, ordinances or codes.

9. Any person aggrieved by a violation of this section may maintain an action in any court of competent jurisdiction for:

   (a) an injunction to enjoin and restrain such unlawful practice;

   (b) actual damages sustained as a result of such unlawful practice; and

   (c) court costs.

Sec. 236. Assignment of lease of a deceased tenant.

Notwithstanding any contrary provision contained in any lease hereafter made which affects premises demised for residential use, or partly for residential and partly for professional use, the executor, administrator or legal representative of a deceased tenant under such a lease, may request the landlord thereunder to consent to the assignment of such a lease, or to the subletting of the premises demised thereby. Such request shall be accompanied by the written consent thereto of any co-tenant or guarantor of such lease and a statement of the name, business and home addresses of the proposed assignee or sublessee. Within ten days after the mailing of such request, the landlord may ask the sender thereof for additional information as will enable the landlord to determine if rejection of such request shall be unreasonable. Within thirty days after the mailing of the request for consent, or of the additional information reasonably asked for by the landlord, whichever is later, the landlord shall send a notice to the sender thereof of his election to terminate said lease or to grant or refuse his consent. Landlord's failure to send such a notice shall be deemed to be a consent to the proposed assignment or subletting. If the landlord consents, said lease may be assigned in accordance with the request provided a written agreement by the assignee assuming the performance of the tenant's obligations under the lease is delivered to the landlord in form reasonably satisfactory to the landlord, or the premises may be sublet in accordance with the request, as the case may be, but the estate of the deceased tenant, and any other tenant thereunder, shall nevertheless remain liable for the performance of tenant`s obligations under said lease. If the landlord terminates said lease or unreasonably refuses his consent, said lease shall be deemed terminated, and the estate of the deceased tenant and any other tenant thereunder shall be discharged from further liability thereunder as of the last day of the calendar month during which the landlord was required hereunder to exercise his option. If the landlord reasonably refuses his consent, said lease shall continue in full force and effect, subject to the right to make further requests for consent hereunder. Any request, notice or communication required or authorized to be given hereunder shall be sent by registered or certified mail, return receipt requested. This act shall not apply to a proprietary lease, viz.: a lease to, or held by, a tenant entitled thereto by reason of ownership of stock in a corporate owner of premises which operates the same on a cooperative basis. Any waiver of any part of this section shall be void as against public policy.

Sec. 236*. Discrimination against children in dwelling houses and mobile home parks.

a. Any person, firm or corporation owning or having in charge any apartment house, tenement house or other building or mobile home park used for dwelling purposes who shall refuse to rent any or part of any such building of mobile home park to any person or family, or who discriminates in the terms, conditions, or privileges of any such rental, solely on the ground that such person or family has or have a child or children shall be guilty of a misdemeanor and on conviction thereof shall be punished by a fine of not less than fifty nor more than one hundred dollars for each offense; provided, however, the prohibition against discrimination against children in dwelling houses and mobile home parks contained in this section shall not apply to:

   (1) housing units for senior citizens subsidized, insured, or guaranteed by the federal government; or

   (2) one or two family owner occupied dwelling houses or mobile homes; or

   (3) mobile home parks exclusively for persons fifty-five years of age or over.

b. Civil liability:

   (1) where discriminatory conduct prohibited by this section has occurred, an aggrieved individual shall have a cause of action in any court of appropriate jurisdiction for damages, declaratory and injunctive relief;

   (2) in all actions brought under this section, reasonable attorney's fees as determined by the court may be awarded to a prevailing plaintiff.

Sec. 237. Discrimination in leases with respect to bearing of children. Any person, firm or corporation owning or having in charge any apartment house, tenement house or other building or mobile home park used for dwelling purposes who shall, in any lease of any or part of any such building or mobile home park, have a clause therein providing that during the term thereof the tenants shall remain childless or shall not bear children, shall be guilty of a violation.

Sec. 238. Agreements or contracts for privileges to deal with occupants of tenements, apartment houses or bungalow colonies.

   1. A contract, agreement or arrangement entered into or executed by and between the owner or prospective owner of an apartment house, tenement or what is commonly known as a bungalow colony connected with common or joint means of ingress and egress, whether such apartment house, tenement or bungalow colony is in existence or in process of construction or to be constructed in the future, or any person in possession or claiming possession of such apartment house, tenement or bungalow colony, or any part thereof, including the common or joint means of ingress or egress, or any of the agents, employees or servants of such an owner or possessors thereof and a dealer in or seller of fuel, ice or food, or his agents, employees or representatives for the purpose of giving to such dealer or seller the privilege of selling or delivering fuel, ice or food, to the persons occupying or to occupy such apartment house, tenement or bungalow colony, or any part thereof, is against public policy and void.

   2. Any person who shall, directly or indirectly, either as the owner or prospective owner of such apartment house, tenement or bungalow colony, or any part thereof, including the common or joint means of ingress or egress, or as an agent, employee or servant of such an owner, or any person in possession or claiming possession of such apartment house, tenement or bungalow colony, or any part thereof, including the common or joint means of ingress or egress, accept any money, property or thing of value for permitting or giving to any person, or his agents, employees or representatives, the privilege of selling or delivering fuel, ice or food, to the persons occupying or to occupy such apartment house, tenement or bungalow colony, or any part thereof, and any person who shall, directly or indirectly, either as a seller of, or dealer in, fuel, ice or food, as an agent, employee, or representative of such seller or dealer, pay or give any money, property or thing of value, for such privilege shall be guilty of a misdemeanor. If a corporation is convicted of a violation of this section, it shall be punished by a fine of not less than fifty nor more than one thousand dollars.

   3. A person occupying an apartment house, tenement or bungalow colony, or any part thereof, to whom fuel, ice or food, shall be sold or delivered by a seller or dealer who has paid or given any money, property or thing of value for the privilege of selling or delivering fuel, ice or food, to the persons occupying or to occupy such apartment house, tenement or bungalow colony, or any part thereof, may recover of such seller or dealer for his benefit a penalty, in the sum of two hundred and fifty dollars, in a civil action brought in a court of competent jurisdiction.

APPENDIX B
EVICTION FLOWCHARTS
AND LEGAL HOLIDAYS

On the next two pages are flowcharts which show each step in the eviction process. The first one is for an eviction for nonpayment of rent. The second one is for evictions based on holdover proceedings.

On the final page of this appendix is a list of the legal holidays in New York. Keep these in mind when calculating time limits for notices.

Eviction Flow Chart—Non-Payment of Rent

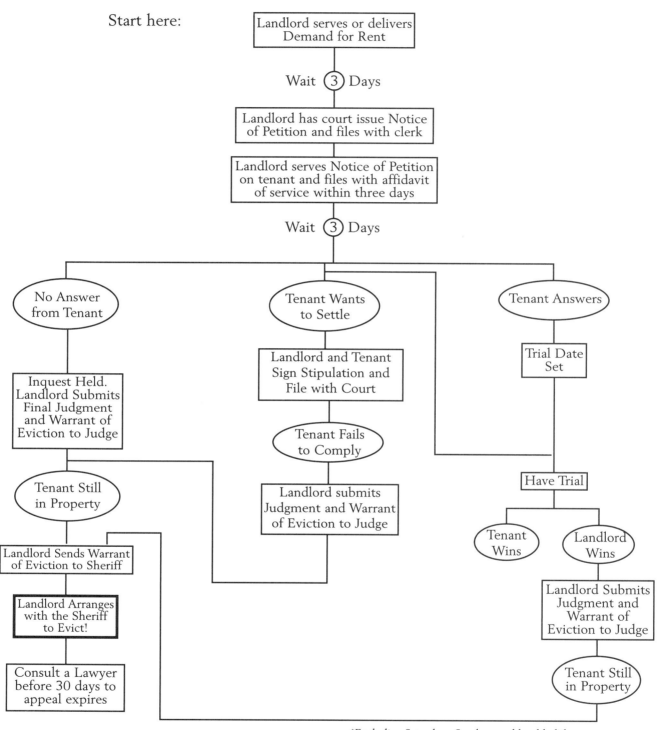

Start here:

Landlord serves or delivers Demand for Rent

Wait ③ Days

Landlord has court issue Notice of Petition and files with clerk

Landlord serves Notice of Petition on tenant and files with affidavit of service within three days

Wait ③ Days

No Answer from Tenant

Inquest Held. Landlord Submits Final Judgment and Warrant of Eviction to Judge

Tenant Still in Property

Landlord Sends Warrant of Eviction to Sheriff

Landlord Arranges with the Sheriff to Evict!

Consult a Lawyer before 30 days to appeal expires

Tenant Wants to Settle

Landlord and Tenant Sign Stipulation and File with Court

Tenant Fails to Comply

Landlord submits Judgment and Warrant of Eviction to Judge

Tenant Answers

Trial Date Set

Have Trial

Tenant Wins   Landlord Wins

Landlord Submits Judgment and Warrant of Eviction to Judge

Tenant Still in Property

*Excluding Saturdays, Sundays, and legal holidays

Eviction Flow Chart—Breach of Lease

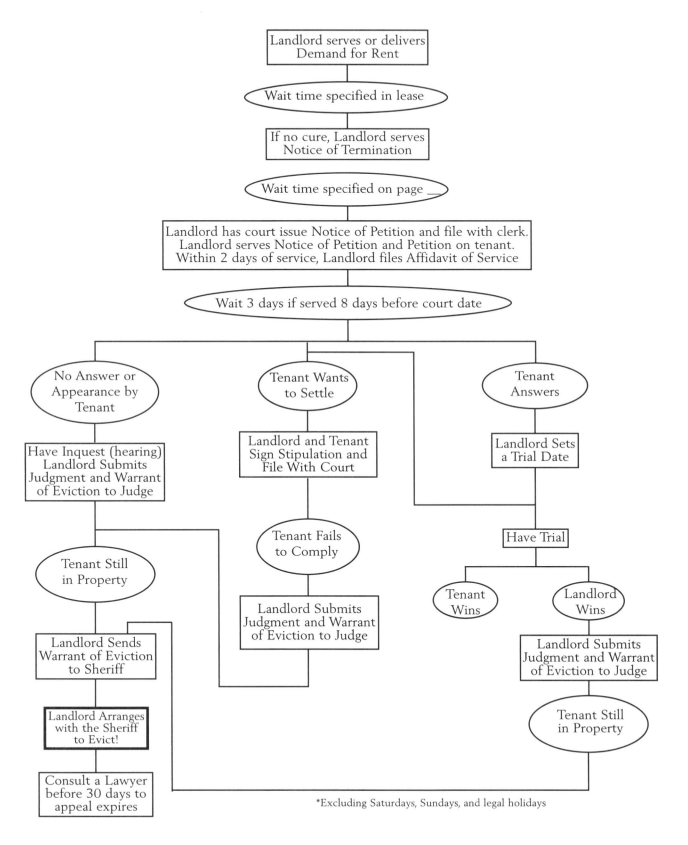

Landlord serves or delivers Demand for Rent

Wait time specified in lease

If no cure, Landlord serves Notice of Termination

Wait time specified on page __

Landlord has court issue Notice of Petition and file with clerk. Landlord serves Notice of Petition and Petition on tenant. Within 2 days of service, Landlord files Affidavit of Service

Wait 3 days if served 8 days before court date

No Answer or Appearance by Tenant

Tenant Wants to Settle

Tenant Answers

Have Inquest (hearing) Landlord Submits Judgment and Warrant of Eviction to Judge

Landlord and Tenant Sign Stipulation and File With Court

Landlord Sets a Trial Date

Tenant Still in Property

Tenant Fails to Comply

Have Trial

Landlord Sends Warrant of Eviction to Sheriff

Landlord Submits Judgment and Warrant of Eviction to Judge

Tenant Wins

Landlord Wins

Landlord Arranges with the Sheriff to Evict!

Landlord Submits Judgment and Warrant of Eviction to Judge

Consult a Lawyer before 30 days to appeal expires

Tenant Still in Property

*Excluding Saturdays, Sundays, and legal holidays

LEGAL HOLIDAYS IN NEW YORK

Every Sunday

New Year's Day   Jan. 1

Martin Luther King, Jr.'s Birthday   Third Mon. in Jan.

Presidents' Day   Third Mon. in Feb.

Good Friday   (varies)

Memorial Day   Last Mon. in May

Independence Day   July 4

Labor Day   First Mon. In Sept

Columbus Day   Second Mon. in Oct.

General Election Day   (varies)

Veterans' Day   Nov. 11

Thanksgiving Day   Fourth Thurs. in Nov.

Christmas Day   Dec. 25

APPENDIX C
FORMS

Use of the following forms is described in the text or should be self-explanatory. If you do not understand any aspect of a form, you should seek advice from an attorney.

Although the forms in this appendix may be grouped according to the type of form, the forms are not necessarily in any particular order. Be sure to read this book to determine which forms you will need in a particular situation. Also, be sure to look at the form's name and form number to be sure you are using the correct form.

LICENSE: Although this book is copyrighted, purchasers of the book are granted a license to copy the forms created by the authors for their own personal use or for use in their law practices.

TABLE OF FORMS

INSPECTION REPORT

Date: _____

Unit: _____

AREA	CONDITION			
	Move-In		Move-out	
	Good	Poor	Good	Poor
Yard/garden				
Driveway				
Patio/porch				
Exterior				
Entry light/bell				
Living room/Dining room/Halls:				
Floors/carpets				
Walls/ceiling				
Doors/locks				
Fixtures/lights				
Outlets/switches				
Other				
Bedrooms:				
Floors/carpets				
Walls/ceiling				
Doors/locks				
Fixtures/lights				
Outlets/switches				
Other				
Bathrooms:				
Faucets				
Toilet				
Sink/tub				
Floors/carpet				
Walls/ceiling				
Doors/locks				
Fixtures/lights				
Outlets/switches				
Other				
Kitchen:				
Refrigerator				
Range				
Oven				
Dishwasher				
Sink/disposal				
Cabinets/counters				
Floors/carpets				
Walls/ceiling				
Doors/locks				
Fixtures/lights				
Outlets/switches				
Other				
Misc.				
Closets/pantry				
Garage				
Keys				
Other				

State of New York
Division of Housing and Community Renewal
Office of Rent Administration

Gertz Plaza
92-31 Union Hall Street
Jamaica, NY 11433

Docket Number:

Tenant's Complaint of Owner's Failure to Renew Lease and/or Failure to Furnish a Copy of a Signed Lease

Instructions to Tenant: Please type or print clearly all information requested on both sides of this form and attach the evidence requested below. Mail or deliver the original plus one copy of the signed form, and one copy of all attachments, to the Rent Office shown above. Keep one copy for your records.

Note: As stated in Section 2522.5 of the Rent Stabilization Code, an owner is required to furnish to the tenant a copy of a fully executed new or renewal lease within 30 days of receipt of the lease, signed and dated, from the tenant. Sections 2522.5 (b) (1) and 2523.5 of the Rent Stabilization Code require an owner to offer a tenant, in writing, the option of a one-or two-year renewal lease. Such offer shall be made not more than 150 days and not less than 120 days prior to the end of the tenant's lease term, and may be served on the tenant by mail or personal delivery. The tenant's acceptance of such offer must be returned to the owner, either by mail or personal delivery, within 60 days.

Part I - General Information

1. **Mailing Address of Tenant:** (Please print or type)

Name: _____

Number/Street _____ Apt. No.: _____

City: _____

State, Zip Code: _____

Telephone Number: Bus. ( ) _____

Res. ( ) _____

2. **Mailing Address of Owner/Agent:** (Please print or type)

Name: _____

Number/Street: _____

City: _____

State, Zip Code: _____

Telephone Number: ( ) _____

Subject Building (if different from tenant's mailing address):

Number and Street	Apartment Number	City, State, Zip Code

Part II - Rental History

3. Terms of apartment rental: Complete either (a) or (b) **and** both (c) and (d)

    (a) I moved into this apartment on _____/_____/_____ under a written lease of _____ years, commencing on
            Date
    _____/_____/_____ and expiring on _____/_____/_____ at a rental of $ _____ per month.
        Date   Date

    (b) I moved into this apartment on _____/_____/_____ without a written lease at an initial rent of $ _____ per month.
                            Date

    (c) The last lease i received for this apartment was for a period of _____ years, commencing on _____/_____/_____ and
        expiring on _____/_____/_____ at a rental of $ _____ per month.   Date
               Date

    (d) I ☐ am ☐ am not up-to-date with my rental payments.

Part III - Nature of Complaint

(Check applicable boxes. If you have additional comments on questions 4-7, please attach additional sheets.)

☐ 4. The owner refuses to give me a renewal lease.

☐ 5. The owner refuses to give me a lease for _____ years as I requested. The owner offered a lease for _____ years.

☐ 6. The owner refuses to offer me a renewal lease on the same terms and conditions as were contained in my expiring lease. The owner has made changes in the new lease. (Identify the clauses in the expiring and new leases below.)

☐ 7. The owner failed to furnish me with a signed copy of my new or renewal lease.

☐ 8. The complaints contained in this application were brought to the attention of the owner or his/her agent:

☐ In person ☐ By phone ☐ By letter or other written notice

Part IV - Evidence

The following evidence must be submitted to support your complaint:

1. A photocopy of your initial lease for the apartment.

2. A photocopy of the current or last lease for your apartment.

3. Proof of payment of rent for the last six (6) months immediately preceding the filing of this complaint.

4. If you are seeking the addition of your spouse as a tenant named on the renewal lease, please submit a photocopy of your Marriage Certificate, together with evidence that your spouse is residing in the apartment.

5. Any other relevant evidence to support your complaint.

Complete this section if you have additional comments on questions 4-7 in Part III:

_____

_____

_____

_____

_____

_____

_____

_____

_____

I have read the above statements and I affirm, under the penalties provided by law, that the contents are true to my own knowledge. It is not necessary that the above be sworn to, but false statements may subject you to the penalties provided by law.

_____/_____/_____
Date

_____
Tenant's Signature

Be sure to date and sign this Form

STATE OF NEW YORK
**DIVISION OF HOUSING AND
COMMUNITY RENEWAL**
GERTZ PLAZA - 92-31 UNION HALL STREET
JAMAICA, NY 11433

Mediation Program - Lease Renewal Violation(s)

The Office of Rent Administration (ORA), has recently expanded its Mediation Program to include new complaints of an owner's failure to renew a lease. By participating in the Program, tenants can benefit by receiving a properly executed lease renewal. Owners can benefit by not having to formally answer a complaint and/or be faced with an extended period of time when the tenant is not required to pay a rent guideline increase. Tenants and owners should be aware that **without** mediation, the current case processing time averages two year.

Here is how the program works:

Upon ORA's receipt of this completed form, the issue(s) raised in the tenant's complaint will be described by ORA's Mediation Counselor over the telephone to the owner. If the owner does **not** agree to participate, the tenant's complaint will be docketed and processed in the normal course of business.

Owners must agree to resolve the issue(s) complained of within 14 days. After 14 days the Mediation Counselor will follow-up with the tenant to determine if the situation has been rectified. If this has not been done, the tenant's complaint, which will already have been date stamped as of the initial date the complaint was submitted to ORA, will then be docketed.

An ORA Mediation Counselor will telephone you upon receipt of this form to review the issues about which you are complaining. The Counselor may not add new conditions not stated in the original complaint. Kindly provide a daytime telephone so that the Division's Counselor can contact you.

Daytime Telephone Number: (   ) _____

Hopefully our mediation services will be helpful to both you and the owner of your building.

Please return to:

New York State Division of Housing and Community Renewal
Office of Rent Administration
Gertz Plaza, 92-31 Union Hall Street
Jamaica, New York 11433
Attn.: Mediation Program - Lease Renewal Violation(s)

RA-ME3 (11/96)

STATE OF NEW YORK
DIVISION OF HOUSING AND COMMUNITY RENEWAL
92-31 UNION HALL STREET
JAMAICA, NEW YORK 11433

Rent Overcharge Application - Information

Attached is the new form RA-89 "Tenant's Complaint of Rent and/or Other Specific Overcharges in Rent Stabilized Apartments in New York City". Please note that you are required to submit **all documentation** in support of your claim or rental overcharge at the time you submit this complaint. Please note that

- all of the requested information/documentation is needed to process your complaint.

- the information requested in this form has always been requested by this agency to process your complaint. However, it is now being asked for at one time rather than in the several periodic requests previously used.

- because of this procedure and the new form, the time required to process your complaint will be shortened significantly.

See Fact Sheet #26," Guide to Rent Increase for Rent Stabilized Apartments in New York City," which summarizes the provisions governing lawful rent increases.

Before you file this complaint:

- Call our Infoline (718-739-6400) to request a computer printout of the Registration History for your apartment. This will show the rent for your apartment as registered by the building owner within the past four years. While this printout **does not** represent a determination of the lawful rent for your apartment, reviewing it in conjunction with Fact Sheet #26 will give you valuable information about how your rent was computed by your building owner.

- If you still have questions, you may discuss them with your building owner.

- If you still feel you need to file a complaint, gather all of the documentation in support of your claim. This may include cancelled checks, leases, previous DHCR orders, rent receipts, written consent for individual apartment improvements and court decisions. Only documentation which relates to the subject apartment is needed.

- Complete all sections of the complaint, and make copies of your documentation. **Submit two copies of the complaint and documentation to DHCR** and keep one copy for yourself. An incomplete complaint will be returned to you.

Once your complaint is docketed, you will receive an acknowledgment in the mail.

RA-89.1 (9/97)

State of New York
Division of Housing and Community Renewal
Office of Rent Administration

Gertz Plaza
92-31 Union Hall Street
Jamaica, NY 11433
(718) 739-6400

Docket Number:

Tenant's Complaint Of Rent and/or Other Specific Overcharges in Rent Stabilized Apartments in New York City

Type or print in ink all information requested (write in the box)

1. Tenant's Last Name   **First Name**   **Middle Initial**

2. Current Mailing Address (Include Street Number and Name)   **Apartment No.**

3. City (Borough or Town)   **State**   **Zip Code**

4. Subject Building Address and Apartment Number (If different from the above.)

5. Telephone Number (Home) _____ (Day time) _____

The information requested is necessary to process your complaint. Your complaint will not be accepted if information is missing.

6. I informed my building ☐ owner ☐ managing agent about my complaint on ____/____/____
    by ☐ letter (attach copy) ☐ phone ☐ in person

7. I am a ☐ prime tenant ☐ sub-tenant ☐ hotel/SRO tenant

8. I live in a co-operative apartment. ☐ Yes ☐ No

9. Number of rental units in the building: ☐ six or more ☐ less than six

10. I moved into the subject apartment on ____/____/____ (Complete (a) or (b) below)

    (a) with a written lease of _____ years, commencing on ____/____/____ and expiring on ____/____/____
        at an initial rent of $_____ per month.

    (b) without a written lease at an initial rent of $_____ per month.

11. My current rent is $_____ per month.

12. Electricity ☐ is ☐ is not   included in my rent.

If you pay your rent to a **Prime Tenant** or any person other than the owner, complete Section 14.

13. Mailing Address of Owner/Agent:

Name: _____

Number/Street: _____
                                    Apt. No.: _____
_____

City, State,
Zip Code: _____

Telephone Number: (___) _____

14. Mailing Address of Prime Tenant:

Name: _____

Number/Street: _____

_____

City, State,
Zip Code: _____

Telephone Number: (___) _____

15. I am complaining about Rent Overcharges arising from the following item(s): (Check all that apply)

☐ Major Capital Improvement (MCI) Increase(s)

☐ Individual Apartment Improvements (IAI)

☐ Rent Reduction Order(s)

☐ Apartment Registration

☐ Others: _____

16. I believe I am being overcharged because: (What are the rental events occurring in the last four years which you believe caused the alleged overcharge? Please list below and submit proof to support your claims).

_____

_____

17. Security Deposits: I am being charged $ _____ as a security deposit, which is more than one month's rent.

A security deposit of $ _____ was paid to the owner/agent on _____/_____/_____.

(a) If you vacated the subject apartment did you use your security deposit to pay part of the rent?

☐ Yes   ☐ No

18. Have you filed any other complaint(s) with DHCR?

☐ Yes   ☐ No, If "yes," list Docket Number(s): _____

(a) Has the complaint in this application been raised in Court? ☐ Yes   ☐ No

If :yes:, ☐ it is pending, Index No. _____

or   ☐ a decision has been made, (attach a copy of the decision).

19. Rental History: List your leases for the last four years or from the date of your occupancy, if less than four years. Start with the current lease. *Information other than for the dates requested will not be considered.*

No	Lease Period(s) From - To	Lease Amount	Additional Security Deposit Charged, Yes or No, If Yes, Write Amount Below
1		$	
2		$	
3		$	
4		$	
5		$	

20. Rental Payments: Last four years or from the date of your occupancy (whichever is less)

Month & Year	Current Year 19_____	Last Year 19_____	2 Years Prior 19_____	3 Years Prior 19_____	4 Years Prior 19_____
January	$	$	$	$	$
February	$	$	$	$	$
March	$	$	$	$	$
April	$	$	$	$	$
May	$	$	$	$	$
June	$	$	$	$	$
July	$	$	$	$	$
August	$	$	$	$	$
September	$	$	$	$	$
October	$	$	$	$	$
November	$	$	$	$	$
December	$	$	$	$	$

21. Major Capital Improvement (MCI) Rent Increase(s): (If none known, state **"None Known"**)

No	Docket Number(s)	Permanent Increase Per Month	Owner Started Collection On	Temporary Increase Per Month	Owner Started Collection On
1		$		$	
2		$		$	
3		$		$	
4		$		$	

22. Individual Apartment Improvement (IAI) Rent Increase(s): (If IAI was before your occupancy and you do not have this information state **"Not Known"**. If IAI was during your occupancy, you must enter all information).

No	Item(s)	Date of Improvement	Before **or** During* your occupancy?	Amount Charged
1				$
2				$
3				$
4				$

*If the improvements were made during your ocupancy, did you sign a written consent?　☐ Yes　☐ No

23. Rent Reduction and Restoration Orders (Only those issued within the last four years):

Docket Number(s)	Did you pay a reduced rent? Yes or No	If yes, when did you begin paying the reduced rent? (month/year)	What was the amount of rent you paid?	If the owner gave you a refund, what was the amount?	Was the rent restored to the full amount? Yes or No	If "yes", when did you begin paying the full amount? (month/year)
			$	$		
			$	$		
			$	$		
			$	$		

24. (*Optional*) Additional Comments or Other Rent Increases (Occurring within the last four years) Not Listed Above: (Attach additional sheets if necessary for this information. Specific dates and documentation must be provided.)

25. Providing the following evidence will make processing quicker and more accurate. Please indicate which of the following documents are attached.

☐ Leases　　☐ Rent Receipts　　☐ Canceled Checks　　☐ DHCR Order(s)

☐ Additional Sheet(s)　　☐ Other: _____

Tenant's Affirmation

I have read all the statements and I affirm that my statements are true and correct to the best of my knowledge and belief. False statements may subject me to the penalties provided by law.

_____
Date

_____
Signature of Tenant

Do Not Write in Space Below
For D.H.C.R. Use Only.

Date complaint received: _____

Tenant's Submissions:

☐ Leases   ☐ Rent Receipts   ☐ Canceled Checks   ☐ DHCR Order(s)

☐ Additional Sheet(s)   ☐ Other: _____

_____

Comments:

State of New York
Division of Housing and Community Renewal
Office of Rent Administration

Gertz Plaza
MBR Section
92-31 Union Hall Street
Jamaica, N.Y. 11433
(718) 739-6400

Docket Number:
(for DHCR Use Only)

Challenge Re: Maximum Base Rent Order

1. Mailing Address of Tenant or Representative:

Name: _____

Number/Street: _____

_____ Apt. No. _____

City, State, Zip Code: _____

Telephone Number: ( ) _____

2. Mailing Address of Owner/Agent:

Name: _____

Number/Street: _____

_____

City, State, Zip Code: _____

Telephone Number: ( ) _____

3. Subject Building: _____

(Number and Street)   (City, State, Zip Code)

4. This form is being filed by the ☐ Owner ☐ Tenant (Complete Item 5 below), against the _____ MBR Order (Enter year)

issued on ____/____/____ under Docket No. _____ , (Check one box only) ☐ Granting

MBR Increases with an Effective Date of ____/____/____ or ☐ Denying MBR Increases.

5. To be completed by Tenant only: Notice of Increase in Maximum Base Rent (MBR) and Maximum Collectible Rent (MCR) Computations (DHCR form RN-26 or RN-26S) was received from the owner on ____/____/____.

Read carefully Notice Form RN-26 or RN-26S, the explanations accompanying those forms, and the instructions below before completing the reverse side of this form.

Instructions

A. File the original of this form at the MBR Section, NYS Division of Housing and Community Renewal, Gertz Plaza, 92-31 Union Hall Street, Jamaica, NY 11433. If the challenge is being filed by the Owner, this form must be filed within thirty-three (33) days of the **issue date** of the Order. If the challenge is being filed by the Tenant(s), this form must be filed within thirty-three (33) days after **receiving** a copy of the Notice of Increase (DHCR form RN-26 or RN-26S).

B. If a challenge affects more than one apartment and identical objections are made, this form should be designated "Master" in Item 1 above. In addition, complete the section titled Schedule of Tenants by listing the names of the tenants and their apartment numbers. When multiple tenants file, they must sign their names and enter their apartment numbers below, and they must designate a representative who must sign the form on the reverse side. (Use additional sheets for tenants' names, apartment numbers, and signatures if necessary.)

C. This form is used only to file objections to an Order of Eligibility or Order Denying Maximum Base Rents. **This form may not be used to register complaints.** Tenants may file complaints of a reduction in essential services on DHCR form RA-81 or RA-84. Complaints of rent overcharge are filed on DHCR form RA-89. Appropriate forms may be obtained at any of the Borough Rent Offices shown below.

D. Until an order is issued determining your challenge, the Maximum Collectible Rent under the MBR Order as computed on the Notice of Increase DHCR form RN-26 or RN-26S remains in effect.

File this form at Gertz Plaza at the address given above. Blank forms may be obtained at any of the following rent offices:

Lower Manhattan	Upper Manhattan	Brooklyn	Bronx	Queens	Staten Island
25 Beaver Street	163 West 125th St.	55 Hanson Place	1 Fordham Plaza	92-31 Union Hall St.	60 Bay St.
5th Floor	5th Floor	7th Floor	2nd Floor	4th Floor	7th Floor
New York, NY 10004	New York, NY 10027	Brooklyn, NY 11217	Bronx, NY 10458	Jamaica, NY 11433	Staten Island, NY 10301

Schedule of Tenants

To the Owner: If filing a "Master" challenge, enter the apartment number and tenant name for all rent-controlled tenants.

To the Tenants: Multiple tenants filing together should sign their names and enter their apartment numbers below and designate their representative on the reverse side. (For rent-controlled tenants only.)

Apt. No.	Rent-Controlled Tenant	Signature

RA-94 MBR (8/98)

Complete the appropriate section below, explaining your objection to the Order:

I/We object to the Maximum Base Rent Order issued for the listed apartment(s), on the following grounds:

Owner of Subject Building complied/failed to comply with all certification requirements. Explain fully:

Effective date of the Order of Eligibility. Explain fully:

MBR Order issued incorrectly. State basis for claim of error:

As a Reminder: To qualify for MBR increases owners must certify that:

1. All rent-impairing and at least 80% of all other violations on record one year prior to the effective date of MBR increases have been cleared, corrected or abated six months prior to the effective date of such MBR increases;
2. 90% of the allowance for operating and maintenance expenses applicable to the building have been expended or incurred; and
3. Essential services have been and will continue to be maintained.

The last two certifications must be made at least 90 days prior to the effective date of the MBR increases. Late certifications result in a delayed effective date. In addition, owners must pay the MBR processing fee and must have registered the stabilized apartments in the subject building with the Division of Housing and Community Renewal.

(If more space is needed, attach additional sheets.)

Required signature of owner, tenant or designated representative:_____

Dated:_____/_____/_____

WARNING: Any person who willfully makes any statement or entry which is false in any material respect or willfully omits or neglects to make any material statement or entry required to be made, shall be guilty of a crime punishable by fine or imprisonment, or both, and, in addition, a civil fine may be levied by the Commissioner for each violation. (See Penal Law, Sections 175.30, 175.35, 210.45; New York City Administrative Code, Sections 26-412e, 26-413a and 26-413b (s) (a))

Designation of Tenants' Representative

The rent-controlled tenants whose signatures appear listed on the reverse side and on any attached sheets, designate:

_____
        (Name)   (Address)

as our representative in this challenge against the Maximum Base Rent Order. We authorize the Division of Housing and Community Renewal to mail all notices and orders to the designated representative with the same force and effect as if such notices or orders were mailed to each of us individually.

Dated:_____/_____/_____

This form need not be notarized; however, false statements may subject you to the penalties provided by law.

RA-94 MBR (8/98)

State of New York
Division of Housing and Community Renewal
Office of Rent Administration

Gertz Plaza
S.C.O.R.E. Intake
92-31 Union Hall Street
Jamaica, NY 11433
(718) 739-6400

| Docket Number: |
| For Office Use Only |

Failure To Provide Heat And/Or Hot Water - Tenant Application For Rent Reduction

Under the Multiple Dwelling Law and Housing Maintenance Code heat and hot water are required. Heat must be provided from **October 1 through May 31 as follows:**

> 6 AM to 10 P.M.:
>
> When the outside temperature is below 55 $^\circ$F, the inside temperature must be at least 68 $^\circ$F.
>
> 10 PM to 6 A.M.:
>
> When the outside temperature is below 40 $^\circ$F, the inside temperature must be at least 55 $^\circ$F.

Hot water is required 365 days per year, 24 hours a day at a minimum of 120°F at the tap .

TENANT INSTRUCTIONS: Please type or clearly print all information requested. Be sure to date and sign the back of the application. Mail or deliver the original plus one copy of the signed application to the DHCR address shown above. Keep one copy for your records.

Part I - General Information

1. Mailing Address of Tenant:

_____
Name

_____
Number/Street   Apt. No.

_____
City, State, Zip Code

Telephone No.: Bus. (____) _____

                 Res. (____) _____

2. Mailing Address of Owner/Managing Agent:

_____
Name

_____
Number/Street

_____
City, State, Zip Code

Telephone Number: (____) _____

3. Subject Building (if different from tenant's mailing address):

_____
Number and Street   Apartment Number   City, State, Zip Code

4. My apartment is: ☐ Rent Stabilized   ☐ Rent Controlled   ☐ Hotel Stabilized   ☐ SRO (Single Room Occupancy)

Complete the following, if applicable:

☐   A Co-op/Condo

   Unit Owner/Proprietary Lessee: _____

   Name of Cooperative Corp./Condo Assn.: _____

   Managing Agent: _____

☐   My building is managed by a 7-A Administrator.

   Name of 7-A Administrator: _____

5. I moved into my apartment on: _____ / _____ / _____ .

6. My current rent is: $ _____ per: ☐ week ☐ month

7. ☐ I have a current lease. The lease term is from _____ / _____ / _____ to _____ / _____ / _____ .

Date
Date

☐ I do not have a current lease.

Part II - Tenant's Statement of Complaint

8. Check appropriate boxes to indicate services not provided.

☐ **Heat - Not Provided/Inadequate**

Date(s) | | | | | |
|---|---|---|---|---|
Time(s) | | | | | |

☐ **Hot Water - Not Provided/Inadequate**

Date(s) | | | | | |
|---|---|---|---|---|
Time(s) | | | | | |

Describe Extent of Reduction of Service: _____

_____

_____

_____

_____

_____

_____

_____

_____

_____

_____

_____

_____

_____

_____

9. The conditions stated in this complaint were brought to the attention of the:

   a. ☐ Owner/Superintendent   ☐ Agent or Co-op Corp./Condo Assn.

   b. ☐ In person: _____ / _____ / _____   ☐ By phone: _____ / _____ / _____   ☐ By Letter: _____ / _____ / _____

Date
Date
Date

   c. ☐ Unable to contact Owner/Agent

Part III - Tenant's Affirmation

I have read the information on this application and I affirm the contents to be true of my own knowledge.

_____ / _____ / _____
_____   _____
Date of Mailing   Tenant's Signature

State of New York
Division of Housing and Community Renewal
Office of Rent Administration

Gertz Plaza
Fuel Cost Unit
92-31 Union Hall Street
Jamaica, NY 11433

Docket Number: (For DHCR use only)

Tenant Challenge To Owner's Report and Certification of Fuel Cost Adjustment (FCA)

Mailing Address of Tenant/Representative:
(Please print or type)

Name: _____

_____

Number/Street: _____ Apt. No.: _____
City,
State, Zip Code: _____

Mailing Address of Owner/Agent:
(Please print or type)

Name: _____

_____

Number/Street: _____
City,
State, Zip Code: _____

Subject Building (if different from tenant's mailing address):

Number and Street	Apartment Number	City, State, Zip Code

Date of receipt of "Notice to Tenant of Fuel Cost Adjustment": _____ / _____ / _____

Filing Instructions: Tenants who were served with "Owner's Report, Certification and Notice of Fuel Cost Adjustment Eligibility," and wish to challenge either eligibility, monthly adjustment, or both, must file an original and one copy of this form with the Division of Housing and Community Renewal (address at the top of this form) within 33 days after receipt of the "Owner's Report".

Multiple tenants may file a single consolidated form with the signature of each tenant and the required information inserted on the reverse side of this form. The tenants must designate a representative who must sign below. Individual tenants may file by inserting the required information on the reverse side and signing below.

I (we) challenge the following item(s) in relation to the Owner's Report and Certification of Fuel Cost Eligibility for the year 19_____:

(Check only those item(s) which apply)

☐ Incorrect room count for apartment.

☐ Incorrect fuel type(s) or quantity(ies) reported.

☐ Incorrect Fuel Cost Adjustment reported.

☐ Incorrect effective date for Increase in Fuel Cost Adjustment.

☐ Rent reduction for lack of heat/hot water is still in effect.

☐ Report not filed or filed untimely by owner.

☐ Tenant(s) not served with "Owner's Report".

☐ Other (Explain briefly: supporting documentation must be included.)

Note: It is not necessary that the above be sworn to, but false statements may subject you to the penalties provided by law.

_____   _____ / _____ / _____
Signature of Tenant or Representative   Date

Designation of Representative

The undersigned, all rent controlled tenants of the housing accommodations referred to in this application, designate

Name	Address

to act as our representative in this challenge to DHCR against the fuel charge on the basis of this Statement. We further authorize DHCR to mail all notices and orders to the designated representative with the same force and effect as if such notice or orders were mailed to each of us individually.

Dated _____ 19 _____ .

Apt. No.	Tenant's Signature	For DHCR use only	

(If more space is needed, use additional sheets)

This form must be filed by the tenant with DHCR

State of New York
Division of Housing and Community Renewal
Office of Rent Administration

Judgment

Under Section YY51-6.0.5 of the Administrative Code of the City of New York and upon the filing of the certified copy of the Order of the New York State Division of Housing and Community Renewal; the certification of the expiration of the period within which to institute an appeal; and the affidavit waiving the choice of offset, it is on motion of

_____

_____

Adjudged that the tenant(s) _____

residing at _____

_____

recover of the owner(s) landlord_____

_____

residing or having its principal place of business at _____

_____

the sum of _____

and that the tenant(s) have execution therefore.

Entered:

_____
Clerk

RN-14.1 (10/92)

State of New York
Division of Housing and Community Renewal
Office of Rent Administration
(718) 739-6400

D.H.C.R.
Gertz Plaza
92-31 Union Hall Street
Jamaica, NY 11433

NOTICE OF RENT STABILIZED TENANT CONCERNING PAYMENT OF PENALTIES WHICH LANDLORD HAS BEEN DIRECTED TO PAY BY AN ADMINISTRATOR'S ORDER

Mailing Address of Tenant:

Name: _____

Number and
Street: _____ Apt. No.: _____

Municipality,
State, Zip: _____

Re: DOCKET NO.: _____

ORDER NO.: _____

DATE ORDER ISSUED: _____

_____
(Number and Street)   (Apt. No.)   (Municipality)

Building _____
(If Different From Tenant's Mailing Address)

TENANT PLEASE TAKE NOTICE:

The owner of your building has been directed to pay you the amount of the penalty as set forth in the Administrator's Order as referenced above.

The owner must pay you this penalty within thirty-five (35) days of the issuance date of the Administrator's Order, unless he or she has served you and filed with the Division a Petition for Administrative Review (**PAR**) of the Administrator's Order. If you have been served with or notified by the Division that a **PAR** has been filed, you should await the decision of the Commissioner before submitting this Notice. Thereafter, you may file the certified copy of the Order as a judgment for the amount specified therein, or as adjusted by the **PAR,** pursuant to the instructions below, unless the owner commences a proceeding for judicial review pursuant to Article 78 of the **CPLR** within sixty (60) days of issuance of the **PAR** Order & Opinion.

If thirty-five (35) days have elapsed and you have neither received a **PAR** from the owner nor been notified by this office that a **PAR** has been filed, you should do the following: Before you take any action to file, this Order as a judgment, mail this Notice to **DHCR** at the address indicated above. It will be returned to you with specific information marked on the reverse side of this form, in either **Part A** or **Part B**.

1. If **Part A** is completed, this means that the review requested by the owner is still in progress; you must wait for further notification from **DHCR** as to the decision and the further action to be taken.

2. If **Part B** is completed, this means that the dollar amount of the penalty is final. **DHCR** will certify one of the following: that the owner did not file a **PAR** within the specified time period; that the owner did file a **PAR** which was dismissed, or modified the Administrator's Order (specific changes will be included): that the owner did not request a court review within the specified time period; that the petition for review was dismissed by the court; or that the court entered a judgment changing the Order, in which case specific changes will be included.

You may then take either, but **not both**, of the following steps to obtain the amount awarded:

a. Deduct from each of your future monthly rent payments an amount not more than twenty percent (20 %) of the authorized penalty, as upheld or as changed by the **PAR** or the court, until you have deducted the total amount of the authorized penalty; or

b. Complete and sign the Tenant's Affidavit (**Part C of the returned Form**) before a Notary Public. Then proceed to file this Notice, together with the certified copy of the Order, with the County Clerk of the county in which your building is located in the same manner as a judgment for the full amount of the authorized penalty.

If you have already sent DHCR a request for information on this Administrator's Order, and have received a reply with information and instructions, please do not mail this Notice as a new request. Instead, follow the instructions in the prior response. Should you have further questions, please contact the **Division's Information Unit** at the address indicated above. When communicating about this matter, please refer to the Order and Docket Number as indicated in the upper right hand section of this page.

(Over)

RN-14 (11/86)

For Completion By The Division of Housing and Community Renewal

(Only applicable portions are marked and completed.)

☐ Part A - Notice of Pending Proceeding for Review

On _____ 19_____ , a judicial proceeding under Article 78 CPLR was instituted to review the Order referred to on the reverse of this form. You will be notified by DHCR when the PAR Order becomes final or when judgment is entered and whether to submit a new Notice for Certification.

Signature: _____

Name: _____

Date: _____

Title: _____

Part B - Division of Housing and Community Renewal Certification

It is hereby certified: (Applicable items are marked)

1. ☐ That more than thirty-five (35) days have expired from the issuance date of the Administrator's Order in this proceeding, _____ 19_____ , and the DHCR has not been served with a Petition for Administrative Review (PAR). Accordingly, the owner is precluded from challenging said Order in an Article 78 CPLR judicial proceeding.

2. ☐ That the (owner) (tenant) did File a PAR to review the Administrator's Determination in this proceeding and on _____ 19_____ , the Commissioner issued an Order and Opinion denying the PAR.

3. ☐ That upon the (owner's) (tenant's) PAR, the Commissioner issued an Order and Opinion which changed the penalty awarded in the Administrator's Order as follows:

4. ☐ That more than sixty (60) days have expired from the issuance date of the Order and Opinion in this proceeding on _____ 19_____ , and the DHCR has not been served with a Notice of Petition and Petition in Article 78 CPLR judicial proceeding to review the Order and Opinion.

5. ☐ That on _____ 19_____ , an Article 78 CPLR judicial proceeding was commenced by (owner) (tenant) to review the Order and Opinion in this proceeding, and on _____ 19 _____ , judgment entered by the Supreme Court dismissing the (owner's) (tenant's) petition.

6. ☐ That judgment was entered on _____ 19_____ , by the court in the Article 78 CPLR judicial proceeding changing the penalty awarded in the Order and Opinion as follows:

Signature: _____

Name: _____

Date of Certification: _____

Title: _____

For Completion by Tenant

Part C - Tenant's Affidavit

State of New York

    County of _____

_____ being duly sworn, deposes and says: I am the tenant in this administrative proceeding. No payment of the penalty has been received by me in cash or as an offset against rent payments as directed in the Order, a certified copy of which is attached.

WHEREFORE, I respectfully request that the Order be entered as a judgment against the owner for the amount directed to be paid as a penalty in said Order and Determination.

Sworn to before me

Signature: _____

this _____ **day of** _____ **19** _____

_____
Notary Public or Commissioner of Deeds

Print Name: _____

RN-14 (11/86)

State of New York
Division of Housing and Community Renewal
Office of Rent Administration

Enforcement Unit
Office of Rent Administration
25 Beaver Street
New York, NY 10004

Docket Number:

Tenant's Statement of Complaint (s) - Harassment

Declaracion Del Inquilino Por Violaciones (Hostigamentos)

Part 1 (Must be filled in completely in every case) (Debe ser llenada completamente en cada caso)

Mailing Address of Tenant:

Name: _____

Number/Street: _____ Apt. No.: _____

City, State, Zip: _____

Telephone Number: ( ) _____ ( ) _____
(Residence)   (Business)

Address of Building   (if different from above):

Number/Street   City, State, Zip Code

(Complete this box in all cases)	Number of	
	Rooms	Occupants
Apt. No. & Location (as "no. 3, second floor front", etc.)		

Mailing Address of Owner:

Name: _____

Number/Street: _____

City, State, Zip: _____

Telephone Number: ( ) _____ ( ) _____
(Residence)   (Business)

Name and Address of Managing Agent (if different from above):

Name: _____

Number/Street: _____

City, State, Zip: _____

Telephone Number: ( ) _____

(Insert an address where you can be reached if you leave your present address)

Are you a SRO (Single Room Occupancy) tenant?   Yes ☐   No ☐

Are you or were you an employee of the owner?   Yes ☐   No ☐

Complete if your unit is in a co-op or condo: (write name and address of each listed below)

Unit Owner/Proprietary Lessee: _____

To Whom do you pay Rent: _____

Managing Agent for Rental Units: _____

Managing Agent for Co-op/Condo Units: _____

President or Chairman of Co-op/Condo: _____

Filing Instructions: Complete an original and two copies of this complaint and include a copy of any attachments to **each** copy. File the original, two copies and any accompanying documents with the Chief, Enforcement Section, at the address indicated above by personal delivery or mail. **Failure to follow this procedure or include all required information may result in the rejection of this application.**

Part II - Definition of Harassment

It shall be unlawful for any owner or any person acting on his or her behalf, directly, or indirectly, to engage in any course of conduct (including, but not limited to, interruption or discontinuance of required services, or unwarranted or baseless court proceedings) which interferes with, or disturbs, or is intended to interfere with or disturb the privacy, comfort, peace, repose or quiet enjoyment of the tenant in his or her use or occupancy of the housing accommodations, or is intended to cause the tenant to vacate such housing accommodation or waive any right afforded under the Rent Regulatory Laws.

There must be a willful interruption in services or a continuing course of conduct, as distinguished from an isolated incident.

Persons using this form may be summoned to testify under oath in court or before this agency in connection with criminal or civil action initiated on the basis of the statements contained herein. Painting complaints, other service complaints, and complaints of violations such as overcharges, bonus payments, furniture tie-in sales, security deposits, lease renewals, etc., should not be filed on this form, but on other appropriate forms which may be obtained at your local Borough or District Rent Office.

Penalties for Proven Violations: Persons adjudged guilty of harassment and/or illegal or constructive eviction may be prosecuted for a crime punishable by imprisonment for not more than one year or by a fine up to $5,000, or both. In addition, a permanent injunction against violation of the Rent Laws may be obtained and the Commissioner may impose civil penalties of up to $1,000 for **each** violation against a rent controlled tenant and up to $2,500 for **each** violation against a rent stabilized tenant. **Each day** such violation continues may constitute a **separate** or **additional** violation.

Part III - General Information

1. Date you took occupancy: _____ Current rent charged: _____ (mo.) (wk.)
   Date current owner of building became the owner: _____

2. Do you have a current lease? Yes ☐ No ☐ If yes, state the term of current lease: From ___/___/___ To ___/___/___

3a. Is rent being paid? Yes ☐ No ☐ Amount paid $_____ , Amount demanded $_____

b. Is rent being accepted? Yes ☐ No ☐ Are receipts being given? Yes ☐ No ☐ Has landlord refused to renew your lease? Yes ☐ No ☐

4a. Give total number of apartments (units) in building: _____ Occupied: _____ Vacant: _____

b. If there are vacant apartments (units) in the building, indicate whether they are left open, locked, boarded up or being altered: (Circle appropriate items)

5. Have you been notified that the building is scheduled for demolition or alteration? Yes ☐ No ☐

6. Has any alteration or construction work taken place at the building in the last six months? Yes ☐ No ☐

7a. Is a "work permit" from the Department of Buildings on display? Yes ☐ No ☐

b. Has the owner filed for Certificates of Eviction or for permission not to renew your lease? Yes ☐ No ☐
   If yes, indicate Docket Nos. _____

8. Is there a tenant's committee in your building? Yes ☐ No ☐ If yes, indicate name, address and telephone number of the Chairman of the Committee: _____

9. My apartment is regulated under ☐ Rent Stabilization; ☐ ETPA; ☐ Rent Control; ☐ Hotel Stabilization (includes Single Room Occupancy (SRO) tenants.)

10. Do you authorize DHCR to communicate with your attorney/representative concerning this complaint?

☐ Yes ☐ No If yes, indicate name, address and telephone number: _____

_____

Part IV - Nature of Harassment
If you need more space for details use Part V

11a.☐ I was offered $_____ by _____ to vacate my apartment by_____ 19_____ .
                         (name)   (date)

b. ☐ I was threatened with eviction if I refused to vacate my apartment. **c.**☐ I was told that essential services would not be provided.

d. ☐ I was offered another apartment. **e.** ☐ After I refused the offer, the services were decreased. **f.** ☐ After I refused the offer, I have received threats of eviction from _____ (Give details in Part V).
                                                      (name)

12. ☐ The owner has brought court action against me: Yes ☐ No ☐ If yes, complete a, b, c & d below.

a ☐ Kind of court action:_____ ; Date of court action: _____

b. Index No. _____ (If more than one court action, list in Part V)

c. ☐ I have retained a lawyer. Give name, address and telephone no.:_____
_____

d. ☐ The claim against me is unfounded for the reasons stated in Part V. **Also give status of legal proceeding.** (In any subsequent conference please bring copies of any court papers)

13a.☐ I filed the following applications with the Office of Rent Administration or other Rent Agency.

Docket No. & Nature of Complaint	Date	Disposition

b. ☐ I have also filed complaints with _____
                                       Name of Agency   Date   File No.

                                             Disposition

14. ☐ I have been illegally evicted, **"locked-out"** or otherwise excluded from my apartment.

15. ☐ I have taken legal action against the owner: Yes ☐ No ☐ If yes, indicate: _____
_____

16. ☐ The owner has intentionally decreased, withheld or interrupted the following services: ☐ security; ☐ heat; ☐ hot water; ☐ cold water; ☐ electricity; ☐ superintendent or janitor; ☐ garbage removal; ☐elevator; ☐other

Part V - Further Statement of Tenant
(Otras Declaraciones Del Inquilino)
(State in this space additional facts which may assist Office of Rent Administration in processing your complaint)
All statements and attachments must be in English.
(Todos las declaraciones y anexos deben estar escritas en ingles.)

I have read the foregoing and I hereby affirm under the penalties provided by law that the contents thereof are true of my own knowledge.
Declaro conforme a la ley que he leido lo antecedente cuyo contenido es verdad.

It is not necessary that the foregoing be notarized, but false statements may subject you to the penalties provided by law. **No es necesario que el documento sea bajo juramento: sin embargo, declaraciones erroneas pueden resultar en un delito de acuerdo con la ley.**	_____ Signature of Tenant - Firma del Inquilino Dated: (Fecha) _____19 _____

This Form and Any and All Attachments Must Be Filed in Triplicate

Esta Planilla Debe De Hacerse Por Triplicado

REQUEST FOR CONSENT TO SUBLEASE

To: _____ (landlord), via certified mail, return receipt requested

1. I am requesting your consent to sublease the unit located at _____
_____, which I am currently leasing
under a lease signed on _____ and due to expire on _____. (a copy of
this lease is attached)

2. I wish to sublease the unit to _____ for the period
_____. The proposed sublessee currently resides at
_____ and has the following business
address_____. A notarized copy of the sublease
agreement is attached.

3.   My address during the sublease will be _____
_____.

4.   I am requesting this sublease for the following reason _____
_____.

5.   If there is a co-tenant or guarantor, his or her consent is attached.

You have 30 days to respond to this request, from the date this request was mailed. Your
consent may not be unreasonably denied. Failure to respond within 30 days is considered to
be consent to the sublease. Any requests for more information must be made within 10 days
of the date this request was mailed and may not be unduly burdensome.

_____ (tenant)

_____ (address)

_____

NOTIFICATION OF ROOMMATE

To: _____ (landlord)

Please be advised that _____ is now my roommate
for the unit located at _____.

_____ (tenant)

_____ (address)

_____

Roommate Agreement

1. This agreement is made on _____ (date) by _____ (Tenant) and _____ (Roommate).

2. Tenant and Roommate agree to share the premises located at _____ _____ for the period beginning _____ and ending _____, during which time Tenant has a valid lease for the premises.

3. Roommate shall pay $_____ to Tenant per month, for rent/utilities OR Roommate shall pay $_____ per month for rent and shall pay _____% of utility bills per month. Payment is due on the _____ day of each month. Roommate shall be responsible as follows for telephone bills:_____ _____.

4. Should Roommate fail to pay the rent due, Tenant may serve Roommate with a Three Day Termination Notice. Roommate will vacate the premises in the time specified in the Notice, but will remain liable to Tenant under the terms of this agreement.

5. Roommate agrees that this agreement covers the use of the following rooms/areas by Roommate:_____.

6. Roommate has read the original lease (attached) and agrees to all of the terms and restrictions contained in it.

7. The parties agree that Roommate shall be responsible for the following jobs/chores/items:_____ _____ _____.

and that Tenant shall be responsible for the following jobs/chores/items:_____ _____ _____.

8. Roommate also agrees to the following requirements and/or restrictions:_____ _____ _____.

9. The parties agree that either Roommate or Tenant may end this agreement with one month's written notice to the other party.

10. Roommate does not have the right to assign this agreement to a third party or to sublet any part of the premises. Roommate has no right to a renewal lease for the premises from Landlord.

11. Tenant remains responsible to the Landlord for the terms of the original lease, but Roommate is responsible for any damage to the premises caused by Roommate and is subject to eviction and liability.

_____   _____

(Tenant signature)   Date

_____   _____

(Roommate signature)   Date

Three Day Notice of Termination

To: _____ (sublessee or roommate)

Date: _____

You are hereby notified that because you have failed to make the rent payment due _____ in the amount of $_____, you are hereby notified that you are to vacate the premises three days after the date of this notice. Failure to do so will result in eviction.

_____ (Sublessor or Tenant)

_____ (address)

_____

AGREEMENT TO SUBLEASE

1.   This sublease is agreed to on _____ (date) by _____ (original tenant, the Sublessor) and _____ (Sublessee).

2.   Sublessee agrees to sublet the premises located at _____ _____ from Sublessor for the period beginning _____ and ending _____. Sublessor has a valid lease for the premises in effect during this time period.

3.   The Sublessee agrees and understands the terms of the original lease, which is attached to this agreement, and agrees to accept its terms as binding on Sublessee, by substituting "Sublessee" for "Tenant" each time it appears in the original lease.

4.   Sublessee agrees to pay Sublessor $_____ per month in rent, due each month on the _____ day of the month.

5.   Sublessee agrees to use the premises for residential use only, unless otherwise agreed to in writing by the parties.

6.   Sublessee will not underlet the premises or assign this sublease to anyone else.

7.   If Sublessee violates the terms of this agreement, Sublessor shall be entitled to serve Sublessee with a Three Day Notice of Termination and Sublessee shall be required to vacate the premises in the time period indicated and shall remain liable to Sublessor as provided for in the lease.

_____   _____
(signature of Sublessor)   Date

_____   _____
(signature of Sublessee)   Date

_____COURT OF NEW YORK

COUNTY OF _____

_____

_____,)

)

  Petitioner,)

_____)

  Address: _____)

_____)

     -against-)

)

)   ANSWER WITH

)   COUNTERCLAIM

           (holdover proceeding)

_____

  Respondent{s}-Tenant{s},)

_____)   Index No. _____

  Address: _____)

_____)

)

Respondent, _____ as answer to the Petition, alleges the following:

1. Denies knowledge or information sufficient to form a belief as to the truth or falsity of the allegations contained in paragraphs number _____ of the Petition.

2. Denies each and every allegation contained in paragraphs number _____ _____ of the Petition.

3. Admits the allegations in paragraphs number _____.

FIRST OBJECTION

4. Petitioner failed to serve the Notice of Petition and Petition in the manner provided by Real Property Actions and Proceedings Law Section 735 in that:_____
_____
_____.

SECOND OBJECTION

5. The notice of termination was legally insufficient to terminate the tenancy. Specifically, the notice was vague, equivocal, and indefinite, and: (i) failed to set forth the grounds upon which the tenancy was terminated, or the facts establishing the grounds; (ii) failed to set forth a specific date upon which the premises were required to be vacated; (iii) failed to set

forth the legal consequences of the tenant's refusal to vacate; and, (iv) was issued by a person lacking authority to terminate the tenancy.

FIRST AFFIRMATIVE DEFENSE

6. During the three-month period following the issuance of the termination notice and prior to the commencement of this proceeding, the landlord accepted, deposited and/or failed to return respondent's monthly rent checks, thereby waiving the alleged default{s}, waiving any termination, and reinstating the tenancy.

FIRST COUNTERCLAIM

7. Respondent repeats the facts set forth in paragraphs "1" through "5," above.

8. The lease agreement includes a provision for the landlord's right to repayment of legal fees, costs, and disbursements.

9. Pursuant to Real Property Law section 234, Respondent is entitled to a reciprocal right to the recovery of such fees and costs.

10. Because of this, Respondent is entitled to a judgment for his/her attorney's fees and costs, in an amount to be determined at a hearing or at trial, but believed to be no less than $_____.

WHEREFORE, Respondent requests that this Court dismiss the Petition, award Respondent judgment on Respondent's counterclaim for attorneys' fees and costs in the sum of at least $_____, and grant such other and further relief as to this Court may be just and proper.

Dated: _____

_____
(Respondent)

_____

_____

_____COURT OF THE STATE OF NEW YORK

COUNTY OF _____

_____

_____)

)

Petitioner,)

_____)

Address:_____)

_____)

          -against-)

)

_____,)

)

Respondent{s}-Tenant{s},)

_____)

Address:_____)

_____)

       ANSWER WITH
COUNTERCLAIMS
(nonpayment proceeding)

Index No._____

Respondent, _____, as answer to the Petition, alleges the following:

1. Denies knowledge or information sufficient to form a belief as to the truth or falsity of the allegations contained in Paragraphs number _____ of the Petition.

2. Denies each and every allegation contained in Paragraphs number _____of the Petition.

3. Admits the allegations contained in paragraphs number _____.

FIRST OBJECTION

4. Petitioner failed to properly serve the Notice of Petition and Petition in the manner provided by Real Property Actions and Proceedings Law section 735, in that: _____
_____.

SECOND OBJECTION

5. Petitioner failed to make a demand of the rent pursuant to RPAPL section 711(2).

FIRST AFFIRMATIVE DEFENSE

6. Upon information and belief, conditions in the premises are, or are likely to become, dangerous, hazardous and detrimental to the life, health and safety of the respondent. These conditions began on or about _____ and continue to the present, and include, but are not limited to, the following: _____
_____

7. The abovementioned conditions are, upon information and belief, in violation of law.

8. The abovementioned conditions have caused Respondent substantial inconvenience and hardship, have made parts of the premises unsuitable for living, and, have deprived the Respondent of the use and enjoyment of all (or part) of the premises.

9. Respondent has given the landlord oral and written notice of these conditions, but landlord has failed and/or refused to correct the conditions.

10.   By reason of the abovementioned, landlord has breached the warranty of habitability, as set forth in Real Property Law s. 235-b, thereby relieving the tenant of the obligation to pay the rent alleged to be due.

FIRST COUNTERCLAIM

11.   Respondent repeats the facts set forth in paragraphs "5" through "9," above, as if fully set forth herein at length.

12.   By reason of the abovementioned, respondent has been damaged by the landlord's breach of the warranty of habitability, as contained in RPL section 235-b.

SECOND COUNTERCLAIM

13.   Respondent repeats the facts set forth in paragraphs "5" through "11," above, as if fully set forth herein at length.

14.   The lease agreement between the parties includes a provision for the landlord's right to be reimbursed for legal fees, costs, and disbursements.

14.   Pursuant to RPL section 234, Respondent is entitled to a reciprocal right to the recovery of such fees, costs, and disbursements.

16.   By reason of the above, Respondent is entitled to judgment for his/her attorneys fees, costs, and disbursements, in an amount to be determined at a hearing or trial, but believed to be no less than $_____.

WHEREFORE, Respondent requests that this court dismiss the Petition and award Respondent the following:

1) a 100% rent abatement;

2) judgment on Respondent's first counterclaim in the sum of $_____;

3) judgment on Respondent's second counterclaim for an award of attorneys' fees in the sum of $_____;

4) such other and further relief this Court may find just and proper.

Dated: _____

_____
(Respondent)

_____

_____
(Address)

VERIFICATION

STATE OF NEW YORK   )

COUNTY OF   )

TOWN/CITY/VILLAGE OF   )

)   ss.:

_____, being duly sworn, deposes and says:

1. I am the Respondent identified and named in the within Petition.

2. I have read the attached Answer and know the contents thereof to be true to my own knowledge, except as to those matters therein stated to be alleged upon information and belief, and as to those matters your deponent believes them to be true.

_____

Respondent

_____

Signature

Sworn to before me

This _____ day of _____

_____

Notary Public

form 20

STATE OF NEW YORK

_____ Court

_____

)
_____)
Petitioner   )
)   NOTICE OF APPEAL
vs.   )
)
_____)
Respondent   )
)   #_____
)
)
)
_____

    PLEASE TAKE NOTICE, that Respondent hereby appeals to the _____
_____, from an Order of the _____ Court
(Hon. _____), entered in the _____ Court Clerk's
Office on _____, and from each and every part thereof (and from
each and every intermediate Order therein entered).

DATED:

               _____ Respondent
               _____ Address
               _____

TO: Court Clerk: _____
       Petitioner(s): _____

_____COURT OF THE STATE OF NEW YORK

COUNTY OF _____

_____	)	
_____,	)	
Petitioner,	)	
Address:_____	)	
_____	)	
-against-	)	
	)	NOTICE OF MOTION
	)	FOR SUMMARY JUDGMENT
_____,	)	
Respondent,	)	
Address:_____	)	
_____	)	
_____	)	Index No. _____
	)	(L & T)
_____	)	

To the above named Petitioner(s):

Please take notice that the Respondent will move this court for Summary Judgment, based upon the attached Affidavit and supporting documents on _____, _____ at _____ A.M./P.M. at the courthouse located at _____, in part _____.

Dated:_____

_____ Respondent
_____ Address
_____
_____ Telephone

AFFIDAVIT OF RESPONDENT

State of New York:
County of _____:
City/Town of _____:
ss:

_____, being duly sworn, swears as follows:

1.   I am the Respondent and tenant in this matter and hereby reassert and reallege all allegations contained in the Answer for this matter (and am attaching a copy of the Answer to this document).

2.   I am the tenant of the property located at _____, which is the subject of this proceeding.

3.   I signed a lease on _____, which expires on _____.

4.   _____

_____

Based upon the above there is no triable issue of fact in this matter and summary judgment should be granted to Respondent with the following relief: _____ _____, and such other and further relief that to the Court may seem just and proper.

Sworn to before me this

_____ day of _____, _____

_____
Notary Public

           _____
           Respondent

_____COURT OF THE STATE OF NEW YORK

COUNTY OF _____

_____)

_____,)

Petitioner,)

Address: _____)

_____)

-against-)

_____,)　　NOTICE OF MOTION

Respondent(s)-Tenant(s),)　　FOR DEFAULT JUDGMENT

Address(es):_____)

_____)

_____)　　Index No. _____

_____

To the above named Petitioner(s):

Please take notice that the Respondent will move this court for Default Judgment, based upon the attached Affidavit and supporting documents on _____, _____ at _____ A.M./P.M. at the courthouse located at _____, in part _____.

Dated:_____

_____ Respondent
_____ Address
_____
_____ Telephone

AFFIDAVIT OF RESPONDENT

State of New York:
County of _____:
City/Town of _____:
ss:

_____, being duly sworn, swears as follows:

1. I am the Respondent and tenant in this matter matter and hereby reassert and reallege all allegations contained in the Answer for this matter..

2. I am the tenant of the property located at _____, which is the subject of this proceeding.

3. I signed a lease on _____, which expires on _____.

4. Landlord has failed to appear, respond or prosecute this action, having been served with the Answer that is herein attached.

Based upon the above, default judgment should be granted to Respondent with the following relief:_____, and such other and further relief that to the Court may seem just and proper.

Sworn to before me this
_____ day of _____, _____

_____
Notary Public

_____
Respondent

_____COURT OF THE STATE OF NEW YORK

COUNTY OF _____

_____)	
_____,)	
Petitioner,)	
Address:_____)	
_____)	
-against-)	
_____,)	JUDGMENT
Respondent,)	
Address:_____)	
_____)	Index No. _____

_____

A Petition having been filed by the Petitioner dated _____ seeking the following relief:_____

_____

in a _____ proceeding and the Respondent having been served on _____ by _____ and Respondent having appeared on _____ _____ and a hearing/inquest having been held on _____, it is hereby ordered, adjudged and decreed:

Dated:_____   _____

ENTER   Hon. _____

_____COURT OF THE STATE OF NEW YORK

COUNTY OF _____

_____)	
_____,)	
Petitioner,)	
Address:_____)	
_____)	
-against-)	
_____,)	STIPULATION SETTLING
Respondent,)	NONPAYMENT PROCEEDING
Address:_____)	
_____)	Index No. _____

_____

The parties stipulate and agree that this proceeding shall be settled as follows:

1. The Petition is hereby amended to include all rent due through the date of this stipulation, _____.

2. Respondent consents to the jurisdiction of this Court, waives any and all jurisdictional defenses and withdraws any counterclaims.

3. The parties agree that Respondent owes $_____ in arrears for rent for the months of _____ through _____ at a rate of $_____ per month.

4. Respondent agrees to pay the arrears by bank check, certified check, and/or money order as follows: _____.

{The need to repair conditions may be addressed at this point in the stipulation. If repairs are not requested, the phrase: "Repairs are not needed" may be inserted. If Respondent states that repairs are required, the following optional paragraphs may be inserted:}

5. a. Repairs are not needed.

    Or

    b. Petitioner agrees to inspect and repair, as necessary, the following conditions: _____.

    c. Respondent agrees to grant Petitioner (its employees, agents, independent contractors and/or assigns) access to the premises for the inspection and completion of repairs on _____ between the hours of _____ and _____.

6. In the event of either parties' default, the case may be restored to the trial calendar on _____ days' written notice to the defaulting party.

Dated:

_____   _____
Petitioner   Respondent

_____COURT OF THE STATE OF NEW YORK

COUNTY OF _____

_____)	
_____,)	
Petitioner)	
Address:_____)	
_____)	
-against-)	
_____,)	STIPULATION SETTLING
Respondent,)	NONPAYMENT PROCEEDING
Address(es):_____)	WITH FINAL JUDGMENT
_____)	Index No. _____
_____	

The parties hereby stipulate and agree to settle the proceeding as follows:

1. The Petition is amended to include all rent owed through _____.

2. Respondent consents to the jurisdiction of this Court, waives any and all jurisdictional defenses and withdraws any counterclaims.

3. Respondent consents to the entry of a final judgment of possession in favor of the Petitioner, with a warrant to issue and execution stayed subject to the terms as set forth herein.

4. Respondent consents to the entry of a money judgment in favor of Petitioner in the amount of $_____, representing unpaid rent for the period _____ through _____ at a rate of $_____ per month.

5. Respondent agrees to pay the arrears by certified check, bank check and/or money order: _____ _____.

6. In the event Respondent defaults in the payment of one or more of the installments due under this stipulation, a warrant of eviction shall be issued, without any further notice other than service of a 72 hour notice of eviction by law enforcement.

7. a. Repairs are not needed.

    Or

    b. Petitioner agrees to inspect and repair, as necessary, the following conditions: _____ _____

    c. Respondent agrees to grant Petitioner (its employees, agents, independent contractors and/or assigns) access to the premises for the inspection and completion of repairs on _____ between the hours of _____and _____.

9. In the event of Petitioner's default or non-compliance herewith, Respondent may restore the case to the calendar on _____ days written notice to Petitioner.

10. Upon the timely payment of all arrears as required in this stipulation, the proceeding shall be deemed discontinued.

Dated:_____

_____   _____
Petitioner   Respondent

_____COURT OF THE STATE OF NEW YORK
COUNTY OF _____

_____)
_____,)
Petitioner,)
Address:_____)
_____)
    -against-)
_____)   STIPULATION SETTLING
Respondent,)   HOLDOVER PROCEEDING
Address(es):_____)
_____)   Index No. _____

_____

The parties hereby agree and stipulate to settle this proceeding as follows:

1. Respondent consents to the jurisdiction of this Court, and waives any and all jurisdictional defenses and withdraws any counterclaims with prejudice.

2. Respondent consents to the entry of a final judgment of possession in favor of the Petitioner, with a warrant to issue forthwith, and execution stayed subject to the terms set forth herein.

3. On or before the date _____, Respondent agrees to do the following: _____ _____ and further agrees to comply with all the terms and conditions of the lease forthwith, including the payment of unpaid rent or use and occupancy in the sum of $_____, which shall be paid to the Petitioner on or before _____.

4. Should the Respondent fail to fully or timely comply with the terms of this stipulation, the warrant of eviction shall execute forthwith, without any further notice other than service of a 72-hour notice of eviction by the {Marshall/Sheriff/Constable}.

Dated:_____

_____   _____
Petitioner   Respondent

_____COURT OF THE STATE OF NEW YORK

COUNTY OF _____

_____)	
_____,)	
Petitioner,)	
Address:_____)	
_____)	
-against-)	
_____)	**STIPULATION AFTER WARRANT**
Respondent,)	
Address(es):_____)	
_____)	Index No. _____

The parties do stipulate and agree as follows:

___ 1. The parties hereby agree to reinstate the lease under the following terms, which include an agreement that Landlord withdraws the warrant ordering Tenant(s) to vacate the premises:

_____

_____

_____

OR

___ 2. The parties agree that Tenant(s) shall pay to Landlord the sum of _____, which shall be in satisfaction of past rent due. They agree and understand that the payment and acceptance of this amount shall not impact Landlord's judgment of possession and the warrant issued by the court.

Dated:

_____   _____

Petitioner   Respondent

form 28

LETTER TO LANDLORD TERMINATING MONTH-TO-MONTH TENANCY

To: _____

_____

_____

From:_____

_____

_____

Date:_____

Dear _____:

Please accept this as notice that I will not be renewing my month-to-month tenancy at the end of the upcoming month for the rental unit you own at _____ _____. I will move out on _____. I would like to schedule a time to do an inspection of the unit with you before I leave. Please call me to arrange this. My new address will be _____. Please forward my security deposit there after the inspection.

Sincerely,

_____

AGREEMENT SUSPENDING LEASE

1. _____, landlord and _____, tenant make this agreement in regard to the rental property located at _____ _____, owned by landlord and occupied by tenant and governed by a lease dated _____ that expires _____.

2. Tenant and Landlord agree to suspend the lease for the period _____ to _____ while major repairs are made. During this period, tenant will reside elsewhere and will not be responsible for rent. Both landlord and tenant shall have access to the unit during this period.

3. When the tenant moves back into the premises, the lease will resume and the expiration date will be the same / will be changed to _____.

_____ _____ _____ _____

Landlord   date   Tenant   date

AGREEMENT FOR REPAIRS BY TENANT

1. _____, landlord and _____, tenant make this agreement with regard to the rental unit located at _____, owned by landlord. This property is governed by a lease between landlord and tenant dated _____ and expiring _____.

2. The parties agree that the following repairs shall be made by tenant to the unit in the manner described:

_____

_____

_____

3. Landlord shall pay tenant for the costs of materials, which shall include the following:_____
_____ and will pay in cash / and will deduct the cost from the next month's rent. Tenant is to provide landlord with original copies of the receipts.

4. Labor performed by tenant at the rate of $_____ per hour to be paid in cash / to be deducted from the next month's rent due after tenant presents landlord with a detailed invoice showing the number of hours worked and the labor performed.

5. The parties agree that all improvements made to the property will be the sole property of the landlord and no other improvements shall be done to the property by the tenant without the permission of the landlord.

_____   _____   _____   _____

Landlord   Date   Tenant   Date

LEASE AMENDMENT

1. _____, landlord and _____, tenant, for the property located at _____ and governed by the lease dated _____ that expires on _____, agree to amend the lease as follows:

_____

_____

_____

_____

_____

_____

_____

2. These amendments shall take effect immediately / take effect on _____.

3. The rest of the lease shall remain in effect and unchanged except for those provisions amended above.

_____   _____   _____   _____
Landlord   Date   Tenant   Date

LEASE BUY OUT AGREEMENT

1. _____,landlord and _____, tenant of the property located at _____ and governed by the lease dated _____ that expires _____ agree to terminate the lease as follows.

2. The lease shall terminate on _____, upon which date possession of the property shall revert to landlord.

3. Tenant agrees to pay Landlord $_____ as compensation for agreeing to terminate the lease at this early date.

4. Tenant shall not be liable to landlord for any further rent after the above mentioned date.

5. All provisions of the lease regarding the security deposit remain in effect until the landlord regains possession of the property on the above mentioned date.

_____   _____   _____   _____
Landlord   Date   Tenant   Date

AGREEMENT TO ASSIGN LEASE

1. _____, Landlord and _____, Tenant of the property located at _____, governed by the lease dated _____ expiring on _____, agree that the lease may be assigned as follows.

2. _____, Assignee, shall take possession of the property on _____ and lasting until _____ and shall accept assignment of the above mentioned lease on the effective date.

3. Tenant shall not be financially responsible for future rent or other matters such as future damage to the property once the assignment takes effect.

4. Tenant shall no longer have the right to possession of the rental property once the assignment takes effect.

5. Assignee will be bound by all of the terms and conditions of the lease that is being assigned.

_____   _____

Landlord   Date

_____   _____

Tenant   Date

_____   _____

Assignee   Date

Letter to Landlord Requesting Repairs

To:_____

_____

_____

From:_____

_____

_____

Date:_____

Dear_____:

As tenant of the rental property you own located at _____, I would like to notify you in writing about some repairs that are necessary on the property. As I told you verbally on _____, the following repairs are needed at the property: _____

_____

_____

_____.

Since these conditions are dangerous and will only get worse with time, I wanted to let you know immediately about the need for repairs. If I do not hear from you by _____, I will make arrangements myself to have these important repairs done and will subtract the cost from my next month's rent.

Sincerely,

_____

NOTICE OF PETITION FOR DEPOSIT OF RENTS PURSUANT TO ARTICLE 7-A

_____COURT OF THE STATE OF NEW YORK
COUNTY OF _____

_____,	
Petitioner(s),	Index No.: _____
-against-	NOTICE OF PETITION
_____,	
Respondent(s) and	

Department of Housing
Preservation and Development,
          Respondent.
_____

    Take notice that a hearing will be held at _____, New York, Room   , Part   , on the   , day of   ___ at   A.M./P.M. on the attached petition which requests a final judgment ordering that:

(1) an Administrator be appointed pursuant to Article 7-A of the New York Real Property Actions and Proceeding Law;

(2) all rent due from the petitioning tenants and from all other occupants, beginning on the date the tenants are served the judgment, be deposited with the Administrator appointed by the Court;

(c) all future rent that will be due from the petitioners and all other building occupants, be deposited with the Administrator as it becomes due;

(d) the deposited rents be used, subject to the direction of the Court to the extent necessary to remedy the conditions complained of at the building that is the subject of this litigation;

(e) along with such other and just relief as to this Court may seem just, proper and equitable, including but not limited to an award of petitioners' attorneys' fees, costs and disbursements.

    Take further notice that if at such time a defense to the petition is not interposed and established by the owner or any mortgagees or lienor of record a final judgment may be rendered as demanded in the petition.

    Take further notice that if this notice of petition is served upon you at least eight (8) days before the time at which it is noticed to be heard, and it so demands, you must answer at least three (3) days before the petition is noticed to be heard, in writing, by serving a copy on the attorney(s) for the petitioners, or if there are none, on the petitioners, and by filing the original of the written answer with proof of service in the office of the clerk of the court at least three (3) days before the time the petition is noticed to be heard. In addition, you must appear in court at the time and place set forth for the hearing.

Dated: _____

VERIFIED PETITION TO APPOINT ADMINISTRATOR PURSUANT TO ARTICLE 7-A

_____

_____ COURT OF THE STATE OF NEW YORK
COUNTY OF _____

_____

     Petitioner(s),   Index No.:

  -against-

                      PETITION

_____

     Respondent(s),

Department of Housing
Preservation and Development,

     Respondent.

_____

     The Petition of _____ alleges as follows:

     1. Petitioners are tenants of apartment units, number _____] in the building located at _____, New York described as follows:

        Petitioner's name: Apartment number:

  a.

  b.

  c.

  d.

     2. The units at issue are part of a multiple dwelling of _____ units.
The petitioners make up at least one third of the buildings tenants as there are _____ tenants total and _____ petitioners.
Upon information and belief, _____ is the owner of the premises at issue in this proceeding..

     6. Upon information and belief, the respondent mortgagee _____ is the first mortgagee and assignee of rents.

     7. Upon information and belief, the respondent _____ is the managing agent of the building on behalf of the owner of the premises.

     8. Various conditions are present in the building at issue which are a threat to the life, health, and safety of the building's occupants.

9. These include, but are not limited to, the following conditions:

a.

b.

c.

d.

10. These conditions have existed for a period of more than five (5) days.

11. Upon information and belief, the work required to remove or correct the conditions described and their approximate costs are as follows:

a. _____ $ _____

b. _____ $ _____

c. _____ $ _____

d. _____ $ _____

11. The amount of monthly rent due from each of the petitioners named in this petition is as follows:

Name of Petitioner/ Tenant:	Apt. No.:	Monthly Rent:	Total Due:
a. _____		$	$ _____
b. _____		$	$ _____
c. _____		$	$ _____

WHEREFORE, it is requested that a final judgment be rendered in favor of the petitioners ordering that:

(a) an Administrator be appointed pursuant to Article 7-A of the New York Real Property Actions and Proceeding Law;

(b) all rent due from the petitioning tenants and from all other occupants, from the date the judgment was served on the tenants, be deposited with the Administrator appointed by this Court;

(c) all future rent that becomes due from the petitioners and all other building occupants, be deposited with the Administrator as it becomes due;

(d) such deposited rents be used, subject to the Court's direction, to the extent necessary to remedy the conditions complained of at the building that is at issue; and

(e) together with such other and just relief this as to the seems just, proper and equitable, including but not limited to an award of petitioners' attorneys' fees, costs and disbursements.

Dated: _____

From: _____

_____

_____

_____

form 37

Order to Show Cause

_____Court of the State of New York

County of _____

_____

_____,   Order to Show Cause

                                                    Index No.: _____

        Petitioner

Against

_____,

        Respondent

Upon the affidavit of _____, Respondent, sworn to on _____ and upon all of the papers and proceedings herein,

Let Petitioner show cause before this court on _____ at _____ A.M./P.M. to be held in the county of _____, in _____ or as soon thereafter as the parties can be heard why an order should not be made:

Granting Respondent's request staying the judgment made by this court in this matter.

And such other and further relief as this Court may deem appropriate.

Sufficient reason therefore appearing, let personal service of this order and a copy of the papers upon which it is granted, issue upon Petitioner on or before _____ be deemed sufficient notice and that answering affidavits if any be served at least two days before the return date of this motion.

ENTER

                                        _____
                                                    J.S.C

Affidavit of Respondent

State of New York   )
County of _____   )
City/Town/Village of _____)

_____, swears the following under penalty of perjury:

_____ is the Respondent in this matter.

Respondent seeks to have the Court stay the Judgment in this matter dated _____.
Respondent gives the following reasons:

_____

_____

_____

_____

_____

_____

Respondent has hereto attached any relevant papers or evidence regarding this matter.

Order to Show Cause: HP Proceeding

_____Court of the State of New York

County of _____

_____

_____,   Order to Show Cause

               Petitioner   Index No.: _____

Against

_____,

            Respondent

Upon the affidavit of _____, Petitioner, sworn to on _____ and upon all of the papers and proceedings herein,

Let Respondent show cause before this court on _____ at _____ A.M./P.M. to be held in the county of _____, in _____ or as soon thereafter as the parties can be heard why an order should not be made:

_____

_____

_____

_____

And such other and further relief as this Court may deem appropriate.

Sufficient reason therefore appearing, let personal service of this order and a copy of the papers upon which it is granted, issue upon Respondent on or before _____ be deemed sufficient notice and that answering affidavits if any be served at least two days before the return date of this motion.

ENTER

                           _____

                                 J.S.C.

Affidavit of Petitioner

State of New York   )
County of _____   )
City/Town/Village of _____   )

_____, swears the following under penalty of perjury:

_____ is the Petitioner in this matter and is the tenant of _____
_____, the respondent landlord.

Petitioner is the tenant at _____, such property which is owned by the landlord.

Tenant leases the property under the attached lease / as a month to month tenant.

Petitioner seeks the court's assistance to :_____
_____
_____

Petitioner gives the following reasons:

_____
_____
_____
_____
_____

4. Petitioner has hereto attached any relevant papers or evidence regarding this matter.

INDEX

Your #1 Source for Real World Legal Information…

SPHINX® PUBLISHING
A Division of Sourcebooks, Inc.®

- Written by lawyers
- Simple English explanation of the law
- Forms and instructions included

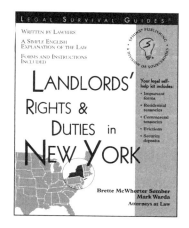

LANDLORDS' RIGHTS AND DUTIES IN NEW YORK

From the tenant application to the sheriff's eviction of the tenant, this book explains everything a landlord needs to know about the laws of renting real property in New York. Explains state and federal laws about discrimination, security deposits, and more!

224 pages; $19.95;
ISBN 1-57071-186-0

HOW TO START A BUSINESS IN NEW YORK

Starting a new business can be a risky venture. This book explains the state and federal laws and regulations that apply to most New York businesses. It includes ready-to-use forms and instructions and covers everything from choosing a name to filing tax returns.

176 pages; $16.95;
ISBN 1-57071-185-2

HOW TO WIN IN SMALL CLAIMS COURT IN NEW YORK

Small claims court can help individuals and small businesses collect money they are owed. This book explains in simple language what types of claims can be filed, how to file and argue your case, and how to evidence and witness. Includes forms and instructions.

160 pages; $14.95;
ISBN 1-57071-187-9

See the following order form for books written specifically for California, Florida, Georgia, Illinois, Massachusetts, Michigan, Minnesota, New York, North Carolina, Pennsylvania, and Texas! *Coming soon—Ohio!*

What our customers say about our books:

"It couldn't be more clear for the lay person." —R.D.

"I want you to know I really appreciate your book. It has saved me a lot of time and money." —L.T.

"Your real estate contracts book has saved me nearly $12,000.00 in closing costs over the past year." —A.B.

"…many of the legal questions that I have had over the years were answered clearly and concisely through your plain English interpretation of the law." —C.E.H.

"If there weren't people out there like you I'd be lost. You have the best books of this type out there." —S.B.

"…your forms and directions are easy to follow." —C.V.M.

SPHINX® PUBLISHING'S NATIONAL TITLES
Valid in All 50 States

LEGAL SURVIVAL IN BUSINESS

How to Form a Limited Liability Company	$19.95
How to Form Your Own Corporation (3E)	$19.95
How to Form Your Own Partnership	$19.95
How to Register Your Own Copyright (3E)	$19.95
How to Register Your Own Trademark (3E)	$19.95
Most Valuable Business Legal Forms You'll Ever Need (2E)	$19.95
Most Valuable Corporate Forms You'll Ever Need (2E)	$24.95
Software Law (with diskette)	$29.95

LEGAL SURVIVAL IN COURT

Crime Victim's Guide to Justice	$19.95
Debtors' Rights (3E)	$12.95
Grandparents' Rights (2E)	$19.95
Help Your Lawyer Win Your Case (2E)	$12.95
Jurors' Rights (2E)	$9.95
Legal Research Made Easy (2E)	$14.95
Winning Your Personal Injury Claim	$19.95

LEGAL SURVIVAL IN REAL ESTATE

How to Buy a Condominium or Townhome	$16.95
How to Negotiate Real Estate Contracts (3E)	$16.95
How to Negotiate Real Estate Leases (3E)	$16.95
Successful Real Estate Brokerage Management	$19.95

LEGAL SURVIVAL IN PERSONAL AFFAIRS

Guia de Inmigracion a Estados Unidos (2E)	$19.95
How to File Your Own Bankruptcy (4E)	$19.95
How to File Your Own Divorce (4E)	$19.95
How to Fire Your First Employee	$19.95
How to Hire Your First Employee	$19.95
How to Make Your Own Will (2E)	$12.95
How to Write Your Own Living Will (2E)	$9.95
How to Write Your Own Premarital Agreement (2E)	$19.95
How to Win Your Unemployment Compensation Claim	$19.95
Living Trusts and Simple Ways to Avoid Probate (2E)	$19.95
Neighbor v. Neighbor (2E)	$12.95
The Most Valuable Personal Legal Forms You'll Ever Need	$19.95
The Nanny and Domestic Help Legal Kit	$19.95
The Power of Attorney Handbook (3E)	$19.95
The Quickie Divorce Book	$19.95
Simple Ways to Protect Yourself from Lawsuits	$24.95
Social Security Benefits Handbook (2E)	$14.95
Unmarried Parents' Rights	$19.95
U.S.A. Immigration Guide (3E)	$19.95
Your Right to Child Custody, Visitation and Support	$19.95

Legal Survival Guides are directly available from Sourcebooks, Inc., or from your local bookstores.

For credit card orders call 1–800–43–BRIGHT, write P.O. Box 4410, Naperville, IL 60567-4410 or fax 630-961-2168

SPHINX® PUBLISHING ORDER FORM

BILL TO:		SHIP TO:	
Phone #	Terms	F.O.B. Chicago, IL	Ship Date

Charge my: ☐ VISA   ☐ MasterCard   ☐ American Express

☐ **Money Order or Personal Check**

Credit Card Number

Expiration Date

Qty	ISBN	Title	Retail	Ext.
		SPHINX PUBLISHING NATIONAL TITLES		
____	1-57071-166-6	Crime Victim's Guide to Justice	$19.95	____
____	1-57071-342-1	Debtors' Rights (3E)	$12.95	____
____	1-57248-082-3	Grandparents' Rights (2E)	$19.95	____
____	1-57248-087-4	Guia de Inmigracion a Estados Unidos (2E)	$19.95	____
____	1-57248-103-X	Help Your Lawyer Win Your Case (2E)	$12.95	____
____	1-57071-164-X	How to Buy a Condominium or Townhome	$16.95	____
____	1-57071-223-9	How to File Your Own Bankruptcy (4E)	$19.95	____
____	1-57248-132-3	How to File Your Own Divorce (4E)	$19.95	____
____	1-57248-083-1	How to Form a Limited Liability Company	$19.95	____
____	1-57248-100-5	How to Form a DE Corporation from Any State	$19.95	____
____	1-57248-101-3	How to Form a NV Corporation from Any State	$19.95	____
____	1-57248-099-8	How to Form a Nonprofit Corporation	$24.95	____
____	1-57248-133-1	How to Form Your Own Corporation (3E)	$19.95	____
____	1-57071-343-X	How to Form Your Own Partnership	$19.95	____
____	1-57248-125-0	How to Fire Your First Employee	$19.95	____
____	1-57248-121-8	How to Hire Your First Employee	$19.95	____
____	1-57248-119-6	How to Make Your Own Will (2E)	$12.95	____
____	1-57071-331-6	How to Negotiate Real Estate Contracts (3E)	$16.95	____
____	1-57071-332-4	How to Negotiate Real Estate Leases (3E)	$16.95	____
____	1-57248-124-2	How to Register Your Own Copyright (3E)	$19.95	____
____	1-57248-104-8	How to Register Your Own Trademark (3E)	$19.95	____
____	1-57071-349-9	How to Win Your Unemployment Compensation Claim	$19.95	____
____	1-57248-118-8	How to Write Your Own Living Will (2E)	$9.95	____
____	1-57071-344-8	How to Write Your Own Premarital Agreement (2E)	$19.95	____
____	1-57071-333-2	Jurors' Rights (2E)	$9.95	____
____	1-57071-400-2	Legal Research Made Easy (2E)	$14.95	____
____	1-57071-336-7	Living Trusts and Simple Ways to Avoid Probate (2E)	$19.95	____
____	1-57071-345-6	Most Valuable Bus. Legal Forms You'll Ever Need (2E)	$19.95	____
____	1-57071-346-4	Most Valuable Corporate Forms You'll Ever Need (2E)	$24.95	____

Qty	ISBN	Title	Retail	Ext.
____	1-57248-130-7	Most Valuable Personal Legal Forms You'll Ever Need	$19.95	____
____	1-57248-089-0	Neighbor v. Neighbor (2E)	$12.95	____
____	1-57071-348-0	The Power of Attorney Handbook (3E)	$19.95	____
____	1-57248-131-5	The Quickie Divorce Book	$19.95	____
____	1-57248-020-3	Simple Ways to Protect Yourself from Lawsuits	$24.95	____
____	1-57071-337-5	Social Security Benefits Handbook (2E)	$14.95	____
____	1-57071-163-1	Software Law (w/diskette)	$29.95	____
____	0-913825-86-7	Successful Real Estate Brokerage Mgmt.	$19.95	____
____	1-57248-098-X	The Nanny and Domestic Help Legal Kit	$19.95	____
____	1-57071-399-5	Unmarried Parents' Rights	$19.95	____
____	1-57071-354-5	U.S.A. Immigration Guide (3E)	$19.95	____
____	0-913825-82-4	Victims' Rights	$12.95	____
____	1-57071-165-8	Winning Your Personal Injury Claim	$19.95	____
____	1-57248-097-1	Your Right to Child Custody, Visitation and Support	$19.95	____
		CALIFORNIA TITLES		
____	1-57071-360-X	CA Power of Attorney Handbook	$12.95	____
____	1-57248-126-9	How to File for Divorce in CA (2E)	$19.95	____
____	1-57071-356-1	How to Make a CA Will	$12.95	____
____	1-57071-408-8	How to Probate an Estate in CA	$19.95	____
____	1-57248-116-1	How to Start a Business in CA	$16.95	____
____	1-57071-358-8	How to Win in Small Claims Court in CA	$14.95	____
____	1-57071-359-6	Landlords' Rights and Duties in CA	$19.95	____
		FLORIDA TITLES		
____	1-57071-363-4	Florida Power of Attorney Handbook (2E)	$12.95	____
____	1-57248-093-9	How to File for Divorce in FL (6E)	$21.95	____
____	1-57248-086-6	How to Form a Limited Liability Co. in FL	$19.95	____
____	1-57071-401-0	How to Form a Partnership in FL	$19.95	____
____	1-57071-380-4	How to Form a Corporation in FL (4E)	$19.95	____
		Form Continued on Following Page	**SUBTOTAL**	

To order, call Sourcebooks at 1-800-43-BRIGHT or FAX (630)961-2168 (Bookstores, libraries, wholesalers—please call for discount)

SPHINX® PUBLISHING ORDER FORM

Qty	ISBN	Title	Retail	Ext.
		FLORIDA TITLES (CONT'D)		
___	1-57248-113-7	How to Make a FL Will (6E)	$16.95	___
___	1-57248-088-2	How to Modify Your FL Divorce Judgment (4E)	$22.95	___
___	1-57248-081-5	How to Start a Business in FL (5E)	$16.95	___
___	1-57071-362-6	How to Win in Small Claims Court in FL (6E)	$14.95	___
___	1-57248-132-4	Landlords' Rights and Duties in FL (8E)	$19.95	___
___	1-57071-334-0	Land Trusts in FL (5E)	$24.95	___
		GEORGIA TITLES		
___	1-57071-376-6	How to File for Divorce in GA (3E)	$19.95	___
___	1-57248-075-0	How to Make a GA Will (3E)	$12.95	___
___	1-57248-076-9	How to Start a Business in Georgia (3E)	$16.95	___
		ILLINOIS TITLES		
___	1-57071-405-3	How to File for Divorce in IL (2E)	$19.95	___
___	1-57071-415-0	How to Make an IL Will (2E)	$12.95	___
___	1-57071-416-9	How to Start a Business in IL (2E)	$16.95	___
___	1-57248-078-5	Landlords' Rights & Duties in IL	$19.95	___
		MASSACHUSETTS TITLES		
___	1-57248-128-5	How to File for Divorce in MA (3E)	$19.95	___
___	1-57248-115-3	How to Form a Corporation in MA	$19.95	___
___	1-57248-108-0	How to Make a MA Will (2E)	$12.95	___
___	1-57248-109-9	How to Probate an Estate in MA (2E)	$19.95	___
___	1-57248-106-4	How to Start a Business in MA (2E)	$16.95	___
___	1-57248-107-2	Landlords' Rights and Duties in MA (2E)	$19.95	___
		MICHIGAN TITLES		
___	1-57071-409-6	How to File for Divorce in MI (2E)	$19.95	___
___	1-57248-077-7	How to Make a MI Will (2E)	$12.95	___
___	1-57071-407-X	How to Start a Business in MI (2E)	$16.95	___
		MINNESOTA TITLES		
___	1-57248-039-4	How to File for Divorce in MN	$19.95	___
___	1-57248-040-8	How to Form a Simple Corporation in MN	$19.95	___
___	1-57248-037-8	How to Make a MN Will	$9.95	___
___	1-57248-038-6	How to Start a Business in MN	$16.95	___

Qty	ISBN	Title	Retail	Ext.
		NEW YORK TITLES		
___	1-57071-184-4	How to File for Divorce in NY	$19.95	___
___	1-57248-105-6	How to Form a Corporation in NY	$19.95	___
___	1-57248-095-5	How to Make a NY Will (2E)	$12.95	___
___	1-57071-185-2	How to Start a Business in NY	$16.95	___
___	1-57071-187-9	How to Win in Small Claims Court in NY	$14.95	___
___	1-57071-186-0	Landlords' Rights and Duties in NY	$19.95	___
___	1-57071-188-7	New York Power of Attorney Handbook	$19.95	___
___	1-57248-122-6	Tenants' Rights in NY	$14.95	___
		NORTH CAROLINA TITLES		
___	1-57071-326-X	How to File for Divorce in NC (2E)	$19.95	___
___	1-57248-129-3	How to Make a NC Will (3E)	$16.95	___
___	1-57248-096-3	How to Start a Business in NC (2E)	$16.95	___
___	1-57248-091-2	Landlords' Rights & Duties in NC	$19.95	___
		OHIO TITLES		
___	1-57248-102-1	How to File for Divorce in OH	$19.95	___
		PENNSYLVANIA TITLES		
___	1-57248-127-7	How to File for Divorce in PA (2E)	$19.95	___
___	1-57248-094-7	How to Make a PA Will (2E)	$12.95	___
___	1-57248-112-9	How to Start a Business in PA (2E)	$16.95	___
___	1-57071-179-8	Landlords' Rights and Duties in PA	$19.95	___
		TEXAS TITLES		
___	1-57071-330-8	How to File for Divorce in TX (2E)	$19.95	___
___	1-57248-114-5	How to Form a Corporation in TX (2E)	$19.95	___
___	1-57071-417-7	How to Make a TX Will (2E)	$12.95	___
___	1-57071-418-5	How to Probate an Estate in TX (2E)	$19.95	___
___	1-57071-365-0	How to Start a Business in TX (2E)	$16.95	___
___	1-57248-111-0	How to Win in Small Claims Court in TX (2E)	$14.95	___
___	1-57248-110-2	Landlords' Rights and Duties in TX (2E)	$19.95	___

SUBTOTAL THIS PAGE ___

SUBTOTAL PREVIOUS PAGE ___

Illinois residents add 6.75% sales tax ___

Florida residents add 6% state sales tax plus applicable discretionary surtax ___

Shipping— $4.00 for 1st book, $1.00 each additional ___

TOTAL ___